MW01519649

There are no scenarios in which the publisher or the original author of this work can be in any fashion deemed liable for any hardship or damages that may befall them after undertaking information described herein.

Additionally, the information in the following pages is intended only for informational purposes and should thus be thought of as universal. As befitting its nature, it is presented without assurance regarding its prolonged validity or interim quality. Trademarks that are mentioned are done without written consent and can in no way be considered an endorsement from the trademark holder.

Table of Contents

Cricut Project Ideas

Amazing DIY Project Ideas to Getting Started with Cricut

Anita Wood

Introduction

Cricut is one of those machines that opens new ways in your art life and fills it with pleasure and amazement. It makes things happen magically due to underlying design space, a free mobile application that certainly helps a lot of work marvelously.

Cricut machines cut different materials into various shapes and designs instead of drawing something. Versatile materials may be used to get the desired product varying from paper or vinyl to wood and even metals. It is an economical way to fabricate multiple art designs than spending money on other means. Other machines come with complex characteristics, offer limited designs, and do the same work expensively.

Cricut machines are known as the die cutter and craft plotter. Images designed on a computer are fed to the Cricut machine, which then moves a blade on host material and cut it into the desired shape instead of simple printing.

Cricut is working criteria based on automation, and it is capable of working on a variety of materials such as paper, metal, vinyl, fabric, and adhesive sheets.

Cricut machine is also very useful in writing texts with different font styles and drawing images using a pen instead of a cutter. One can design different kinds of party and wedding invitations.

The Cricut image library is fed with thousands of images and art designs. Moreover, designed images are stored in the memory—making the user can pick any of these designs and utilize them again with edited patterns and new style. Thus, a Cricut machine makes the user work with the versatile dimensions of art and craft.

However, a Cricut machine offers a user-friendly interface for working in a creative environment with new materials, tricks, and tips. The massive user base of Cricut always shares the latest with the greatest.

Cricut offers unlimited features as it is a computer-aided crafter. If you are an art lover and want to develop new creative things, there is nothing to worry about.

Just broaden your imagination and turn it into reality with this beautiful art machine. For this purpose, this book will help you to start with the Cricut and get an idea to step into the new art world.

If you think of purchasing this wonderful art and craft machine, you will need a user guide to understand its features and work. In that case, this user manual will help beginners start with Cricut as this guide is composed of easy and understanding directions to work with Cricut.

The mentioned chapters will help create compatibility with Cricut and explain how you can use it to create artwork.

It will be good for you to read this book as it provides the reader with step-by-step information to use the machine and exciting ideas for some projects. Each chapter has been composed specially to get familiar with and learn more about this art machine.

Moreover, by purchasing this book, you are heading in the right direction as you appreciate our hard work and helping hand in the world of art as it provides the reader with quality knowledge and understanding of the Cricut machine. So, let us start with this user guide.

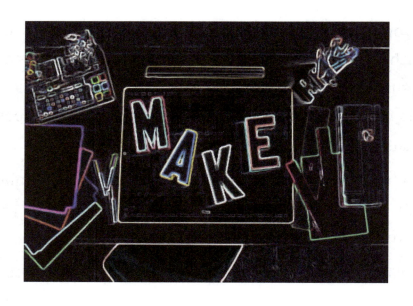

Chapter 1: Knowledge of the Cricut Machine

What Is a Cricut Machine?

The Cricut machine is the cutting machine that can cut various shapes out of many materials such as cardstock, paper, fabric, wood, leather, and many more. Thus, the Cricut machine helps you out in crafting different desired objects from your chosen material.

How Does Cricut Machine Work?

Software

Every machine runs on software like your computers and laptops; they run on windows, the operating software. Similarly, design space is the software that the Cricut machine uses to operate itself. You need to install design space software on your PC or even can download it on your smartphone.

Using design space, you can not only import your required design from the internet or any other system, but it also provides you with the provision that you can create your design using different tools available in the software.

Construction

The Cricut machine is very simple. Its main parts are the small blade, pen, or rotary cutter (The one to be used depends on your design requirements) over the railing over which the cutter can move in x-axis and y-axis to complete its tasks.

Under the cutter is the space provided to hold the material you like to cut your design. Behind the cutter is the Cricut machine's circuit, which receives the input from software, translates it to the cutter, and moves it according to input design.

Working

First, transfer the design from software to the machine, subsequently, place the material to be cut over the cutting mate. Press the start button; the machine will start cutting the selected material according to its design.

What Can You Make Using a Cricut Machine?

There is no limit on products you can make using this wonderful machine. However, to give an idea, a few examples are given below:

1. Custom bags, T-shirts, blazers, or hats by using iron-on vinyl.

2. Make custom invitations for parties, weddings, and even thank you cards.

3. Make paper envelopes with distinctive designs.

4. Etched products, i.e., door glass, mugs, and jugs.

5. Print stickers and cut them into desired shapes.

6. Make ornaments for weddings and annual festivals like Christmas.

7. Make vinyl decals in a variety of shapes and designs for glass, mugs, and shirts.

8. Make leather bracelets.

9. Make monograms of different materials.

10. Design different pillows, bed sheets, and covers.

11. Make bracelets.

12. Shapes and letters for the scrapbook.

13. Make window clings.

14. Make wall stickers and many more.

No other tools available work similarly as the Cricut do to some extent, but their usability is limited because of their finite features. Although they are being launched every year with modified versions, Cricut has secured a superior position over other means because of its versatile usage in art and craft.

Due to the simple user interface applications, the professionals recommend the Cricut machine for newcomers. In case users face any difficulty generating new ideas, the Cricut product library provides multiple sample design ideas and easy tasks for learners, from greeting cards and photographs to improved customer services. It is a machine that can work with different host materials without any struts.

Cricut Machine Benefits

There are multiple options available for the Cricut machine, and if we are not patient, we will end up with the wrong decision. That is why it requires a detailed study about anything before purchasing it. Because of this some benefits of the Cricut machine are mentioned below to make your work easy.

- **Cricut is Quick and Time-Saving:** One important factor of being Cricut so popular among the public fond of doing artwork is its flexibility in usage. You do not need much time to learn how to start with a Cricut unit. The setup of Cricut is very simple and can be organized by anyone easily. Directions to make its setup are always available with the package, and the consumer can easily manage to arrange it at any suit space in his/her workplace.
- **Cricut is captivating:** We are not too concerned with appearance and beauty for working purposes, but it is necessary to make things appealing as they play an important role in

enhancing workability. Cricut successfully secures a higher position than other craft machines in this regard as it provides the best user compatibility, working feasibility, and natural affection due to its easy use.

- **Cricut machine is easy to use:** Generally, in troubleshooting the problems while working with other computer-aided systems, people download different malware too, which corrupt the whole system and cause irreversible and devastating damage, but there is no such case while working with Cricut. You need to go to an online website, and things are ready to continue.

- **Simply attainable:** Cricut machine mechanism is available to be used as conflicted by any of the other equipment. This is since once you decide to use Cricut, you need to be online. But at the same time, it may be a downside as it is widely available on the website. It would help if you were connected with an internet connection anytime you decide to use this software.

General Questions about Cricut

Which Cricut Model Is Best for Use?

As suggested by the professional experts, the best choice to work with is Cricut Builder. With this, you may be able to work with a broader perspective. You are free to use it in any aspect as you wish according to your creative skills. It is like a flagship platform that works on almost all types of sheets to wood products.

Moreover, Cricut Builder is incorporated with versatile tools' collection, i.e., scoring tool, ink, and cutter. When a user is aimed to work on clothes, then there are motor cutters available that fit with Cricut maker from which you can cut any type of cloth material very easily and precisely.

If we have heavy and thick fabric and want to do creative artwork, then there are knife blade cutters available for this purpose.

If you are confused about the design, then there are various visual patterns available to use in your design and extract something creative and unique.

All the designs from the library can be made by the Cricut very quickly and easily. Thus, it helps in making beautiful embroidery on the fabrics. What we need to do is just select the design and finish our task.

We still have another option to make our real craft ideas. It just requires import with the Cricut application and use.

Why Is Cricut Worth Buying or What Benefits Does the Cricut Secure?

Some reasons why Cricut is important for artwork and beneficial for quick, easy, and unique crafts, without any doubt, it is a wonderful product and equally beneficial for decorative purposes.

Some main reasons that why the Cricut machine has its unique place in the art world are mentioned below:

- User attains access to more than 8000 designs at relatively low prices and gets updated designs regularly.

- More than 400 font styles along with composing fonts are accessible to the consumer.

- Cricut provides a quick and most efficient user guide for its members.

- Ten percent saving on all the transactions of Cricut.com, including all Cricut tools, devices, fabrics, and many more.

- Almost ten percent saving on special luxury fonts that are certified. Not only fonts but all kinds of tools, graphics, and devices.

- Cricut offers special discount offers and deals for its customers. This is the one more special characteristic of Cricut, thus bringing a revolution in the world of art.

- Cricut offers surprise packages and joy pack for the users at surprisingly low rates.

- If you have designed something extraordinary and want to conduct it in the design industry, it will provide you with the best tax exemption.

- There is also an application room for Cricut so that you may purchase different connectivity plans via smartphone and Android or IOS.

Is Cricut Difficult to Use?

You do not need to be very smart about using the machines and such kind of computer-aided systems.

What you need to do is to get a basic knowledge of the computer system—Basics things like how to open a tab and enter the Design Room of Cricut. This is the window where the item which is required to cut is organized.

If you want to work with a mobile application, you need to have some basic software knowledge. You do not need to be afraid of the fear like you cannot do it. Everything is possible with passion and true spirit if you are committed to doing it.

With the different tool products available at economical rates, Cricut devices come with well-elaborated user manuals, making things easily understandable. Moreover, many other helping materials are available online. Consumers do not need to get any high level of expertise in graphics to start with the Cricut.

Cricut Design space contains a catalog of different designs and photos used to construct a new project.

Chapter 2: Cricut Machine Models Overview

A few types of Cricut machines do all basic functions, but some with advanced and unique functions.

Similarities

Listed below are some commonly found features in every Cricut machine, regardless of their type and version.

- **Cutting and writing:** The first feature that a very Cricut machine possesses is that it can cut and write because all the Cricut machines have a blade fitted in them that is used to cut various crafting material, and this blade can be replaced with markers or pen according to the need of the user. Thus, the universal function of cutting and writing is possessed by all the Cricut machines.

- **Material cutting:** A second common feature of the Cricut machine is that it can cut limitless materials. Only your imagination can stop you. The fine blade built in every type of Cricut machine is capable of cutting various designs on different materials. Furthermore, some advanced versions of Cricut machines use some much more advanced cutting tools apart from blades to cut the material better.

- **Software:** The third feature is the software. All the types use the basic design space software to translate the design into the machine. This software is available for every user type and can be used with any device such as windows and smartphones. Regardless of the type of Cricut machine you are using, you can use design space to create the desired design and export it to the machine.

- **Image library:** The design space software provides you with an infinite library of built-in designs that you can use. But if there is something not there that you want, it also lets you create your design using different designing tools and export it to the machine. Moreover, uploading the machine's design or making a new design using design space stays the same with all machines.

- **Wireless connection:** Another most attractive feature shared by all the Cricut machines is that they can be wirelessly connected with computers, laptops, or smartphone, and you don't have to plug in different wires with the machine and the device to transfer the design and give a command to the machine, you do it with great ease provided by wireless communication.

Differences

With advancements in technology and competition, the Cricut machine designers have worked on their product to keep updating to stay in the market with their magical product. Thus, mentioned below are some unique features by which the Cricut machine has various types.

- **Size:** The biggest difference is the size of the machine. Cricut explore air and Cricut maker are 24*8*8 dimensions, the desktop size almost with 16 lb and 24 lb weight. Thus, designed to be used as tabletop machines. At the same time, Cricut joy is 8*4*4 dimensions with a 4 lb weight. Thus, Cricut Joy is more portable than its ancestors

- **Cutting mats:** The other difference is the cutting mat that gives a platform for the material to be placed under the blade. In exploring and Maker for fragile materials such as tissue, delicate paper, light grip cutting mat is placed under the blade to grip these delicate materials, thus avoiding any damage caused due to mat during the cutting process and for fabric materials fabric grip cutting mat. Moreover, material like vinyl and paper standard grip cutting mat is recommended, and for tough materials such as strong leather, grip cutting mat is used. These cutting mats are available in two standard sizes, 12*24 and 12*12 inches. While in a joy machine, the use of a mat is optional; if you want to use it, you can, but joy machine can also work without cutting mats too when cutting smart materials such as smart labels, smart iron-on materials, and many more. Furthermore, the joy machine's cutting mats are available even in smaller sizes, 4.5*12 and 4.5*6.5 inches.

- **Cutting size:** Another difference between Cricut explore and Maker from Cricut joy is the size of material they can cut. Because of their large size, explore and Maker can cut large pieces of 24 inches while joy can cut pieces of 6.5 inches' length.

- **Tool holder:** The carriage of explore and Maker can hold two tools simultaneously, thus proficient in performing two similar or different tasks simultaneously. They have two tools mounted space available in a carriage in which a user can fix blade and pen at a time and can cut and write in parallel. While Cricut joy lacks such a feature, it has only one tool holder capacity at a time. Thus, if you have to cut and write using Cricut joy, you need to change the tool to attain the desired results.

- **Tool system:** In explore and Cricut joy, the holder is programmed such that when it has to at a specific point, then it goes down and touches the target material and cut the desired design, and when it has to move to another point, then it moves up, breaking the contact with the material and moves side wise to the new location. Thus, it can be said that the holder in Cricut joy and Cricut explore can move up and down to perform its task. But Cricut

Maker has a unique feature of adaptive tool system in it which is absent in Joy and Explore because of which Cricut Maker is said to be more controlled with intricate and clean cuts.

1. It provides ten times greater force to cut the material as compared to other machines of its type.

2. Its steering system controls the movement of the blade, thus making the blade more efficient.

3. The pressure of the blade is automatically adjusted to give a desired cutting effect on the material.

4. It provides the space to work with different cutting tools such as knife blade, engraving tools, and much more.

- **Card mat:** The card mat feature is unique to Cricut Joy. With the card mat option, you can place the folded card of the desired size on the cutting mat to get your desired design cut on it, thus getting your customized card for any occasion, which is not the case in other machines because, in them, you have to place the flat piece of card over cutting mat to get required design and to fold the card later on which might not get adjusted in the envelope—Thus saving you from the hassle of folding and fitting the card in an envelope.

- **Print then cut:** The eye sensor positioned above the cutting tool helps it to recognize the material's marks to cut it. Using the print and cut command, you send the design to print and print it on the desired material. Afterward, the image is exported to the Cricut machine, which will cut the printed image. This print and the cut option are available for exploring and Maker but is absent in Cricut Joy.

- **Fast mode:** Cricut Explore and Maker are furnished with a fast cut option using which you can cut a repeated design multiple times on the material with a very fast speed, double the speed than normal. This helps the user cut a lot of design in a much shorter period, saving time and energy.

- **USB mode:** You need to connect your machine with the physical cartridge to get some additional pre-made designs for your library. Cricut Explore has the advantage of providing a pot to connect or attach a physical cartridge with it while Joy and Maker lack this option, and from them, you have to buy a new USB cartridge set up to connect with your machine.

- **Accessories:** When you buy the machine, different accessories are also part of the package, and for some accessories, you have to make another purchase. What and how many accessories are present in the package and the machine, varies from machine to machine and company to company.

Model Overview

In this section of the book, three main types of Cricut machines will be discussed to give you an idea about all of them with their pros and cons to help you decide which is the best suited for your needs.

Cricut Joy

Cricut joy is the die-cutting digital machine and considered the updated version of the Cricut machine introduced in early 2020, which can write using a joy marker and pen and cut through a fine tip blade. It has the features to make customized items because of its small size and enhanced features. Thus, if someone is looking for a Cricut machine with an affordable price and a portable device, he can go for it.

Listed below is the summary of Cricut Joy benefits:

1. Automatic writing and cutting.

2. Offers to cut more than 50 different materials.

3. Provides the option to cut with mat and without mat through smart material.

4. Can make personalized cards.

5. Portable, light in weight, with compact size.

6. Wireless connection.

7. Built-in the library for pre-made designs in addition to the option of self-creation of design.

Everything in this comes with its shortcomings, and it is up to our needs that whether the benefits suppress the limitations or vice versa. Thus, the limitations of the Cricut machine are given below to ease your decision:

1. Please limit the size of material that can be cut, 4.5 inches due to its compact size.

2. Perform one function at a time, either cut or write. The user has to switch the mode from cut to write during the process.

3. Limits the users regarding the tool that can be used and offers to use a blade or pen/marker only.

4. Lack print then cut option due to unavailability of sensor eye.

5. No option to cut fabric material.

6. No USB slot available.

Cricut Explore Air

It is a die-cutting machine of desktop size. If you are looking for a machine to use for commercial purposes, it is best suited for your needs due to its fast mode option, which allows you to perform tasks faster and cut multiple copies of a single project.

Furthermore, the deep fine blade can cut 100 various materials. Moreover, it has an additional feature to speed up your work by providing a double tool holder option, which saves your time from manually shift the mode from cut to write during the process.

Some more advantages are listed below:

1. Automatic scores, cut, and write.

2. Double tool holder feature.

3. A fine sharp blade can cut more than 100 different materials.

4. Wireless connection through Bluetooth mode.

5. Fast mode option to cut and write repeated projects with increased speed.

6. Print then cut feature.

7. Design your project and also provide built-in pre-made projects.

8. Built-in cartridge option to connect the additional physical cartridge.

Limitations

1. No option to cut fabric without any modification.

2. Adaptive tool accessories option is missing.

3. The desktop size needs a proper place to work

4. A cutting mat is needed.

5. The size of material to be used to cut and write is limited, can cut 24 inches long piece.

6. Personalized cards cannot be made because the card mat option is missing.

Cricut Maker

It is the smart die-cutting machine, best suited for professionals. It can cut and write on more than 100 various materials, including wood, paper, fabric, and much more. Its state-of-the-art features outshines it among other Cricut machines.

Its most impressive feature is an adaptive tool system that allows you to use diverse tools to perform your tasks efficiently and cleanly.

Following are the tool accessories options that can be used because of the adaptive tool system feature:

1. **Rotary blade:** can cut paper, fabric like delicate materials without any bunching and raveling.

2. **Knife blade:** can make intricate cuts through hard and thick materials like leather and wood.

3. **Scoring wheels:** can make score lines on any material with any thickness.

4. **Engraving tool:** can use it for décor purpose, design jewelry, nameplates, and much more.

5. **Perforation blade:** make perforated lines and make raffle tickets, journals, and many more.

6. **Fine debossing tool:** can make debossed patterns on any material.

7. **Wavy blade:** help to create wavy edges to décor any design and material.

Advantages

1. Scores, cut, and writes robotically.

2. Adaptive tool system: can use various tools to perform and design projects apart from commercial tools such as blade and pen/marker.

3. Can cut more than 250 various materials.

4. Have the ability to create and cut sewing patterns.

5. Double holder tool.

6. Wireless connection through Bluetooth mode.

7. Fast mode option.

8. Pre-made projects.

9. Can create your projects using design space software.

10. Print then cut feature.

Precincts

1. Expensive.

2. Bulky.

3. Need specific, dedicated space.

4. Material size is a limitation.

5. Cutting mat requirement.

6. Lack of card mat option.

7. No, in the built slot to connect physical cartridges.

Chapter 3: Cricut Design Space Tutorial

Cricut Design Space

In the Cricut design space, we arrange and design our creations. This is where you can do all kinds of magic in your art before making the machine ready to cut the material.

In Design Space of Cricut, you can not only upload your favorite images and fonts, but you can use Cricut's premium designed images by individually purchasing them at cheaper rates as compared to the other relatively complex and expensive machines.

This is an excellent tool for beginners to start with the Cricut during their learning phase. They can easily make new creative artworks and enhance their exposure to this wonderful machine.

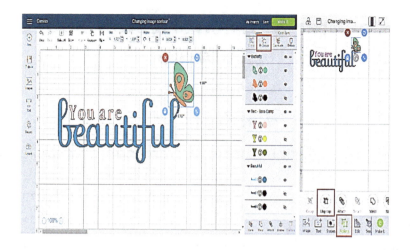

If the user has not experienced any other graphic design software like adobe Photoshop, then though the user is less confident about this new working machine after doing few projects, it will be a pleasure to work with this wonderful machine. Contrary to it, if the consumer is already familiar with the design software, this is just like a breeze for him/her.

Design space is basically for touching up the projects and construct new artistic designs with a variety of shapes, styles, and fonts. As the user gets involved with this device more, it becomes like a joy game for him/her. Thus, making the consumer habitual of creativity and variety of new unique artwork. If someone wants to create more sophisticated designs, then it will require special access to a supergiant design library of design space, which you can get at very affordable rates.

There is a window named Canvas where the user will work. Whenever he/she desires to make something new first, he/she will be required to log into his/her account and start/edit the new project.

Canvas is the space where a consumer does all the designing activities, whether he/she works from scratch or edit any of the projects already available in the gallery before cutting.

There are various options and buttons available on Canvas. If you are a beginner, it won't be very clear for you to start with it. You do not need to worry, as it will demand very little effort from your side to learn and get used to it. Just cheer up and start with a fresh active mind without any hesitation.

Break all the chains and start working with Cricut with new excitement and enthusiasm. It will be an enjoyable tenure for you. For easy understanding, I am going to divide the Canvas into four major areas.

1. **Editing area** – top yellow panel.
2. **Insertion area** – left blue panel.
3. **Panel for layers** – purple panel on right side.
4. **Green Canvas area**.

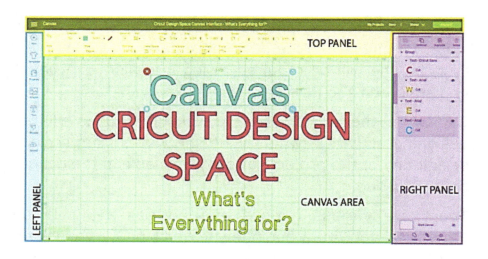

Design Space—Top Panel

In the design space, the top panel area of Canvas is for arranging and designing the elements to construct new interesting and appealing projects. In this panel, you have multiple options for selecting the font style and size, design alignments, and many more. As you will start using Canvas more, you will learn about it as practice makes a man perfect. We can do this through this guidebook to give you a brief knowledge about CRICUT's versatility so that you may be able to break your chains and work with the diversity in the world of art and make new horizons.

This top panel is further divided into different small sub-panels. The first one is to save the file and name the project; moreover, the cut command is also available. The second sub-portion will allow you to edit the designs and control the projects on the Canvas area.

Sub-Panel Number 1 Name & Cut Your Project

This part makes the user enable to navigate with Canvas to his/her profile and projects. Moreover, it also conveys the projects which are completed to cut.

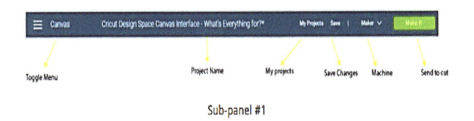

Sub-panel #1

Toggle Menu in Canvas

When a user clicks on this button, then it will open a completely new menu. It is a handy menu, but at the same time, I must mention that it is not part of Canvas.

That is why I am not going to discuss it in detail. This is the place from where you can jump onto your profile and change the photo.

You can play some more interesting and technical tactics using this menu; for example, you can recalibrate your machine's blades and update the software, thus incorporating new features and specifications in your working means.

Secondly, subscriptions can be managed quickly and easily by accessing the Cricut, the account details, and many other related things.

I recommend the user to click and check each option available. This will make the user able to explore new things and get an excellent experience with Cricut. Users can alter the visibility and the measurements of Canvas too.

- **Name the project.** When we start making any project, it always initiates with an 'untitled title.' So, this is the Canvas area from where you can name the project according to your wish. It is possible only when you have entered at least one image or shape in Canvas working space.

- **My Projects.** When the user clicks on my projects' option, it will redirect to the library where constructed designs are saved earlier. This is very useful as sometimes when required to complete the work in a limited time; it gives an accelerating effect by giving us space to edit the previously made projects and convert them into new designs. Thus, the user does not need to recreate the project with the same features again and again.

- **Save command.** The user will use this command after placing at least one element on the Canvas working area. It is highly recommended for a user to save the project first as sometimes accidentally we close the window—thus wasting all the hard work done to create a new design. That is why it is necessary to save the project first and then continue further.

- **Joy, Maker, or Explore options.** These options are available in the menu depending upon the type of Cricut machine the consumer uses to create his/her projects. It becomes necessary to mention here that we have three different versions (Maker, Joy & Explore) of Cricut available, having their characteristics. Although basic features are the same, they slightly differ from each other. So, it is very much necessary to select the option that matches your machine type; otherwise, you will not accomplish your project as it will cause certain limitations.

For example, if you are available with the Cricut Maker version and are designing with the Joy option, it will not be possible to trigger the tools.

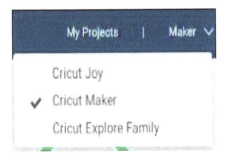

- **Make it.** Once the user has uploaded the files after successfully designing the project and ready to cut so that the required product may be achieved from host material, click on the 'Make it' command. For better user learning, I am attaching a screenshot that will help develop a better understanding.

If a consumer wants to cut more than one piece of the same design, this can also be done from this window as Cricut can create multiple copies of the same design simultaneously, thus saving capital, time, and potential.

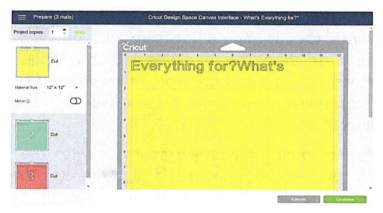

When you click on Make it. This is what you see

Sub-Panel Number 2 Editing Menu in Cricut

This is an extremely wonderful feature available in the Cricut Canvas workspace. By using it, one can organize and set images and fonts with different styles.

Top Panel – Editing Menu

Undo and Redo Commands

Usually, while designing a project, we make sudden mistakes that are necessary to remove; otherwise, our whole project may be compromised, which is not acceptable at any cost. But we do not need to worry, as this problem can be solved using these commands.

Clink on undoing when we create something that is not right and creates trouble and redo when we accidentally remove/delete ant thing from the Canvas working space.

Line Type & Fill

These options give the user a choice of the kind of blades he is going to use during cutting.
It depends upon the machine type which the user selects in the first step before further proceeding, whether it is Joy, Maker, or Explore.

Depending upon the machine type, the user will be available with different options.

The line type option tells the machine which kind of tool will be used during cutting; there are eight different options available for some specific purpose.

These commands include score, cut, engrave, draw, foil, wave, perforation, and deboss. Each of these eight commands has its specification.

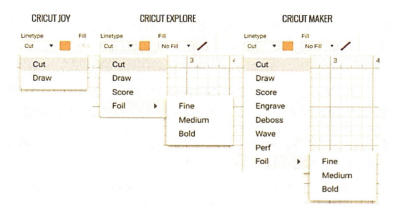

LINETYPE FOR EACH CRICUT MACHINE

If we are using Cricut Maker, then all these commands will be available, but some of these commands are excluded from it if we have Cricut Explore. Commands which will be available in Maker are draw, foil, cut, and score, and if we are using Cricut Joy, then the only available options are draw and cut.

Cut

'Cut' is a default line type that will cut the host materials according to the Canvas design. When we enter the command Make it, then Cricut starts cutting the designs. By selecting the Cut option, we can alter the fill.

Score

This option is located on the left panel, and it is the strongest version of the scoring line. When we decide to apply this command as a result, we get the designs that appear dashed, or we may say scored.

And when we select this command, it will cause our material to be scored instead of cutting. For such kind of projects, we need a wheel for scoring. But we should keep in mind always that this wheel works only with the Cricut Maker.

Draw

If we write something on our designs, then this is also possible by the Cricut machine. We can use any of the line types available in our Canvas. With this command, when we select it, Cricut will start drawing the shape instead of cutting the material. But this is the option that is not for coloring the designs.

Engrave

As the name suggests, this command will neither cut nor draw any design but will engrave the different shapes and quotes on the host material. By using these features, we can make monograms on the sheets of aluminum to reveal silver beneath.

Deboss

This is a tip that pushes the host material in and creates amazing and wonderful designs on it. Through this command, users can customize the designs up to a new level of creativity. It is a captivating feature.

You can now imagine a marvelous gift box with stars, flowers, and different kind of stickers on it, along with the different love and care notes, etc.

Perforation

This tool allows the user to cut the material with multiple uniform small lines to create an exact and crispy tear effect similar to raffle tickets, cards, coupons, etc.

Wave

This is a tool used to create wavy effect lines on the material instead of making exact straight lines. To get curvy lines is a complicated task, but this tool makes Cricut make the task to accomplish interestingly with very little effort.

Foil Tool

This is the latest tool incorporated in Cricut, which allows it to create magnificent foil finishing on his/her project. For this purpose, there is a kit for foil transfer in Cricut. While using this feature, user is allowed to select any line type, i.e., bold, fine, or medium.

Fill Tool

If the user is aimed to have printing patterns on the designs, then he/she may use this tool in Cricut. This tool will be triggered only when the user has cut like a line type, and if one selects the no fill option, it means that the consumer does not want to print anything on the cutting host material.

Print

One of the most interesting features of Cricut is the Printing feature as it allows the user to print beautiful design patterns on the material and then cut it into the desired shape depending upon the design. It is a fabulous feature—and believe me— you will also love it once you start using the Cricut Canvas.

Another interesting option available along with the printing is the pattern. When we select the options to fill, then after clicking on the make it option, what happens is that the user first sends the files to the basic printer and then to Cricut to do all the lifting means cutting.

This option is so cool. We can add pattern to any layer of our design. It depends on our choices to modify and create our pattern according to the demand to make our artwork captivating and worthy.

It all depends upon your imaginations of how you will create the patterns beyond the boundaries of thinking. Skills can be improved by practicing and regular trial activities. Gradually, with time, the circle of imagination and creativity continues to expand, making you a true artist, and this task becomes easier and more interesting due to Cricut's wonderful features to its users.

Select All Tool

When we want to move all our elements inside the Canvas area, instead of moving them one by one, we may use all options to make our task easy and time-saving.

Edit Feature

This feature contains a drop and down menu. It will make the user able to cut any unwanted thing from Canvas and add something new.
Its copy and cut options will be activated when the user chooses more than one element from Canvas.

Align

Align is a complete menu, and if the user has previous experience with other graphic software like adobe photoshoot, he/she will be aware of these options. But if you are a beginner and have no idea about it, then it is enough to know that Align commands are used when you are required to do some perfections in your designs.

Through practice, you will learn better. As you select multiple items or I can say more than two items, then this command activates.

- While using the align-right command, all elements will be organized on the left side.
- The center horizontal option will align all the elements in the horizontal direction.
- Align the right option will shift all the elements on the right side.
- The top align command will arrange all the elements of your design elements on the top side.

- The vertical center command will organize the elements in the vertical direction.
- Bottom align selected elements will be aligned at the bottom.

The center option is a very cool one. When a user clicks on this option, it brings all the horizontal and vertical elements in the center, i.e., it arranges both horizontally and vertically. It is used when the user wants to arrange the text in a square shape.

Distribute command is operatable when the user wants uniform spacing between the elements. If we start doing it separately, it will be a time-consuming process that is not favorable at any cost.

That is why, by using the distribute command, we can arrange the different design parts at equal spacing. For the distribute command to be activated, one must select at least 3–4 elements in Canvas.

The vertical distribution command will distribute the design parts in the vertical direction. The top and bottom elements determine the length of distribution. Other central items will be arranged between these two elements.

The horizontal distribution will arrange the elements in the horizontal direction. The most right and left elements decide the length of distribution.

Thus, the central elements are arranged between these distant elements on the right and left sides.

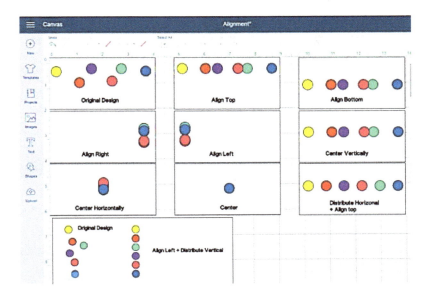

Flip

This command will do your work if you want to reflect our design in the Cricut Canvas design space. It has two choices 1-horizontal flip & 2-vertical flip.

Flip horizontal will arrange the image or any designed project in a horizontal direction.
It's like a mirror image, when you try to make the left and right images by yourself, it becomes a very hectic and tiring activity and time gaining. So, the best solution for this is to use the flip command and arrange the design according to your wish within no time.

Flip vertical will work in the same way as the flip horizontal, but it will give the mirror image in the vertical direction, making the task easy and fast.

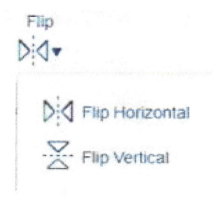

Rotate Command

This is also a very useful command in the Cricut Canvas area, where one can quickly manage things with the greatest ease. Some project designs required to set at some specific angle. This rotate command does it very easily. I will recommend the user to utilize this command if he/she plans to do something like this.

Fonts in Cricut Canvas

There are a variety of fonts available in Cricut Canvas in different styles and sizes. User is free to select any of these fonts depending upon the style which suits his/her design.

When a user clicks on the front panel, all the fonts open in front of the user on the working space's top side. If the user has a Cricut membership, he/she can easily use all the available fonts; otherwise, try to use the system's fonts.

In other cases, the user may be charged once he completes his/her project and finally decides to send the project for a cut. The two most important factors in font selection are size and style.

Font Style

A user can change the font style anytime he selects any font to work with. There are some specifications regarding font style. For example, the regular font is the default setting, and the font's appearance will not change with this setting. With the bold option selected, the whole font will give a thicker look than before. If the user selects an italic style, then the font will be tilted on the right side. And similarly, the bold italic style will keep the font in tilted form but with a thicker look.

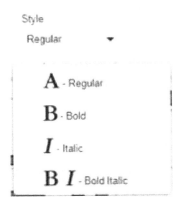

Other options available for font settings are size, space, and letter. If set properly before designing any craft, these options give an amazing look to the final designed product.

Font size can be changed manually. Its options are available in the Cricut Canvas working space area.

Some fonts are such that the space between them is more than required, so the letter space option is available to solve this issue. Users can easily reduce the space between the letters. Thus, keeping in view the characteristics explained so far, I can confidently say that Cricut is a game-changer in the art and craft world with amazing features and learning ease.

Like the letter-spacing option, the line space option will adjust the space between the lines to get the desired output with an amazing and wonderful final look—thus creating a fascinating artwork.

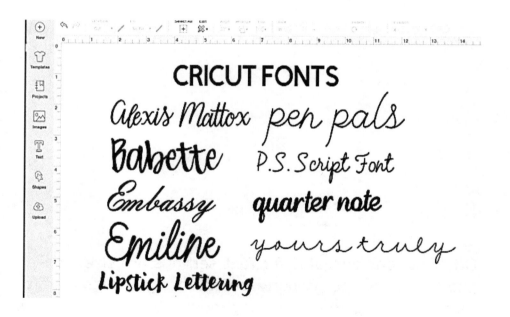

Alignment of Lines

An alignment is explained earlier, but this alignment differs from that, if only for adjusting the paragraphs. There are some options available for paragraph alignment, including left, right, and the center. As suggested by their names, left option will align the paragraph on the left side, right will adjust the paragraph on the right side and the center in the middle.

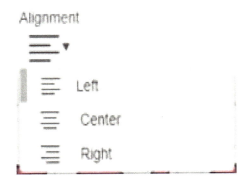

Curve Option

This option is incorporated in the Cricut Canvas to do some more creativity with the text. By using this option, we can easily give our text a cervical look by sliding the slider. When the slider is moved to the left, the text will be curved upward, and when it is moved to the right, the entire text will be curved inwards. One more interesting factor is that if we entirely move the slider in the left or right direction, the whole text will be arranged in a circular shape.

Arrange Feature

When we are working with multiple pictures and texts, then we usually find a problem. Whenever we enter a new image, it will appear as a top layer, i.e., on the top of the whole design image. But we must arrange the image according to our wish, so this 'Arrange' will help us in this regard.

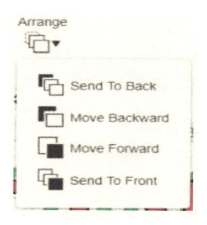

There are multiple sub-options available in the arrange feature. With this command, we can easily adjust our images in the Canvas window. We are free to decide and then arrange what item should be in front or back. The options available under the Arrange command are explained below:

- Send to the back option will send the selected image to the backside.

- Move backward option should not be confused with send to back as this option moves the image just one step back.

- The move forward option will shift the selected image, just a single step forward. We use this option when we have multiple images and want to put them in a specific arrangement.

- Sent to the front command will shift the selected image to the front from any design layer.

Advance Option in Cricut Canvas

This is the last option available on the edit panel of Canvas. Once users learn how to use all these commands, then he/she will enjoy working with Canvas, and it will not be hard anymore. This advance menu has the following commands available:

- Ungroup letter option is used to make the letters separate from each other in a single layer.

- Ungroup to lines option is somehow exceptional, and it is used to separate the individual lines from a paragraph. Type the paragraph first and then apply this command. Now user can modify every single line separately.

- Ungroup to layers is the trickiest command. You will be able to activate this command if using a multilayer font. And such kind of font is accessible if you have secured membership on Canvas. Multilayer fonts possess a fascinating attribute with different colors and shadows around them, which adds more to your work.

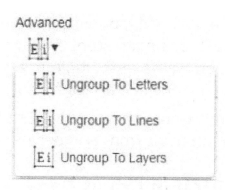

Advanced

The Left Panel on Canvas

This panel secures the authority of inserting all kinds of images, shapes, and design projects which are ready to cut and many more. There are almost seven options available in this panel, which are briefly explained below:

1. The new command is used to create a new project in the Cricut Canvas area.

2. Templates allow the user to get a guide on the types of designs to be cut.

3. Project commands add ready to cut designs from the Cricut access.

4. Images commands pick the single images from the Cricut access and magazine to create a project design.

5. Click on the text command to add text to your design.

6. You can add all kind of shapes by using the shape command in the left panel.

7. The upload will add the images and cut the files to the program.

Now we will explain step by step the characteristics of each command.

New

When a user clicks on this command, then there are two possibilities.

First, if a user is working on a certain project, then he/she will receive a warning message that whether he/she wants to keep the project or replace it. Now it depends upon his/her own choice.

The second possibility is that simple if you are just logged on to your account and start creating a new project; in this case, we will never receive any warning alert.

Templates

To see how the project will fit into a particular surface, the user can use this Template command. If someone wants to customize his/her project, then this is a marvellous tool available in Canvas.

This template command is just for visualization. It has nothing to do with readiness, drawing, or cut.

Projects

This command is specifically used to make finally the project design practically, i.e., when the project is ready, click on the "make it" command; it will cut the host material's design.

Tip

If someone has no time to draw any project from scratch or edit the previously made project, then there is a wonderful facility for the Cricut Canvas user to have their accounts and memberships. They can purchase customized projects available online at cheaper rates.

Images

Through this command, one can add new shapes and images to the project, thus adding a more appealing effect and a fascination with the artwork. Not only this, but Cricut also provides free designed images each week.

You can honestly say that there are no such useful means available where you have all kinds of products and facilities available at cheaper rates. Moreover, there are multiple filters available in Cricut Canvas to add beauty to the designed project.

Text

If the user wants to write something on his/her project, he/she can use this text command.

When a user clicks on this command, a blank box is opened in the window. He/she is free to write anything according to the demand to accomplish the project.

Shapes

To use the shapes available in Canvas, one should generate creative ideas and interestingly compose those shapes to make any fascinating project. Canvas's multiple shapes provide its user, for example, square, circle, triangle, octagon, star, heart, and line. Practice can make the user better at creating new ideas on Cricut practically. Once the user starts using this wonderful machine, then he/she falls in love with it.

Upload

If we want to upload the separate files and images, then Canvas provides its user a separate command for this purpose. It is compulsory to have an internet connection, as millions of designers upload wonderful new designs every day. Thus, you can also enter a global circle where you can get new creative marvelous ideas.

Right Panel on Cricut Canvas

In this section, you will be able to learn about the layers. Layers tell the designer about every single component present in the Canvas area.

In my opinion, each part of the project design and elements are part of layers. It is the choice of the designers that in how many layers does he/she divides the designs.

For example, there may be three different layers of text but keep in mind the fact that once designers divide the project into layers, he/she will not be able to do any editing. In this guidebook, I can verbally tell you about the layer, and I am trying my best to convey as much as I can. But still, you will learn more by just doing the practice.

Delete, Group, Ungroup and Duplicate Commands

While moving the Canvas working area components, these commands will make things easy for the user. Only one thing is necessary: to know how to play with these commands, and again, I will say that these things can be learned through practice.

- The Delete option will delete the selected item from the Canvas.

- The Duplicate command will make the duplicate copies of the layers and components selected.

- To ungroup the layers or project design, Canvas provides a separate 'Ungroup' command for this.

- Group command will be used to group the layers. This command will help the user while designing a complex project.

Fill or Line Type

Each item in the layer panel indicates what kind of line, or you may call fill, is being used in the design, i.e., whether you are using cut, wavy, write, print, or score, etc.

Blank Canvas in Cricut

If the user wants to change the Canvas color, then the option available for this purpose is blank Canvas. More you will learn by using it practically.

Slice, Weld, Contour, Attach and Flatten

These are wonderfully amazing tools available in Canvas. If users learn to use them smartly, then there are many wonders that a consumer can do using them. I will not explain them in detail.

The reader can go for the online tutorials because they need a detailed elaboration, which is not suitable. It will be a little bit boring to read a whole book on these commands separately. That is why I am leaving this responsibility on the reader's shoulders. What I can do is to give a visual presentation through a picture:

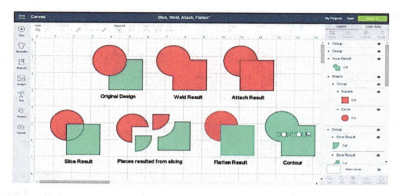

Color Synchronization

In the layer panel, this is the last option available. Each color represents a material color separately. You can use a single color in different shades, too. There are limitless wonders one can make from Cricut Canvas working space.

Grid & Measurements in Canvas

To make a fine project design with maximum accuracy, the Canvas working area is divided into grid lines. These grid lines help in selecting the size of the cutting mat.

These grid lines are variable from cm to mm etc. there is also a toggle menu available in the window; as you click on this, a window popped up with multiple options.

Zoom in Zoom out Options in Canvas

As names suggest, these options are available to make the design available to see in the required size, i.e., large, small, or extra small. Keep in mind one thing, these commands do not affect the actual size of the design.

Chapter 4: Cricut Design Projects

You can make a lot of items using a Cricut machine with any material.

Listed below are some ideas about Cricut design projects with different materials:

- Variety of cards.
- Décor items such as things for wall décor, utensil décor, gift warps.
- Face masks.
- Customized T-shirts.
- Jewelry items such as earrings, bracelets, necklace, and hair accessories.
- Different types of holders such as mobile holder, key holder, etc.
- Wallet/clutches, bags.
- Household items like cord keepers, vase wrap, mat.
- And much more.

In the following section, a step-by-step guide is given for beginners to do it yourself (DIY) projects.

Make a Birthday Card at the Last Moment with Cricut

Let us make a situation. Consider that you are getting ready for office and suddenly it notifies you that your friends' birthday today, your colleague, and you did not purchase a gift or best wishes card for him. What should I do now? This is the first question which arises in our mind. This is not possible to purchase even a bouquet in such a short period. If you are the owner of this wonderful machine, you should not be worried about anything as you can make a fascinating birthday card within 10 minutes. How you can make it, the steps are described below:

Select a Design

There are multiple sample card designs available in the Canvas design space. Open the design space and select one of the best designs according to your friend's choice.

Just pick a fascinating, colorful design and trigger the command of Make it.

As the Make it command activates, the Cricut machine starts working on the host material.

The host material may be of any type available for example, in this case, suppose you have a card, so the blade will start cutting this card into the final shape and color.

Insertion of the Card in the Mat

Multiple options are available in the design space for selecting the cards' type and size. It is necessary to set these parameters before starting the cutting by any Cricut version, i.e., Maker or Joy.

Draw a Shape on the Card before the Cut

To enhance the look, we see that sometimes cards are included with the pen drawing. It looks amazing and wonderful that it takes my heart with it as it looks like a handmade material. Whenever we want to write some goodwill on the card, it will require shipping on the pan before cutting.

Decorative Card Insertion

Once we are done with the card making, then remove this card from the mat. We still have other options available to make it more magnificent. One simple way is to slide the card's corners and make a beautiful birthday card. Similarly, we have the option to make an envelope and decorate it.

Making of the Customized Coffee Mug Using Cricut Canvas Design Space

The first step is to log in to your Cricut Canvas design space and make a project. It will be a blank space where you will further work to design your coffee mug. Just keep in mind that you are in your world while working with the Canvas; thus, feel free and design with an open mind.

If you do so, then it definitely will be a pleasant experience working with Cricut.

Your exam is to write or draw anything using all the interesting and valuable bale tools available in the Canvas working space, as explained in the whole user guide.

You may create your design or, if not, want to invest time in creating from scratch then; as explained earlier, Cricut Canvas gives you space and opportunity to select online designs available.

Moreover, there are some sample designs available in the Cricut design library. The user is free to pick any of them and start working with them. Do some addition to increase the beauty of your design, and then go to the next step.

It will be a wonderful idea to play with different font styles and sizes to get your will's final product. You may leave it simple or may use the curve option to enhance beauty. It depends upon your choice.

After doing this, in the next step, you will click on the attach option. Attach your design means avoiding misinterpretation of design, and all the letters are cut together instead of separately.

If you want to customize your design, you need to the Unlock Design option; otherwise, you will not be able to do it.

After unlocking the design in the next step, you will select your design dimensions to be placed on your mug. All options are available in the toolbar, as explained earlier. For example, if you have an eleven-ounce mug, five by five will be enough for it.

After successfully selecting the dimension, you will finally click the Make it commands. And as I have explained earlier, once you have triggered this command, you will not undo it as it starts cutting your host material.

After this, make the transfer tape ready to be placed.

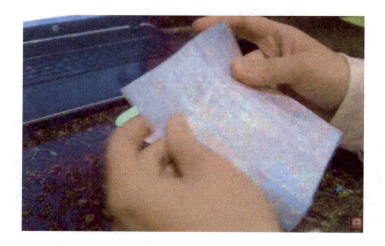

Just cut a piece of the tape to attach with the prepared design so that you may be able to paste it on your mug. Stick it well on the mug. And finally, your mug is ready to use.

Make a Customized Bag with Cricut

The first step is to gather all the necessary components for designing a customized bag. For example, a sample plain cloth bag or bag of any material, i.e., leather or plastic. It depends on you. Moreover, the color selection will be yours.

Then log into your Cricut Canvas account; it will open a blank plain working space in front of you where you will design for your bag. Now create your design. Feel free to work and design with a broad imagination. It will add quality to your work if it is done with zeal and zest.

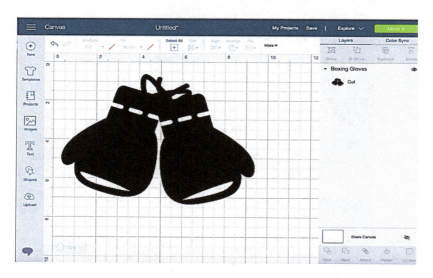

If you want to add some text, you can also do it; as I have explained earlier, there are multiple types of font styles available in the Canvas design space. Just pick any of them matching your design and theme and start doing work with that.

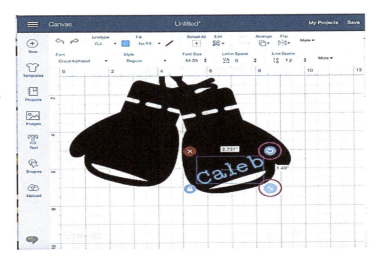

After you are done with your design, press the "make it" command. It will cut the material you are using in your design. But before doing this, you need to adjust your dimensions according to the size of your bag.

After that, take the prepared design and start weeding it, i.e., remove the unnecessary parts you do not want on your bag. Remember, you are using vinyl material in this project.

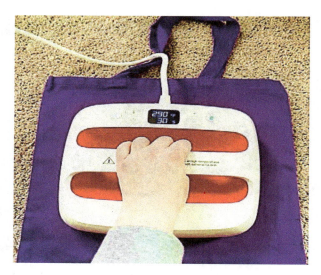

Now place it on your bag, and iron it to have it on your bag. Your customized bag is ready now. I hope that now you have got enough knowledge to design any project using Cricut Canvas. However, I would like to mention again that 'Practice makes a man perfect.'

Start using Cricut; you will fall in love with this wonderful art and craft machine.

How to Print and Cut the T-Shirt

The feel of wearing our designed customized T-shirt is awesome and is one of the triggering factors because people buy a Cricut machine. Thus, here is a step by step for you to design and cut your personalized T-shirt in a much simpler way:

- The first step is to create a design for your T-shirt.
- For this purpose, follow these steps.
- Open Cricut design space software.
- Go to a new project.
- Find template option on the top left corner of the taskbar.
- From the template, pop-down menu, select the classic T-shirt tab, and from here, choose the color, the size, and the style of your T-shirt.

- In the Cricut design space image library, you will have many designs that you can choose from.

- Now, paste the selected design onto the shirt.

- Resize the design to fit the T-shirt by clicking and dragging the resize option in the lower right corner of the design. You can also change its orientation if you like this.

- Once you are satisfied with the image, size, and position, hit the make-it button in green at the top right corner. Don't forget to hit the mirror button because all the iron-on images have to be mirrored so that the correct orientation is pasted on the T-shirt.

- Now, it's time to cut the design.

- Place the iron-on vinyl on the cutting mat with the shining surface facing downwards.

- Remove all the unwanted vinyl portions of the material through which the design will transfer to your project.

- For this, first, start removing the unwanted edges and then move towards the other portions. You have to use a sharp tool to remove the vinyl to keep your design intact on the carrier sheet.

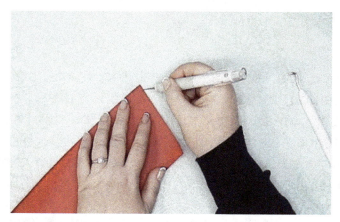

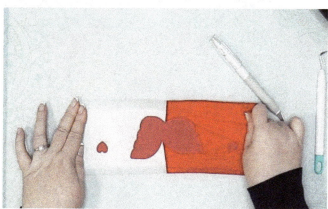

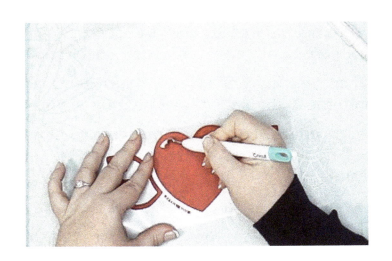

- After getting rid of all the extra material from the carrier sheet and getting only your selected design on the sheet, preheat your iron.

- Lightly preheat your project too so that to get a good print.

- Place the incorrect design orientation and in the desired position.

- Use a heated iron to heat the design using gentle pressure to not burn the carrier sheet and T-shirt.

- When you think the design has been transferred onto the T-shirt, then let it heat for a while.

  Don't remove the sheet. You can also flip the shirt and do ironing on the opposite too to get better results.

- Remove the carrier sheet from the T-shirt.

- **Tip:** Don't wash the shirt before 24 hours of imprinting.
  Wash your shirt inside out to avoid the fading of the design. The design will withstand 50 washes.

How to Make a Leather Wallet Using a Cricut Machine

- Go to design space.

- Find the tab for projects using a fold-up leather case.

- Select the cutting template.

- Press the Make it button; the template will be uploaded.

- Place your material on the cutting mat designated for leather cutting "strong grip," the smooth side facing downwards.

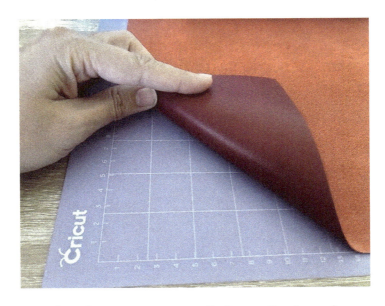

- Press leather to ensure it is well placed over the cutting mat without any bumps.

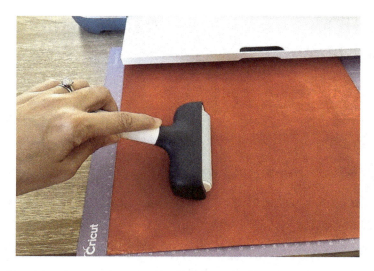

- Now, place the cutting mat with leather on it into the machine. Press the C button to command the machine to load the mat.

- Select the leather option in the design space's material section and fix the tool holder's deep cut blade.

- Command the machine to cut the selected design.

- Make the design is cut on the leather before removing it from the machine. Gently separate the leather from the cutting mat.

- The machine has cut the wallet's outline into the leather, and now your work has started.

- Fold the wallet in the shape you selected and let it dry out for a while to gain permanent shape. You can use Bayer too to fold it.

- Apply glue to the flaps of the wallet to stick them properly. You can place some heavy objects on the glued section of the wallet.

- Now make your wallet a little fancy, select the iron-on design in design space and upload it onto the machine.

- Press the make it button. Don't forget to press the mirror flip option because you want to paste the wallet's design.

- Choose the iron-on vinyl option in the design space.

- Load a fine tip blade.

- Place the vinyl carrier sheet onto the cutting mat and load it into the machine by pressing the C button.

- Weed out the extra vinyl material from the carrier sheet.

- Put the carrier sheet with the design onto the wallet where you want a design.

- Preheat the iron.

- Place butter paper over the carrier sheet and wallet to avoid burning of leather.

- With gentle pressure, heat your carrier sheet using preheated iron for half a minute and then flip the side of the flap and press the opposite side for another half a minute.

- Let the design to cool down.

- Separate the sheet from leather.

- Your designed leather wallet is ready.

Tips and Tricks to Make Cricut Machine Easier and Efficient

The new machine is always a challenge for beginners. Because the experts, due to a lot of experience, know the machines' hacks or shortcuts.

Thus, some of the most important beginners' tips are to make the most out of their Cricut machine.

If you want to use a Cricut machine for commercial purposes, then the Cricut machine's pro will recommend you to subscribe to the Cricut access because it will save you time and money.

If you are not a subscriber, you have to purchase the images and projects that will cost a lot. With Cricut access, you can have more have 400 fonts, projects, and much more.

Place the material on the cutting mat first before placing and fixing it in the machine.

After every project or use, don't forget to cover your cutting mat to keep it dust-free and keep it sticky for a longer time.

Use baby wipes to clean your cutting mat after completing your project.

Keep a whole set of tools such as spatula, weeding tool, scraper, and many more like this, with you to make the most out of it.

For card projects, the scoring stylus is very important to ease your work. Buy it.

It is recommended that beginners start working on Cricut machine with the cheapest material and simplest design to get familiar with the machine. This will help to save time and money. Never start with the actual project and material.

The mat should be positioned correctly under the rollers before starting with cutting, writing, engraving, or any other option.

In case of working with the most expensive material for the sensitive project, start with a test run using the same design on the cheapest material to see if you are on the right path or not.

The most important tip. Make sure to reset the machine and replace the tool holder, especially the pen or marker, because the pen or marker will dry off if you forget it inside the machine for a longer time.

The physical cartridge can only be linked to one device. So, make sure that the cartridge you are buying is not linked to any other device before.

In case of sticking the mat with the project, always peel away the project's mat, not the project, to avoid curling the project.

Design space software is not the only option for you to upload and create your design. You can create customized SVG files. So, buy free SVG files and enjoy working with the Cricut machine.

Conclusion

Cricut machine is a smart die-cutting machine that has revolutionized craftsman's world by translating its complex imaginations into reality most efficiently and simply saving its time, energy, and money. The machine can cut unlimited designs on hundreds of various materials to make endless unique products in the least time frame.

After reading the whole book thoroughly, you are no more a beginner. This material has given all the basic knowledge about the Cricut machine types and their different versions available in the market.

What features are incorporated in them?

How they differ from each other?

What are commands available in them separately? How can you activate the desired version from Canvas compatible with the Cricut machine type?

In which panels can the Canvas design space be divided, and what options are available in each part of the panel separately?

In the end, some examples of DIY projects are also given. These examples will help create a more understanding and compatibility level with this wonderful art and craft machine. Now, it comes under your responsibility how you will beneficially take this knowledge. The user must still do a lot of practice to have an open hand with this magnificent tool.

Cricut Explore Air 2

A Beginner's Guide to Getting Started with The Cricut Explore Air + Tips, Tricks and Amazing DIY Project Ideas

Anita Wood

Introduction

In the present age, everyone is an artist. Everyone is into making stuff, either stationery or fashion or any other craft. Making stuff is not easy. It takes huge effort to turn your imagination into reality.

The final product you see in the market or on Pinterest is not made instantly; it takes several hours of hard work to sketch, cut, draw, glue, color, and pack.

Cricut machines are available in the markets to reduce the extra tiresome work of cutting. It is a new-age machine for the crafters as it helps to cut down various materials with precision and without any error.

Several Cricut machines are in the market, and crafters never hesitate to try them to enhance their craft and make things.

This book provides complete details regarding the machine's know-how and the things it can cut, and some beginners' project ideas.

Chapter 1: Cricut Machine

A Cricut is a machine that helps you cut and make exquisite crafts from materials you didn't even know existed. That's the short explanation.

You can also draw, emboss, and manufacture folding lines to create 3D projects, greeting cards, boxes, etc., based on the model you have.

For people who enjoy crafting and for people who need to cut a lot of stuff and various kinds of materials, the Cricut is the best tool. In markets, various brands of Cricut machines are available.

Apart from the machine, various other accessories are available to make it more reliable for cutting more complex materials and fabrics with precision. Not only cutting, but the machines can do a lot more like coloring, designing, engraving, etc., on the desired material.

Chapter 2: Cricut Explore Air 2

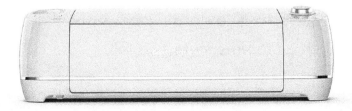

In late 2016, the Cricut Explore Air 2 was launched, packed with features that made it the most versatile and fastest cutter in the market. It quickly sold out and proved to be a long-lasting favorite among crafters.

Over time, it's gotten even more accessible and has become one of the best deals on a home vinyl cutter one can get. With a double rapid mode to cut the materials, the Explore Air 2 is the fastest home cutter you can find anywhere and is one of the best cutters in the market. It looks great and is a joy to use.

The Cricut Explore Air 2 is a beautiful tool with helpful features, such as the double tool holder and double fast mode, to make your cutting tasks a success. From vinyl and cardstock, it can cut complex and challenging, and consistent designs and can also withstand thicker materials such as foam sheets and felt.

For crafters, it's a perfect pick, and it makes a beautiful gift, too. But what exactly is the Cricut Machine Explorer? The best answer is that the Cricut Machine Explorer is an automated cutting unit that looks kind of like a printer, but it uses an exact blade and a set of rollers to cut out nearly everything you might conceive, including vinyl stickers, decals for clothes, paper crafts, and more, instead of printing the designs on paper.

The Cricut Explore differs from the older Cricut devices (like the Expression, the Gypsy, etc.) You will have access to Cricut Access and their vast library of cut files instead of cartridges. Your files can be uploaded and split. On your device or phone, online or off, you can use the app. About 100 different materials are cut. With it, you can also sketch, rate, and compose.

This machine is indeed masterfully engineered, and the accuracy with which it cuts materials never fails to amaze. At its most simple, the Cricut Design Space program can design something you want to cut; all you are required to do is position the material on the cutting pad, validate the settings and Eureka!

The applications are well beyond the scrapbooking domain for the Cricut Explore unit. Cricut Explore Air 2 is best for you to build new creations in a fun way. You can cut as well as write up to two times faster with this speed machine.

This device has it all, perfect for beginners and seasoned crafters alike. Laden with the latest features for a job done right with every use, these devices encourage you to take control of your artistic side in vivid detail to bring your dreams to life.

This book helps you know everything you need to know about these machines and provides you with the projects you can easily make with them.

Chapter 3: Setting up Cricut Explore Air 2

Items in the Packaging Box

The package includes the following items:

- Cricut machine.
- A user's manual.
- A cutting mat.
- An accessory adapter.
- A cutting blade.
- Power cable.
- Pen.
- A cardstock.
- USB cords.
- Vinyl samples.

Configuration of the Machine

The machine is a box that has the following attachments:

1. **Tool cup:** It holds the scissors, pins, pen, threads, or other things that are in use.

2. **Smart set dial:** To pick the material you will be cutting; you must rotate the dial. With two times quick mode, it feels nice to transform and shows which materials you should cut.

3. **The mat for cutting and holding:** This is used as the base to load the materials into the Cricut machine. It's sticky on one side for holding the material securely.

4. **Clamp a-accessory:** This is the part where the accessory adapter is installed and where one can insert a pen for drawing when one is not cutting.

5. **Clamp b-blade:** The blade is already installed, and if you need to replace it or remove vinyl bits, this is where you have to look.

6. **Accessory storage compartments:** Besides the tool cup, there are two storage places in the Explore Air 2. The smaller chamber is used to hold the additional blade housings, blades, and the accessory adapter. For holding longer tools/pens, the larger compartment is used.

What Comes in Addition to Machine Setup?

Apart from the machine set, the package includes many to make easy for you to start with your projects. Some items that come in the box with the Cricut machine are stated as under.

Basic Set of Tools

- Three packs of cutting mat variety.
- A deep cut blades.
- Gold multi pen set.
- Some vinyl pieces.
- Dry erase vinyl.
- Black multi-point pens.
- Scoring stylus.
- German carbide replacement blade.
- Window cling material.
- Trimmer tool.
- Outdoor glossy vinyl.
- One metallic poster board.
- Pieces of faux leather.
- Washi sheets.
- Printable iron-on.
- Chalkboard vinyl.

How to Connect the Machine to Your PC/MAC/iPad for Designing

Although the Cricut Explore Air 2 can be used wirelessly, it is convenient to set it up with a USB cable.

Start by putting it behind it on a surface with at least 10″ available as the cutting mat travels within the unit back and forth. Then follow the following steps:

For the Windows/Mac

- Plugin the device and then turn it up.
- Link the unit to your device, or pair it with Bluetooth with a USB cable.
- Use the browser to go to design.cricut.com/setup.
- Upload Design Space for Desktop and install it.
- Sign in or build your Cricut ID, obey the on-screen instructions, and set up your new device.
- When you are asked to make a test cut, you will know the setup is completed.

For iOS/Android

- Plugin the device and then turn it up.
- Pair your Android or iOS smartphone via Bluetooth with the Cricut screen.
- Download the Design Space software and install it.

- Start the program, then log in or generate a Cricut ID.

- Tap the menu and pick the System Settings.

- To complete the configuration, pick your machine model and follow the on-screen prompts.

- When you are asked to do a test cut, you will know the setup is completed.

Chapter 4: Essential Accessories

The Cutting Mat

The cutting mat is the essential attachment, which is how most material is inserted into the unit. On the one hand, it's sticky enough that whether it's sliced, dyed, or etched, the substance is tightly fixed in place.

The basic mat is available in three kinds. Each is used for a distinct set of products, or depending on what you normally work with; you may pick all three.

Light Grip (Blue)

The blue-colored mat has a light grip, and the following materials stick to it before letting them into the machine.

- Construction paper.
- Light cardstock.

Scrapbook paper

- Printer paper.
- Vellum.

Standard Grip (Green)

The green-colored mat has a standard grip and is used to hold the following materials:

- Regular and embossed cardstock.
- Regular vinyl.
- Window clings.
- Heat transfer (iron-on).
- Vinyl.

Strong Grip (Purple)

The purple-colored mat has a firm grip and is used for holding the following mentioned materials:

- Backed fabric.
- Corrugated cardboard.
- Leather.
- Suede.
- Foam.
- Posterboard.
- Chipboard.
- Wood.
- Magnetic material.

Craft Basic Set-Cricut Tools

This is the bundle of valuable tools that the machine needs when working with it. The following are included in this pack:

- **Scissors:** It is well known to all what the scissors do. As per the specifications, they are used to cut the cloth and the paper sheets.

- **Tweezer:** They are reverse gripped, which means the handle is twisted to open and released to close. It is used to tie the materials together until they dry and perform several other minor tasks.

- **Scraper:** It is used for dealing with vinyl and even for cleaning the cutting pad, which is vital.

- **Spatula:** It is used to lift gently the material off the cutting mat before applying it anywhere else.

- **Weeder:** It helps to strip the vinyl from the liner or to remove tiny cuts.

Chapter 5: Starting up the Design Space

The machine works wonders when it gets a particular command. But how exactly it gets its command. The answer is simple- through the Design Space.

After you bring the machine home and set it up, you need to connect it with your computer, and hence you'll need to download and install Design Space on your computer to let your machine work more efficiently.

How to Download and Install Design Space

This designing application can be easily installed on the Windows or Mac computer and both iOS or Android devices.

Instruction to download and install the Design Space app on your Windows computer:

- Open the web and go to design.cricut.com.

- Download the app.

- Double-click the file in your update folder when the download is over.

- The window opens and asks for approval from you. Give your consent.

- Afterward, a configuration window will display the status of the installation.

- Now, sign in.

- A Design Space for desktop icon will add to your desktop screen.

- Enjoy using your Design Space.

Instruction to download and install the Design Space app on your Mac computer:

- Open the web and go to design.cricut.com.
- Download the app here.
- When the update is complete, in the downloads folder, double click the .dmg file.
- To begin the installation, drag the Cricut icon onto the applications folder icon. You immediately assign design space for desktop to the applications list.
- Double-click on the Cricut Design Space in your applications folder to launch Design Space for desktop.
- It will appear that a Mac note asks if you want to access the downloaded program from the internet. To proceed, click open.
- Now, sign in.

Instruction to download and install the Design Space app on your iOS devices:

- Head to the iOS device's app store.

- A white square with a green "C" logo in the middle appears as the Cricut Design Space app.

- To download the app and check the download with your iTunes password, press the get button.

- The app will open and display options for completing the latest system configuration or continuing to the app summary until the update is completed.

- Simply press the "X" in the upper right corner to reach the landing page, sign in, and start creating on the go if you don't want to do either.

Instruction to download and install the Design Space app on your Android:

- Use the Google Play Store app on your smartphone to download the app.

- A white square with a green Cricut "C" logo in the middle appears as the Cricut Design Space app.

- To download and update the software, press the Install button.

- The app will appear on your app home screen until the installation is completed.

- To open the app, tap on the button, sign in, and start designing on the go!

System Requirements for Using Design Space

Design Space is a free design software available for Windows, Mac, iOS, and Android for Cricut's smart cutting machines.

For the program, below are the latest minimum device specifications. The requirements change with time. The below stated are the recent requirements.

Device Configuration

- Operating System-Windows 8 or later is optimum.
- CPU-Intel Dual-Core or equivalent AMD processor is efficient for the machine to work properly.
- 4 GB of RAM.
- 2 GB free disk space.
- A USB port or Bluetooth connection.
- 1024px x 768 pixels of screen resolution-Display.

Internet Requirements

- Broadband connection.
- Minimum 2–3 Mbps Download speed.
- Minimum 1–2 Mbps Upload speed.
- Standard data rates may apply.

Working with the Design Space

Design Space is the designing app that is compatible with your Cricut Explore Air 2 machine and does most of your work. It's an easy-to-use application and, as stated earlier, can be downloaded and installed on your respective computer devices.

After you install and sign up for the Design Space app, you are good to go. Follow the below-mentioned steps to work on the Design Space app:

- First, you need to download the design you want to cut or engrave on the desired material. You can even take pictures of your day-to-day life via your camera or mobile phone. Then import it into the device through which you are using your Design Space app.

- Afterward, open the app and select the desired image or the design you need to work on.

- The selected design would appear on your work screen, and from there, you will find various tools and options to edit the design as per your liking. You can change the color, the contrast, the hue, the sharpness of the design.

- After editing the design, load the material on the cutting mat in the machine.

- Then select the settings for the material and the blade.

- Arrange the design on the virtual mat that would appear on your screen.

- Then press continue, the machine would start working, and you will get your design in no matter of time.

- Carefully remove the material from the mat, and voila!

- It is highly recommended for you to save your design for further usage.

Chapter 6: Materials Your Cricut Machine Can Work with

Your Cricut machine can cut several materials and can do a lot more things on them. Every material can be cut with a specially designed blade that comes with the machine. All you need to do is attach the right blade, fix the material on the right cutting mat, and set all the required material and blade settings on the mat and go.

Papers

Paper is an easy alternative because it has been the key material used for too long, but a wide range of papers can be cut and designed with your Cricut machine. It will help if you use a standard grip mat to hold these.

These can be cut using a fine pony blade. Some are listed below:

- Adhesive cardstock.
- Watercolour paper.
- Cereal box.
- Wax paper.
- Flat cardboard.
- Construction paper.
- Flocked cardstock.

- Paper board.

- Cardstock.

- Scrapbook paper.

- Solid core cardstock.

- Flocked paper.

- Craft board.

- Shimmer paper.

- Glitter paper.

- Kraft board.

- Foil embossed paper.

- White core cardstock.

- Copy paper.

- Foil poster board.

- Freezer paper.

- Glitter cardstock.

- Kraft paper.

- Post-its.

- Poster board.

- Rice paper.

- Parchment paper.

- Pearl cardstock.

- Metallic cardstock.

- Notebook paper.

- Pearl paper.

- Photographs.

- Metallic paper.

- Metallic poster board.

- Photo framing mat.

- Paper grocery bags.

Iron-On Vinyl

Iron-on Vinyl is prominently used on fabric based in some way, such as t-shirts, totes, napkins, etc. For iron-on vinyl, use the iron-on setting on the Cricut.

Iron-on Vinyl, also known as the heat transfer vinyl or HTV, is the most favorite material for Cricut users. These are also cut using a fine point blade. Some types of vinyl cut with the Cricut machine are stated as under:

- Sister heat transfer vinyl.

- Firefly heat transfer vinyl.

- My vinyl direct.

- Fame heat transfer vinyl.

- Cricut heat transfer vinyl.

Adhesive Vinyl

Adhesive vinyl is very similar to the HTV. There are many uses for adhesive vinyl, such as mugs, wall decals, containers, ornaments, wall art, etc.

Below mentioned are some of the best brands of adhesive vinyl that you can use in your projects. For it, you will always use the vinyl setting on your Cricut machine.

- Oracal vinyl.
- Expression's vinyl.
- Cricut adhesive vinyl.
- Happy crafters.

Apart from the vinyl mentioned above, following can be worked upon in the Cricut machine:

- Matte vinyl.
- Metallic vinyl.
- Outdoor vinyl.
- Chalkboard vinyl.
- Dry erase vinyl.
- Glitter vinyl.
- Glossy vinyl.
- Holographic vinyl.
- Printable vinyl.
- Stencil vinyl.

Fabric and Textiles

Fabric is a very fun material to work with on the Cricut machine. With their fabric mat, one can easily cut so different materials, including faux suede, cotton duck, burlap, and leather.

The type of blade to be used will depend on the material. The deep point blade or the rotary blade can be used to cut various types of fabric. This makes cutting fabric easy.

Following stated are some fabrics the Cricut Explore can cut:

- Burlap.
- Flannel.
- Cotton fabric.
- Faux suede.
- Denim.
- Fleece.
- Linen.
- Duck cloth.
- Metallic leather.
- Faux leather.
- Seersucker.
- Felt.

- Silk.
- Terry cloth.
- Muslin.
- Tulle.
- Jute.
- Knits.
- Printable fabric.
- Leather.
- Moleskin.
- Tweed.
- Velvet.
- Wool felt.
- Oil cloth.
- Polyester.

Other Materials

You can use many different materials, including birch wood, balsa wood, corkboard, magnet sheets, and so much more. If you wonder if the material you have can be cut, check out the list below.

For woods, stiff fabrics, thicker materials such as magnet chipboard, stiffened felt, foam sheet, and cardboard, the deep point blade is used.

You can use the Rotary Blade for lighter Cricut Explore Air 2 materials such as tissue paper, light cardstock, and acetate. You can also use the rotary blade for the corkboard and tissue paper. In terms of the mat, you will want to use the Fabric Grip Mat for these.

You can also use the Knife Blade for Balsa Wood, mat board, and chipboard. Use the Fabric Grip Mat or the Strong Grip Mat for this.

Some materials that Cricut can cut are listed below:

- Adhesive foil.
- Printable magnet sheets.
- Shrink plastic.
- Aluminum sheets.
- Cork board.
- Washi tape.
- Duct tape.
- Printable sticker paper.
- Window cling.
- Corrugated paper.
- Embossable foil.
- Balsa wood.
- Wood veneer.

- Craft foam.

- Aluminum foil.

- Wrapping paper.

- Birch wood.

- Metallic vellum.

- Foil acetate.

- Stencil material.

- Glitter foam.

- Magnet sheets.

- Paint chips.

- Transparency film.

- Adhesive wood.

- Plastic packaging.

- Soda can.

- Tissue paper temporary tattoo paper.

- Vellum.

- Washi sheets.

Chapter 7: How to Earn Money with Your Cricut Machine

The people who purchased the Cricut machine had the impression that it could be expensive for this machine. But what if I told you that you could make money easily from your Cricut machine?

Yeah, a one-time investment for you to start earning is the Cricut machine.

Everyone who buys Cricut is an artist, and you will become an entrepreneur with this machine. What you need to do is start selling the creations you make with the machine.

Nowadays, everybody is a craft lover and buys everything original and artistic. You can begin your start-up with the aid of this machine.

You can create an online page or website and highlight your designs. You will then seek orders for the ventures easily and gain simple money by selling them.

Via Cricut Explore, making money is not limited to selling the goods you produce from the machine. You may also market the designs to be used by other individuals.

You make out of the machine. You can also sell your designs for other people to use.

Offer your creativity a boost and design as many files for SNG and PNG and sell them for using by other Cricut users online. It's a good sales stream.

You can start writing your blog on using the Cricut machine because it is not an old idea, and more and more people are eager to learn about the Cricut machine's features, use, and functionality.

It is a rising topic, and as more people are interested to learn new topics in the modern period, the reach is increasing.

You can invest conveniently in the machine and yearn income from it, whether you are a mother or a craft enthusiast. It's a no-lose gamble, and it's a simple money game from a market point of yours.

After making products and selling them, all you have to do is have fun.

It's a no-brainer and quick method to make fast money, so this is for you if you love to make things. So, go with it. Oh, good luck!

Chapter 8: Pros and Cons of the Cricut Machine

Every machine has both its benefits and drawbacks.

The following stated are some pros and cons of using a Cricut Explore Air 2:

Advantages of Cricut Explore Air 2

The following is stated in terms of Cricut Explore Air 2 benefits:

1. This machine cuts, writes and scores easily on the suggested fabrics.

2. It has a double accessory clamp.

3. It has a built-in Bluetooth

4. It can cut dozens of materials.

5. It can work in a fast mode.

6. It provides free access to the Design space.

7. It easily cuts SVGs and prints them.

8. You are free to upload your images in the Design Space to work.

9. It has a separate cartridge slot.

10. It is less expensive than its contemporary Cricut Explore Air.

Disadvantages of Cricut Explore Air 2

Some drawbacks of Cricut Explore Air 2 are listed under:

1. It requires bonded fabrics.

2. It is not compatible with the rotary blade, knife blade, and scoring wheels.

3. It doesn't have the best long-term value. It requires regular maintenance.

4. It cannot cut very delicate materials like crepe paper.

Thicker materials like wood cannot be cut as clean as other materials.

Chapter 9: Suggestive Tips

The following provided are some tips you might find useful while using your Cricut Explore Air 2:

1. All you need to do is pull open the lever and pull out the metal housing to remove the blade or the accessory clamp. The blade is on the inside, and the top has a small plunger. To show the blade, hold down on this one. They can stick out the blade. Take it out now and then lower the other blade.

2. Open accessory clamp A to use the pen, lower it, and then close the clamp. The pen is going to be ready for use.

3. Your sign-in recalls the Design Space app. You will not have to sign in any time you launch until you have signed out of the last session.

4. There is no auto-save from the Design app. Save your projects often when you plan the program and before you leave.

5. The Cricut Design Space app can also be downloaded from the Play store and conveniently used with your android cell phone.

Chapter 10: Frequently Asked Questions

How Is Cricut Explore Air 2 Different from Cricut Explore Air?

The Explorer Air and the Explorer Air 2 look the same and have the same features.

The only differences between the two models are color and speed.

The Explore Air 2 has a double fast mode, which works with vinyl, iron-on, and cardstock.

Can Explore Air 2 Be Used Without Bluetooth?

Yes, it can. Just follow the step-by-step instructions given in the user's manual.

Is a Bluetooth Adapter Needed for Explore Air 2?

No, it is not needed as it has a wireless module built-in.

Is the Design Space App Compatible with All the Devices?

Design Space application is not compatible with Chromebooks or Unix/Linux Computers.

Is Cricut Machine Expensive?

To be quite frank, a Cricut machine can be expensive depending on the model you buy, but it's completely worth it, and you can also earn via your Cricut machine.

Are Cricut Materials Expensive?

Cricut supplies can be relatively expensive, depending on the projects you choose to cut.

This is why the unit that will also enable you to buy items to cut should be bought.

Materials such as basswood can also be very expensive. Therefore, you should use paper if you are a beginner.

Paper is the safest way for you to master the machine, and it's all paper if you cut anything incorrectly.

Can Off-Brand Materials Be Cut Using a Cricut Machine?

Yes, they can. You don't have to be limited to the materials that Cricut makes.

There are many amazing materials you can work with the machine.

Chapter 11: DIY Projects for Beginners

Crafting and imagination have no limit and are inexhaustible.

You can start using the Cricut Explore to define your imagination and craft.

In this chapter, some project ideas have been provided for you to learn the use of Cricut.

The ideas are not restricted to what is provided in this chapter, but you can use your skill in designing various designs and SVG files.

You can also click pictures and turn them into PNG files and transfer them onto your respected fabrics.

Below provided are some projects you can try with ease and learn the Cricut machine's working.

Christmas Tea Towels

Materials/tools:

- Cricut Explore Air 2 cutting machine

- Cricut Design Space account

- Cricut fine point blade

- Iron-on

- Leaf cut design

- Easy press mini

- Kitchen towel

Instructions:

1. Open the Design Space cut file of your liking or make your own design and scale it to suit your tea towel.

2. Put the iron on a cutting mat, don't forget to mirror the cut and place it on the polished mat side.

3. Cut the project.

4. Delete the iron-on waste.

5. From the cutting mat, remove the file.

6. Press on a smooth tea towel with the pic.

7. Cut the sheet from the carrier, and you are finished.

Love You, Gift Tag

Materials/tools

- Cricut Explore Air 2
- Design Space account
- Card stock
- Gold colored glitter pen

Instructions:

1. Draw and cut each layer as needed by first designing it in the app and then cutting the material after required settings.

2. Glue the two layers of paper together, aligning the opening at the top of the tag that is heart-shaped.

3. Attach the vinyl to make sure it is cleaned so that it adheres thoroughly.

4. To the tag hole, apply a ribbon or twine and tie the tag to the gift.

5. Draw on the gift-tag using your glitter.

Iron-on Vinyl on Wood

Materials / Tools

- Wood Plaque
- Iron-On Vinyl
- Weeding Tool
- Cricut Explore Air 2
- Cricut Easy Press
- Love Grows Here SVG

Instructions

1. Download the SVG file from the web or use the Cricut Design Space app or some other design app to build the design.

2. Set the iron-on machine to

3. Lay the glossy side of iron-on vinyl flat on the mat

4. Mirror your image

5. Then cut the picture, and the residual vinyl is weeded out.

6. For iron-on vinyl-300 ° and 40 seconds, turn Simple Press on and set it to the right wood configuration.

7. Then use the Simple Button to press the vinyl flat. Between Quick Press and the vinyl, using a cotton cloth piece makes sure you have all the movement parts.

8. The backing plastic is then gently stripped off. If the vinyl pieces haven't adhered to the wood, just give them an extra press.

Valentine's Day Garland

Materials/tools:

- Heart cards and envelope

- Cricut Explore Air 2

- Mega runner

- Foam dots

- Scissors

- White glitter cardstock

- Twine

Instructions:

1. Lay the twine over the fold and open the card.

2. To add some adhesive to the top of the heart and the foot, use your super racer.

3. Fold-out the closed card.

4. Cut the XO photos out of the cardstock shimmer by using the Design Space App.

5. Add foam tape to each letter's back and stick to it.

6. And voila!

Love is Our Religion Pillow Cover

Materials/tools:

- Cricut Explore Air 2
- Cricut tools
- Cricut Design Space
- Cricut mat
- Pillow cover
- Png image
- Cricut glitter iron-on vinyl; red
- Cricut bright pad
- Cricut easy press
- Linen cloth

Instructions:

1. Upload the PNG file "Love is our Religion" to Cricut Template Space Scale the picture on your pillow to how big you want it (or even a shirt or a bag or whatever you want to place this on).

2. Then pick the picture to be sliced. Since you are using iron-on vinyl, remember to mirror the pic.

3. Let your Cricut Explore Air 2 do the next job.

4. Pull the pattern from the mat carefully. Start to weed the negative from the iron-on vinyl using Cricut methods such as the flat spatula and weeding tool.

5. First, fire up the Quick Press Cricut and stick your template to your pillow cover. Make sure the push directions for pressing the pillow are followed.

6. The pillow cover, simple as that, is over.

Thanksgiving Kitchen Towel

Materials/tools:

- Cricut Explore Air 2
- Easy press
- Cricut Design Space account
- Leaf design
- Iron-on
- Kitchen towel

Instructions:

1. To suit your kitchen towel, first open the designing app, download a file, design it, and scale it.

2. Put the iron on the cutting mat, mirror the image, and place it down on the side of the shiny mat.

3. Send a cut to the project.

4. Remove the iron-on waste.

5. Remove the photo from your mat.

6. Press it on your kitchen towel.

7. Take the sheet from the carrier, and you are done.

Personalized Phone Case

Materials/tools:

- Cricut Explore Air 2

- Clear phone case

- Foil adhesive vinyl or standard permanent vinyl

- Transfer tape

- Cricut design space files for cherries, pineapples, and watermelon

Instructions:

1. Open and size the template space cut file that you downloaded from the web or designed on your own to fit your phone case.

2. Place the iron on a cutting pad and do not forget to mirror the cut and place it down on the side of the shiny mat.

3. Cut the project.

4. Remove the iron-on waste.

5. Remove the photo from the cutting mat. By separating the mat from the tags, keep your tags from curling. There are pliable pads.

6. Use your clear phone case to click the image.

7. Take the sheet from the carrier, and you're done.

Don't Let it Snow Mugs

Materials/tools:

- Clear mug
- Design Space
- Cricut Explore Air 2
- Adhesive vinyl
- Transfer tape
- Scraper tool
- Weeding tool

Instructions:

1. Download the SVG file from the web or use the Cricut Design Space app or some other design app to build the design.

2. Set the vinyl mode on your computer.

3. Place the vinyl on your mat.

4. Mirror your image.

5. Then cut the picture, and the residual vinyl is weeded out.

6. Then add and brush the transfer tape over the pattern until it adheres to it.

7. Then add it and rub it over on the transparent cup so that the logo gets stuck on the cup.

8. The backing plastic is then gently stripped off. If the vinyl components haven't adhered to the cup, just give them an extra press.

Multiple Layer Snowflake Winter Crafts

Materials/ tools:

- Cricut Explore Air 2 cutting machine

- Cricut Access

- Snowflake SVG file

- Light blue felt

- Holographic iron-on vinyl

- White glitter iron-on vinyl

- Twine

- Iron or Easy Press

Instructions:

1. To Cricut Design Space, upload the snowflake SVG file.

2. Resize the 3" large style, ungroup the layers and cover all the drawing lines.

3. For blue felt, set the backdrop sheet.

4. For holographic iron-on, set the precise top layer pattern.

5. For white glitter iron-on vinyl, set the leaf shape info.

6. To cut the multiple layers, obey on-screen directions.

7. At least 10'' high cut a slice of twine. Place the blue felt twine next to the tip of one of the arms of the snowflake.

8. As you click it, Iron-on, the holographic iron-on vinyl means that the twine is between the felt and the vinyl.

9. Iron the vinyl with a white glitter in place.

10. At the top of the snowflake, tie the twine into a little bow. For your decoration or gift tag, tie a knot at the end of the twine to make a hanging loop.

11. Cut out a little card and a selection of envelopes.

12. To match the front of the card, cut a piece of silver-glitter vinyl. Place the vinyl on the card's front.

Friends Thanksgiving Shirt-Here Comes the Meat Sweats

Materials/tools:

- Cricut Explore Air 2
- Cricut Easy Press, heat press, or iron
- Heat transfer vinyl
- Cricut Design Space
- Weeding tool
- Plain shirt

Instructions:

1. Download the SVG file from the web or use the Cricut Design Space app or some other design app to build the design.

2. Set the iron-on machine.

3. Lay the glossy side of iron-on vinyl flat on the mat.

4. Mirror your image.

5. Then cut the picture, and the residual vinyl is weeded out.

6. To iron vinyl, do so at 305°F for 30 seconds, switch on easy press, and set it to the right wood setting.

7. To get the moisture out, preheat the clothes.

8. Then use the simple button to press the vinyl flat. Between quick press and the vinyl, using a cotton cloth piece makes sure you have all the moving parts.

9. The backing plastic is then gently stripped off. Only give them an extra press if pieces of vinyl have not adhered to the fabric.

Infusible Ink Tote Bag

Materials/tools:

- Cricut Explore Air 2
- Cricut mat
- Blank tote bag
- Easy Press 2
- Easy Press 2 Mat
- Transfer sheet
- Tweezers
- Heat-resistant tape

- White cardstock
- Butcher paper
- Lint roller

Instructions:

1. Build your idea in the Design Space app.

2. Resize it so that it suits your tote.

3. In the upper right corner, press Make It. Make sure to mirror your picture. Select continue.

4. Pick the infusible ink transfer sheet as the make screen content.

5. Ensure that you have inserted the fine point blade.

6. Place the liner on the side of the infusible ink transfer sheet on a green cutting pad.

7. Then insert and cut into your machine.

8. You need to pack your tote bag before you do your transfer. With a white piece of cardstock on top, begin by placing your Easy Press Mat inside your tote bag.

9. Then use a lint roller to clear your tote bag from any dust and dirt.

10. For cricut infusible ink switch, use the simple press.

11. Next, cover the butcher paper that came with the transfer sheet with your blank tote bag.

12. Before applying for your transfer, preheat your bag to flatten your surface and dry some moisture in the bag itself. Press and let it cool absolutely for 15 seconds.

13. You can add your transfer until your bag is fully cooled.

14. On top of the move, put the butcher paper back. Then press your simple press carefully (or use your heat press) with light but constant pressure on your project.

15. Be sure that the Easy Press protects the whole move.

16. Let the transfer cool and pick it up carefully.

Pinecone Earrings

Materials/tools:

- Cricut Explore Air 2

- Strong grip cutting mat

- Masking tape

- Deep cut blade

- Cricut wood veneer

- Pinecone earrings SVG file

- Scraper or tweezer tools

- Fish-hook earring findings

- Jump rings

- Jewelry pliers

Instructions:

1. Start by uploading or making your own design of the pinecone earring in Cricut Design Space.

2. By using the edit toolbar, resize it according to your likings.

3. If you're about to make your earrings on the upper left, click Make It. You'll see the two mats for this project on the prepare screen.

4. To build your idea, click on continue.

5. For your earrings, cut your wood veneer.

6. You'll set your material on the make screen to veneer.

7. Using the brayer to get it to stick uniformly, put the veneer on the Cricut mat with the grain running from the top of the mat to the bottom. If your mat is on the older side, to help prevent the veneer from moving, you should put masking tape on all four sides of your project.

8. Ensure that your deep cut blade is in your unit, insert your mat, and cut your veneer with your Cricut.

9. Cover from the mat the veneer.

10. It can be tricky to extract any project from a Cricut mat, but you don't want to crack the veneer project.

11. Using your hand to hold the veneer flat on the surface, you will put the mat face-down on the table and gently peel the mat away from the veneer. If you choose, you can use a scraper, spatula, or tweezers.

12. It's time to assemble your earrings until you get all layers cut. Stack the two pieces of the veneer earring together, then slip into the hole with the hop ring.

13. Add the finding of the fish-hook earring (make sure it's in the correct direction).

14. Using the pliers, snap the jump ring closed. You would most likely have to twist the bottom of the fish-hook earring 90° with the pliers so that the earrings hang properly.

15. You are done.

Cookies for Santa Tray

Materials/tools:

- Cricut Explore Air 2
- Cricut cutting mat
- Weeding tool
- Scraper
- Vinyl-black and red
- Transfer tape
- Metal tray

Instructions:

1. Upload the file from the web to Cricut Design Space or make your very own design.

2. Afterward, make sure that the settings of the machine are on vinyl.

3. Cut the pieces from adhesive vinyl, load it on the mat, and then let it slide in the cutting machine.

4. After the machine is done with the cutting, weed your adhesive vinyl pieces.

5. Use transfer tape to adhere the two layers to the tray. And you're done.

Hot Cocoa Mug Gift

Materials/tools:

- Cricut Explore Air 2

- Blue or green cutting mat

- Three colors of permanent vinyl

- Weeding tool

- Transfer tape

- White mug

- Hot chocolate ingredients

- Crinkle paper filler

- Ribbon for decoration

Instructions:

1. Download the SVG file from the web or use the Cricut Design Space app or some other design app to build the design.

2. Set the vinyl mode on your device.

3. Place the vinyl on your mat.

4. Mirror your image.

5. Then cut the image, and the residual vinyl is weeded out.

6. Then add and brush the transfer tape over the pattern until it adheres to it.

7. On the clear mug, then add this and rub it over so that the design gets stuck on the mug.

8. The backing plastic is gently stripped off. If the vinyl components haven't adhered to the mug, just give them an extra press.

9. Fill the paper filler at the bottom of the mug, and you cannot miss the goodies to make the hot chocolate—hot chocolate mix, mini marshmallows, and a candy cane. String a bow and you are ready to give your present.

Faux Leather Cross Earrings

Materials/tools:

- Faux suede

- Fishhook earring findings

- Cricut Explore Air 2

- SVG image

- Poker

- Needle-nose pliers

Instructions:

1. Start by uploading or making your own faux leather earring design in Cricut Design Space.

2. By using the edit toolbar, resize it according to your likings.

3. If you're about to make your earrings on the upper left, press Make It. You'll see the two mats for this project on the prepare screen.

4. To do your project, click on continue.

5. Set the material settings and put the material in your machine.

6. Remove it from the mat until the material is cut.

7. Then cut a tiny hole in the top of the teardrop shape with your poker. It should be from the top around 1/16''.

8. Open the ring at the bottom of the fish-hook earring with your needle-nose pliers. Using the hole, you just punched, slip the teardrop onto the earring and clamp the ring back in place.

9. They are up and ready to wear!

Funny Christmas Socks with the Cricut

Material/tools:

- Cricut Explore Air 2

- Green Standard Grip Mat

- Weeder

- Cricut Easy Press Mini

- Pressing mat

- Iron-on vinyl

- Socks

Instructions:

1. Upload the socks design from the web to your designing app or create your very own design.

2. As per your likings, select the color and size of the socks to fit your socks.

3. Afterward, load the material on the mat, set the material settings on the machine, and let the machine do its work.

4. After the machine is done cutting, cut the pieces from the vinyl.

5. Weed the iron-on vinyl pieces.

6. Adhere to the iron-on decals at the base of the socks.

7. You are done.

Gift Card Holder

Materials/tools:

- Cricut Explore Air 2

- Green standard grip mat

- Scoring wheel or scoring stylus

- Supplies

- Scrapbook paper or cardstock four colors

- Tacky glue

- Glue dots or another adhesive

Instructions:

1. In Cricut Design Space, set up the gift card file, so it scores accordingly. You can also make your own design in the app that suits your likings.

2. Afterward, load the material on the mat, set the material settings, and let the machine do its work.

3. After the machine is done cutting, remove the mat, and remove your material.

4. To create the envelope, fold and glue the cardstock.

5. Apply the insert piece to a gift card.

6. Glue and place the bow around the envelope. A gift to anyone.

New-born Footprint Ornaments

Materials/tools:

- Cricut Explore Air 2

- Green standard grip mat

- Weeding tool

- Easy press mini or iron

- Pressing mat

- Supplies

- Iron-on vinyl brown

- Wood slice ornament 3.5" or larger

- Ribbon or twine

Instructions:

1. Upload your footprint ornament to your designing app from the web, and by using the tools, remove the background.

2. You can either make your own design or have the baby's real footprint; you can add life to it. To do this, you need to paint the foot and get the foot mark on a sheet and then click its picture via your camera. Then upload the image of that clicked image to the design space app and edit it however you wish.

3. Save the image in the app.

4. Separate the footprints and reposition them to suit an ornament by using the contour tool.

5. Cut out the iron-on vinyl bits.

6. Weed the vinyl bits with iron-on.

7. Adhere the iron-on bits to the ornament of the wood.

8. Afterward, hang it with a ribbon.

Teacher Koozie

Materials/tools:

- Cricut Explore Air 2

- Pre-made blank cozies

- Cricut iron-on lite

- Iron or Cricut Easy Press

- Ironing board or Cricut Easy Press Mat

Instructions:

1. Collect supplies.

2. Download and upload an SVG, DXF, EPS, or PNG file to Cricut Design Space from the web, or you can make your design.

3. Dependent on the scale of your koozie, size the picture

4. Make sure a mirror image is used, put the shiny side down on the mat, and then cut the frames.

5. Then weed the image out.

6. To iron the koozie, use an iron or a simple press. Hold the Easy Press down at 250ºF for about 5 seconds. It takes no long at all.

7. Attach a drink or, as-is, offer to your teacher.

Halloween Welcome Door Mat

Materials/tools:

- Cricut Explore Air 2

- Cricut Cutting Mat

- SVG file

- Cardstock

- Plain doormat

- Fabric paint

- Stencil brush

- Painter's tape

- Gloves (optional)

Instructions:

1. Collect supplies.

2. You're going to need a plain doormat.

3. Download and upload the SVG file to Cricut Design Space or make your own design in the app.

4. Scale the image according to your doormat's size. Cut and weed the image (remove the negative part of the cut image, in this case, you will remove the letters inside).

5. To secure it, arrange the image on the doormat using painter's tape. When spreading paint in those places, you will need to be very patient.

6. To paint inside the cutout, use paint and a stencil brush.

7. To show the completed project, peel off the stencil. You don't want to leave the stencil on for a long time. The cardstock might otherwise adhere to the mat. You should fill up any spot with a black sharpie or with a small brush with more color.

8. Until putting it outdoors, let it dry for 24–48 hours

Customized Pot Holders

Materials/tools:

- Cricut Explore Air 2

- Green standard grip mat

- Weeder

- Easy press mini

- Pressing mat

- Iron-on vinyl in white

- Pot holders

Instructions:

1. Upload the file to your designing app and choose the photos according to your preferences or make your own design.

2. Weld each image so that it's cut as a single object.

3. To suit your potholders, paint the images white and resize.

4. Cut out the iron-on vinyl bits.

5. Weed the vinyl bits.

6. Adhere to the potholder, the iron-on decal.

Christmas Countdown Calendar

Materials/tools:

- Cricut Explore Air 2

- Green standard grip mat

- Weeder

- Scraper

- Magnetic chalkboard

- Adhesive vinyl white, dark pink, light pink, yellow, green, blue

- Transfer tape

Instructions:

1. To Cricut Design Space, upload the file or make your design and weld parts for cutting.

2. Break the adhesive vinyl parts.

3. Weed the vinyl adhesive bits.

4. To stick to the bigger bits on the chalkboard, use transfer tape.

5. Hand-place the tiny vinyl lights like stickers on the chalkboard.

Burlap wreath for Fall

Materials/tools:

- Straw wreath or pool noodle or foam wreath

- Burlap ribbon

- Cricut Explore Air 2

- Weeder

- Free printable or your embellishments

- Glass head sewing pins

Instructions:

1. Collect the supplies.

2. Using the burlap cloth to wrap the straw wreath.

3. For the straw wreath, pin the ends of the ribbon.

4. Cut the printable free by hand or your Cricut machine to cut the design.

5. Using push pins to tie the wreath to flowers or bats and the sky.

6. You can add ribbons and hang them anywhere in your house.

Leather Key Fob

Materials/tools:

- Cricut Explore Air 2

- Key fob designs

- Cutting mat

- Faux leather in silver, brown, and beige

- Paper crafting set

- Key rings

- Rivets

- Gorilla glue

Instructions:

1. In the designing app, open up key fob models or design your own model.

2. Select your design and set the dial to custom on the Cricut, then choose faux leather.

3. Poke holes where the rivet would go, using the piercer. For the rivet base to go in, make the hole wide enough.

4. Slip the key ring into the key fob. From the back of the key fob, drive the longer end of the rivet into all the layers. Place the top of the rivet over the rivet's base, directly place the rivet mallet on top of the rivet, and hit the mallet.

Leather Cuff Bracelet

Materials/tools:

- Small piece of leather

- Cricut Explore Air 2

- A Bracelet chain or cording

- Round nose jewelry pliers

- Deep cut blade for your Cricut Explore

- Small jump hoops (2) (Optional)

Instructions:

1. To create the design, look for lace, pick a picture from the design space gallery.

2. Set the acceptable size afterward and first cut it on paper. Then cut the design on your leather until you believe a suitable size has been cut.

3. Remove the leather gently from the mat.

4. Take the chain or chord afterward and assemble the bracelet. With little hoops, tie the chain to the leather.

5. All you'll get after you tie the chord with the leather pattern is a pretty bracelet that you can give to anybody.

Stencil Design

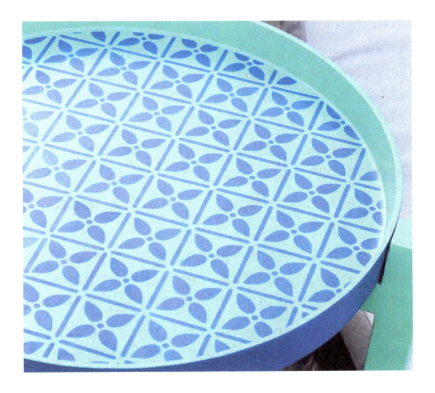

Materials/tools:

- Cricut Explore Air 2

- Standard grip cutting mat

- Cricut stencil vinyl

- Essential tool set

Instructions:

1. In a new project inside Design Space, incorporate a square shape.

2. To turn a square into a thin bar, activate the square (click on the padlock icon on the square's bottom). Insert and connect a rounded triangle from the photos in Cricut to the end of the bar.

   Duplicate the triangle, turn it (a mirror image) horizontally and tie it to the other end of the bar.

3. Choose the bar and all triangles and weld together the forms.

4. Switch to a 45° angle and duplicate the newly shaped pointed end bar three times. Flip horizontally and put 2 of the bars into a rectangle.

5. Insert a loop and a teardrop from the photos on Cricut. Three times, repeat the teardrop and resize and align the teardrops, and circle accordingly. To build the tile, solder all the elements together.

6. Duplicate the tile and line it up in the center by overlapping the bars. Weld together the two tiles.

7. Continue to duplicate and weld tiles together until the appropriate size is the custom stencil style.

8. Insert a rim shape (in this situation, you will insert a 13″ circle) to make a round stencil. To pick them and then slice the image, click on the circle and the stencil design.

9. You can remove the design outside of the circle until the custom stencil design is cut and delete the circle itself.

10. You are now ready for your unique stencil pattern to be cut. Switch the dial to custom on your Cricut Explore Air and pick stencil content from the drop-down menu.

Working with your custom stencil:

1. On a standard grip cutting mat, cut the stencil on your Cricut Explore Air 2, carefully peel back the mat from the stencil material, and trim it with scissors to size.

2. With the Cricut weeder tool, weed out negative space.

3. Take the stencil gently from the backing, and position it on the surface to be painted.

4. Ensure that by pushing it down softly with the Cricut scraper tool, the stencil is snug to the surface and free of bubbles. You're good to paint then.

Floral Monogram Letters

Materials/tools:

- Cricut Explore Air 2 with rotary blade and knife blade

- Cricut fabric grip mat and strong grip mat

- Masking tape

- 1/16" basswood

- Assorted colors of felt

- Cricut patterned iron-on

- Cricut Easy Press 2

- Hot glue gun

- Brayer (optional, but helpful)

Instructions:

1. First, for the monogram letter, we have to create the floral designs, and for that, use the Design space app and use a rotatory blade to cut the shapes for the flowers.

2. Next, using the Knife Blade, cut the monogram letter from basswood.

3. After you cut both the flower content and the monogram's letter, assembling them is all you need.

4. Each flower is made from six separate parts, then stacked to create a beautiful flower, using hot-glue to assemble the peony flowers.

5. Glue together the four basswood layers and use clothespins to keep the edges in place when drying the glue.

6. Afterward, arrange the flowers according to your imagination on the basswood letter and verify how many flowers you need to create for the design.

7. Heat the Fast Press for 25 seconds at 285ºF and make the vinyl adhere to the basswood's letter.

8. Offer the edges of the letter monogram a coat of white paint to complement the vinyl's background color.

9. Now apply the monogram to the flowers and let them dry.

Harry Potter SVG Marathon Blanket

Materials/tools:

- Polyester fleece blanket

- Cricut infusible ink transfer sheet in black

- Cricut Explore Air 2

- Cricut Easy Press 2

- Cricut Easy press mat

- Butcher paper

- White cardstock

- Heat resistant tape (optional)

Instructions:

1. Open Cricut Design Space (or other software programs) to create your Harry Potter marathon blanket and upload the Harry Potter marathon's SVG file or design your own.
2. To cut the infusible ink transfer layer, use your Cricut unit.
3. Weed the infusible ink attentively. Gently bend the backing paper to "crack" the cuts open and remove the extra bits either with hands or tweezers.
4. Do not use conventional weed infusible ink weeding tools as this may allow bits of ink to be trapped in the transfer sheet, which can result in your project being moved to unnecessary ink!
5. Place a sheet of cardstock on top of the Easy Press mat and then place the blanket corner on top. Brush the entire blanket's fabrics in the same direction with your palm and put the outline of the Infusible Ink face down on top of the blanket.
6. Use heat resistant tape to help hold the pattern in place if needed.
7. Heat 2 to 400ºF on the Easy Press. Cover the Infusible Ink outline with a sheet of butcher paper and use light pressure to press with the Easy Press for 40 seconds. Please enable it to fully cool.
8. To show your cool new Harry Potter marathon blanket, peel off the transfer sheet. To become part of the cloth, the Infusible Ink fuses and mixes with the blanket.

Rock Art with Vinyl Word Art

Materials/tools:

- Cricut Explore Air 2

- Cricut Design Space account

- Rocks—washed and dried

- Paint and paint-brushes

- Sealer

- Permanent vinyl

Instructions:

1. Paint your rocks according to your liking with different colors and allow them to dry.

2. Use your Cricut machine and Cricut Design Space to cut out your vinyl word art.

3. Seal it after you've added your vinyl template.

4. Using the transfer tape until the design is finished to adhere the design to the stones you have painted.

5. To decorate painted rocks, use permanent vinyl cut with your Cricut.

6. These stones may be used as presents or as paperweights, or only as decorations.

Homemade Christmas Ornaments

Materials/tools:

- Cricut Explore Air 2

- Cricut Design Space app

- Ornament SVG cut file or your design

- White cardstock

- Glue

- Twine

Instructions:

1. To Cricut Design Space, upload the ornament cut file from the web or make your own via the app tools.
2. Ungroup the decorative sheet you'd like to use and resize it. In Design Space, make sure to set a scoreline to score.
3. Send to the mat the plan. To cut five copies of the pattern, change the cut number. Arrange as much as you like on the mat.
4. Along the scoreline, fold each cut pattern.
5. To one side of a split shape, add glue. Line up the form of the second cut, click, and keep in place to stick together.
6. Repeat until the entire cut shapes have been applied into a single 3D decoration.
7. You have two choices for adding the twine to your ornament for the application of the twine. At the neck of the ball shape, use either loop and tie the twine around the top of the ornament, or you can extend a piece of twine to the middle of the ornament until the final two sides are glued together. Be sure to build a knot at the top and bottom of the twine if you chose this form so that the twine doesn't fall out of the middle of the ornament.
8. You can hang the ornament as per your liking. You can also experiment with the designs and colors.

Wood Sign

Materials/tools:

- Cricut Explore Air 2

- Hello wood sign cut file

- Orchard patterned vinyl

- Knife blade

- Frame

- Basswood

- Masking tape

- Mini glue dots

Instructions:

1. In your designing app, open the Hello image. To your taste, adjust the scale. Click Make it and pick basswood as the material for cutting.

2. Until cutting, you can reposition your picture so that you can monitor specifically what portion of your content is cut.

3. Onto basswood, place pattered vinyl. Load the blade of the knife to make sure the star wheels are being moved to the right and cut.

4. Push carefully back on the wood around the pattern until the cut is finished and before unloading the mat to make sure it's cut all the way through. You can push the machine's go button to cut another pass if the wood doesn't seem to be cut all the way through.

5. Move the pattern softly after the mat is unloaded to release it from the rest of the wood.

6. Use tiny glue dots to stick the wood salute to the poster, and you're done.

Cork Labels

Materials/tools:

- Cork

- Cricut Explore Air 2 machine

- Vinyl

- Dollar store glass container

- Transfer tape

Instructions:

1. Begin by uploading the design to the Design Space App.

2. By simply writing the label names in various fonts of your choosing, you can create your design.

3. To weld the word together, highlight the word and press "weld" so that the Cricut will cut it in one movement.

4. Configure the cork cut second. Break the vinyl into circles such that its same dimension is the font size that is to be applied to the cork cover.

5. To stiffen it up, apply the transfer tape underneath the cork to make the cut straighter.

6. Break the vinyl afterward and then clean the excess content out.

7. Then stick the font on the cork top with the aid of the transfer tape and voila.

Unicorn Bookmarks

Materials/tools:

- Cricut Explore Air 2 machine

- Design space

- Colored paper

- Weeder tool

- Tweezers

- Black pen

- Glitter pens

- Glue

Instructions:

1. First, cut all the pieces on your Cricut machine that you will assemble at a later stage. They are:

   - **White** – Face with ears.

   - **Gold** – Horn, and star.

   - **Light pink** – Snout, inside ears and mane.

   - **Glitter purple or pink** – Flower.

   - **Teal and purple** – Mane.

2. Curl the triangular ends, so they establish the outline of the bookmark.
3. One ear of the paper is cut off, but both ears will show up when you fold it.
4. Glue the top flap's back to the front so that it is easy to attach a book page.
5. To keep the pieces properly, glue all the pieces on with the help of tweezers.
6. Attach the horn, next.
7. Then glue three layers of mane, which are slightly different sizes, so make sure that the smallest portion is first glued on top of the medium and large parts.
8. End with the star and the flower.
9. To draw the nostrils and pupils, use a thin-tipped black pen, and you are done.

Diamond Hanging Planters

Materials/tools:

- Cricut Explore Air 2

- Strong grip cutting mat

- Deep cut blade

- Chipboard

- Leather cording

- Glue gun

- Foam brushes

- Light masking tape

- Acrylic paint, sea glass & grey sky

- Wire, optional

Instructions:

1. Build the diamond design images first and submit them to the Design Space app. 2.3 wide x 2.82" should be measured by the bottom triangle panels, while the top trapezoid panels measure 2.3 wide x 0.76". You will need six panels each

2. On the cutting dial, choose the custom mode. Then pick and press GO with chipboard hard, 0.7mm.

3. Hit GO again after the first cut is completed and send it for a second time to cut properly.

4. Assemble them for gluing until all the panels are removed.

5. Line up the six triangle panels as close as possible, with a thin masking tape securing them in place.

6. Now, apply the trapezoid pieces to the top in the same manner.

7. With another sheet of light masking tape, seal off the diamond form. Often, gently tape together all the trapezoid parts so that the entire diamond form is completed before gluing.

8. Glue the diamond's outer seams with either a glue gun or rapid dry glue. The taped parts should be on the inside; make sure that any leftover adhesive is washed up. Let dry everything.

9. Take off all the tape from the inside until it's dry

10. Now, build the leather cording holes to mount them.

11. Afterward, color the entire diamond according to your choice.

12. Install the leather cording when the paint dries.

13. On the inside of the diamond planter, hot glue it or tie a knot at the end that goes on the inside of the planter.

14. For hanging, add some wire to tie the two strands together at the end.

15. Place live or artificial succulents, whatever's available, and you're done.

Wreath Slat Sig

Materials/tools:

- Cricut Explore Air 2

- Design space app

- Slat wood board

- Paint

- Vinyl

- Weeder

Instructions:

1 Start by uploading the image from the web to the space app, or you can create your own.

2 On a cutting pad, put the vinyl in the machine, set the settings, and cut out the vinyl pattern.

3 Sanding it and paint it in a tan color, get the slat wood board primed. Place the vinyl on it until the tan paint has dried.

4 Start to paint white on top of the vinyl.

5 Paint over the exterior in at least a few coats of paint.

6 Before peeling up the stencil, let it dry momentarily.

7 Peel off the vinyl stencil until it's dried and voila!

Cricut Supply Organisation

Materials/tools:

- Cricut Explore Air 2

- Vinyl storage bins

- Cricut supplies organization cut file

- Vinyl in colors of your choice

- Weeder tool

- Cricut transfer tape

Instructions:

1. Open the cut file for Cricut supplies organization in Design Room via web or create your very own file.

2. Switch the vinyl button on the Cricut Machine and cut pictures and lettering.

3. With the Weeder tool, weed out negative space.

4. Over the lettering, press transfer tape to smooth any bubbles out. Peel the vinyl liner away and add the transfer tape to the front of the vinyl pictures with the words. Smooth out the bubbles and softly peel back the design's transfer tape.

5. To add the full labels to the bins, use the same procedure, and you're done.

Treat Yourself Breakfast Tray

Materials/tools:

- Wooden breakfast tray

- Treat yourself, hand-lettered design or make your own on the Design Space app

- Cricut Explore Air 2

- Adhesive vinyl

- Transfer tape

- Pencil and paint maker

Instructions:

1. Design the font in the design space app first.

2. In the Cricut machine, put the vinyl, set the controls, and then let the machine cut the vinyl.

3. Scrape out the excess content until the machine is finished with the cutting.

4. Move the font to your wooden tray using the transfer tape and let the logo stick to the tray, and you are finished.

Team T-Shirts

Materials/tools:

- Cricut Explore Air 2

- Plain t-shirts

- Cricut Cutting Mat

- Cricut Design Space

- Iron-on vinyl

- Iron or Cricut Easy Press

Instructions:

1. In your browser, open Cricut Design Space.

2. In the top-right corner, click on new project.

3. Begin with the text. On the left-hand side, press the 'Text' button, which will generate a new text box. By using the box at the top of the mat, you can select your font. Both Cricut fonts and the fonts you have on your machine can be used.

4. First, type the team's name like mega beast and then create a second text box for "The."

5. Next, click on the picture on the left-hand side and scroll through the Cricut image library until, like a monster, you find some image of your likes. Pick the preferred image and click insert photos.

6. Click on it and then click on the weld to turn the image into a silhouette. This will combine into one of all the layers.

7. To fit the letter, turn the welded monster dark. In Design Space, find the monster layer and click on it to do so. Select the ideal hue.

8. Resize the thumbnail and put it where you want it to go. Then pick the whole template and press the Connect button.

9. In the upper right-hand corner, click on 'make it' and then click mirror. Select continue. Click Continue.

10. Set the Cricut Explore dial to load your heat transfer vinyl into your machine and onto a Cricut mat. On Cricut design room, click Go.

11. Remove the unit's mat, weed out the unwanted vinyl, and then it's time to follow the instructions on the heat transfer vinyl to adhere the pattern to the tee.

Farmhouse Style Wood Truck Sign

Materials/tools:

- Cricut Explore Air 2

- Cricut knife blade

- Strong grip mat

- Basswood

- White iron-on

- Cricut Easy Press

- Masking tape

- Paint for truck and hearts

- Hot glue

Instructions:

- Upload the truck design from the web or use the designing app to make your own.

- On the Strong Grip mat, put your basswood firmly, and tape the edges.

- Press Make it. From the content list, pick basswood and be sure that your knife blade is inserted.

- When it's carving, keep an eye on the machine. The concept takes about 20 to 30 minutes to cut off. Brush little splinters of wood down, so they're not standing in the way.

- Remove the tape gently and remove the bits which you have taken off.

- Split the white herb, iron-on, and put aside.

- Paint the bits of your truck. Give time to dry for them.

- Hot your easy press and follow the instructions in the manual for ironing on wood.

- To tie your truck and heart to the tag, use hot glue, and then you are done.

Kitchen Towels

Materials/tools:

- Cricut Explore Air 2

- Kitchen towel cut files

- Light grip cricut mat

- Cricut everyday iron-on in black

- Printable iron-on

- Cricut weeder tool

- White flour sack kitchen towels

- Easy Press or iron and press cloth

Instructions:

1. Open the Design Space app and design your kitchen towel layout.
2. Change the size of the font according to your towel size.
3. There will be three mats for the project; two for printing, then cutting images (two images per mat), and one for the text to be cut.
4. Since we're using iron-on, make sure to mirror the photos and text.
5. On the iron-on printable stuff, print the pictures.
6. Enable 5 to 10 minutes to dry before cutting.
7. Set the dial to 'Custom' on the Cricut and pick 'Iron-on, Printable' from the drop-down menu; cut photos.
8. Return to the mats for the pattern and mirror the terms. Switch to "Iron-on" the dial; cut words.
9. Remove the excess material around the cuts using the weeder tool.
10. Set the iron to a high degree. Pre-warm the iron towel and place the photo on the towel. Over iron-on, put a press cloth and press tightly with iron for 25–30 seconds. Continue to lift the whole construction area and press over it. Slowly peel back off; if any corners rise, click again. Repeat with words.
11. For the remaining three towels, repeat, and you're done.

Conclusion

Thanks for reading the book. I hope the designs have been enjoyable and easy to work with for you.

Cricut Explore is worth it, giving your inner artist a lift and encouraging you to play with fabrics and colors.

This book has offered you the information you need, and I hope all your questions about the machine are clear.

I hope you've enjoyed the book.

The projects are not exhaustive in the book. As for the artistic creativity and the availability of resources, you can modify them.

Keep cutting, continuing to craft, and keep creating stuff; many thanks and good luck.

Cricut Joy

A Beginner's Guide to Getting Started with the Cricut JOY + Tips, Tricks and Amazing DIY Project Ideas

Anita Wood

Introduction

A Cricut is an electronic cutting instrument that helps you cut and makes elegant and glorious creations from materials you did not even realize existed. It will cut many different materials for your art projects, including paper, cardstock, and vinyl.

A few Cricut machines can cut various materials, including leather, thin wood, fabric, and more. You can also emboss, draw, and produce folding lines to create 3D projects, greeting cards, boxes, etc., based on the model you own.

With the help of the Cricut machine, not only you can cut out and print a variety of etching, vinyl, or stenciling designs. But also cut fabric and more than 100 other types of materials.

For people who love crafting and for people who need to cut a lot of stuff and various materials, the Cricut is an excellent machine. It is like a combination of a laser cutter and a craft plotter (which has a knife).

The Cricut machine enables us to cut with precision since it does not cut with an x-acto or scissors, enhancing overall quality and speed. This small power tool streamlines the creative process, making it more efficient than ever before. Therefore, a Cricut machine is a dream find when it comes to crafting.

You can download their vast library of design via subscription, via purchase on a per-project basis, or upload your own files.

The guys at Cricut have revolutionized the industry as they provide a revolutionary new product for crafters called Infusible Ink!

The arrival of Infusible Ink heat transfer products has revolutionized the way your designs can be permanently imprinted. They last in the same way the project itself does. No flaking or peeling, with no cracking or wrinkling.

How Does the Cricut Machine Operate?

You can wirelessly connect a Cricut to the computer, use it to create and print project instructions, and use it to cut the project. Cricut has software known as Design Space (available for Windows, MAC, and smartphones) that enables you to produce and import machine-cut designs.

The Cricut has a blade (or a pen or a rotary cutter or a scoring tool) inside it. Once you have gained a design prepared to cut in Design Space, you can send that design from the computer to the Cricut wirelessly. Now into your machine, load your material. You will begin cutting your project with the click of a button.

What types of Cricut machines are available?

Currently, three devices fall under the Cricut family.

1. Cricut Maker

2. Cricut Explore Air 2.

3. Cricut Joy

A. The Cricut Maker

It is Circuits' top products. Although it presents a similar appearance to explore models, it has been extensively redesigned. It includes all functions of Cricut Explore but comes with additional features. The model was introduced, including the new batch of blades, allowing for the cutting of heavier materials like wood and leather. It's one of the strongest members of the Cricut family.

Cricut Maker can cut unbounded fabric, therefore doesn't need stabilizers like those required for the Cricut Explore line. It is an excellent machine if you are trying to look to go for felt crafts due to its cutting capabilities.

Cricut Maker cuts thicker materials like balsa wood and thick leather with the Knife Blade, and the blade cuts at a lower feed speed. It can provide scoring for various materials with the Scoring Wheel.

B. The Explore Family

These were the most popular models until they were discontinued last year.

The Explore One is a newer version of the Cricut machines' family, but it only sports one tool holder. This device is now no longer accessible from Cricut but could be found on a second-hand market.

Explore One is the least expensive Cricut machine to date. It has all of the cutting, writing, and scoring features of the Explore Air machines, such as paper, card stock, and more.

It is not Bluetooth-enabled (means you will need a USB cord to connect it to your desktop), and it does not come with a double tool cartridge, so you won't be able to cut or write and score in the same pass.

The Explore Air is the second generation of the Cricut brand. In this version, the cutter has a double tool holder, so you can draw and cut simultaneously. This machine adds wireless Bluetooth connection, though this machine has been discontinued but can be bought second hand.

Cricut Explore Air is a downgrade from Air 2, but it gives you the two qualities that Cricut Explore One below doesn't—Bluetooth-enabled it's so you do not have to plug it into your device, and it also has a secondary tool holder; therefore, you can score and cut or write and cut at the same time.

Explore Air 2 has the same basic features and functions as the previous versions, but it is twice as fast, and some users report that it is slightly less noisy. It can cut iron-on, vinyl, cardstock, faux suede/leather, Cricut felt, and more than 100 other products. It is an incredible workhorse machine.

Furthermore, it comes in a variety of colors to complement any craft room.

C. Cricut Joy

Cricut announced its latest cutting machine, Cricut Joy, in February 2020. Cricut Joy is a small compact cutting machine, only about half the Cricut Explore size and the Cricut Maker. The machine is pared down to just a single blade and pen holder. The cut is 4.5 inches in width.

Don't let the product's small size fool you—it's got some exciting new features! The two prominent features are 1) mat-free cutting and 2) cutting up to twenty feet of the Smart vinyl in a single go.

Cricut Joy is also a card making tool that makes it easy to create cards of all sorts.

The Joy is perfect for many of your basic Cricut projects, including iron-on vinyl, adhesive vinyl, writeable labels, and cardstock. If you are concerned about your lack of time or space or about the level of dedication needed to own a Cricut device, you should set aside all of these fears today!

Cricut Joy is for everyone, whether a beginner or a veteran crafting enthusiast.

Discontinued Cricuts

Legacy machines that are no longer being manufactured include Cricut Gypsy, Cricut Personal, Cricut Cake, Cricut Expression, and Expression 2. The machines are no longer under new and improved versions.

There has been the discontinuation of all Cricut Explore family. These three Explore devices still work with Cricut Design Space and are supported by Cricut.

Note that Cuttlebug Cricut, an entirely different machine type, is mainly used for embossing and die-cutting. The machine was discontinued in spring 2019.

What Model of the Cricut Machine Should You Get?

Personally, it depends mainly on what materials you're looking for if you're only planning to use for a paper-craft and vinyl cutting. The Cricut Explore family is sufficient for your budget. However, Cricut Joy is a great educational tool for beginners. It is practical, efficient, and easy to maintain. It's quick and easy.

There are no physical buttons to control the machine. It works on your desktop, phone, or laptop computer via Wi-Fi with space for Cricut Design. There are tons of available patterns and templates, or you can also subscribe to receive even more.

If your plans include cutting thicker materials like wood, leather, or fabrics without a stabilizer, the Cricut Maker would be the right choice.

But you will not need a cutting mat with the Joy Cricut Machine. There is now smart vinyl with thicker backs, which feed correctly in the printers. However, you may choose to use whatever kind of vinyl you have due to the variety of Cricut mats available to cut almost any surface.

Once you have a large supply of scrapbook paper and cardstock, you can make unique cards and give or sell them to friends. Cards help get you other things you can create and sell on the Web.

Even if you are not an artist, business owners can use this tool for a logo.

You can make vinyl cut lettering that displays your logo, slogan, or company name. Select and personalize your tools, equipment decor, staff shirts, and gear.

You can even use your own created designs.

It comes with a cutting blade and a range of pens to be used for drawing designs!

The Joy is lightweight, easy to carry or move. It can save you money AND make you money.

Chapter 1: The Cricut Joy

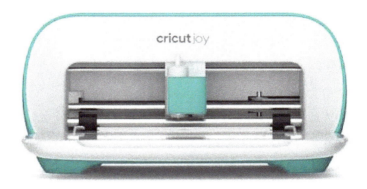

A compact crafting machine built to make crafting fast and simple is the Cricut Joy. The Cricut machines are best popular for precise cutting, but they even draw and compose if you change the blade for ink.

The Cricut Joy is the smallest device in the Cricut lineup, a scaled-down Cricut system that can be used to manufacture personalized stickers, decals, clothes, home decor, tags, paper crafts, and much more.

Cricut Joy is a small cutting machine, which is less than half of Cricut Explore and Cricut Maker size—making it ideal for those without a designated craft area. Cricut Joy is the right machine for those who want to test the Cricut to see if it works for them.

If you're like me, you've undoubtedly heard people speak about the Cricut devices; seeing "svg. Files," "layers," "weeding" all the various projects and language, it sounds overwhelming and fascinating as well.

I used to believe that markers, scissors, glue were everything I wanted, and that stuff goes a long way. Yet this little gadget will help boost your imagination, and when you display your finished workpieces, you will have profound "WOW" feelings.

Cricut Joy is crafted to be a partner device to the already owned Cricut.

Use it to create fast projects without taking out your Cricut Maker or Cricut explore or getting it working at the very same moment as your other devices.

I've got too many readers who're so worried about having to use a Cricut. Are they going to be able to work it out? Are they going to grasp all the mats, knives, equipment, and materials? Are they really going to *use* it? Cricut Joy is the right machine for entirely new Cricut users searching for a way to create fast creations without a lot of commitment.

And if you've had a Cricut for years or only took your Cricut Joy out from the package, you will love it. It's compact and light enough to fly with, making it easier to function with buddies on weekends, work on organizing tasks, or even just all over the house to make it more fun to build projects.

Looking at the Machine

Let's get to know the fundamentals first! With under 4 pounds of weight and a petite 5″ x 8″ closed dimension, the Cricut Joy packs a Lot of incredible strength inside of this tiny unit!

The absence of dials buttons on the unit is among the first things you could note about Cricut Joy. It has a super smooth, compact, and lightweight profile, and the Design Space program of Cricut manages all or most of the functions.

Only plug the unit in, and you are good to go!

What Would You Cut with the Cricut Joy?

Cricut Joy's launch also comes together with the debut of several groundbreaking new cutting products.

The complete lineup of Smart Materials, like Smart Vinyl, Smart Sticker, Smart Iron-On, and is built for even quicker and more effective cutting without a mat (I stress, WITHOUT A MAT!!!)

Cricut also sells Infusible Ink Transfer Papers, Adhesive-Backed Paper, and Transfer Tape, all of which are ideally sized to match Cricut Joy together with small-sized mats for Cricut Joy for items like paper that need one.

What's New with the Cricut Joy?

Mat-free cutting is not the only new development arriving with Cricut Joy's release, too! Now you can even make long cuts of up to 20 feet in total

Cricut Joy can create continuous figures up to 4.5'' width by 4 feet of length, and up to 20 feet long can cut repeated forms! That means you can cut a whole room full of vinyl wall stickers with one single cut! It's awe-inspiring, and it's a big time-saver.

Does Cricut Joy Draw and Write?

Cricut Joy provides far more than the opportunity to cut material, like other famous Cricut machines! A customized line of various pens (in an extensive range of colors and tips) and markers for Infusible Ink enable the device to write and draw accurately.

Just put the pen into the holder, and with ease, you can produce professional-grade cards and labels! Use pens provided with Cricut Joy on all-new Smart Label content to make decorative stickers organize your whole existence!

What Are the Card Inserts and Card Mat?

One of my absolute favorite things about Cricut Joy is its outstanding (quicker and easier!) ability to make cards. The new Cricut card and insert package allows users to make cards in minutes, ideal for all of those last-minute party scenarios!

Could You Use Cricut Joy with Infusible Ink?

If you ever decided to give Infusible Ink a shot, here is the perfect chance! For Cricut Joy, its Infusible Ink Transfer Sheets are already-sized and perfect for producing Infusible Ink projects and other stuff!

Infusible ink is a way of decorating clothes and home decor, identical to iron-on vinyl (heat transfer), but it uses a nontoxic and non-hazardous substance.

Instead, it is merely ink. When added to the cloth (or ceramic), it is fully infused into the fiber. Over repetitive cleaning, it won't peel off or rub off.

The Cricut Joy's Main Features

The Cricut is the smallest unit of the Cricut family. Yet there's so much this little unit can do!

Portable & Compact

Joy is the smallest electric smart cutting unit ever! It fits or looks fantastic on a counter and even in a cubby. Joy quickly packs up and immediately sets up, making going from room to room super convenient. Combined with the reduced material scale, not needing to carry a mat renders the entire device lightweight and versatile—no need for a craft room.

It's great for setting up parties quickly and easily! Carry the Cricut Joy to the party and decorate the table in a manner that eliminates additional decoration.

A Great Partner to Bigger Machines

Cricut Joy is the best companion for Air 2 or Your Maker! You can instantly and conveniently personalize everything with one color and one cut, only in 15 minutes or even less, right from your coffee table or kitchen counter, with this new machine. It is enjoyable, practical, and easy to use. Practical, routine projects have never been more straightforward or more available!

Joy unlocks additional artistic possibilities with exclusive features if you already have an Air 2 or a Maker and is the ideal companion for simple, mat-free, and long-lasting projects.

Optional Mats!

Joy has a complete range of innovative materials that do not need a mat, allowing fewer purchases, fewer steps, and quicker outcomes. New Smart vinyl is available in expanded sizes, with a repeated cutting capacity of up to 20' and the need to swap out several mats.

The Comparison of the Cricut Maker and Cricut Joy

Cricut Joy has certain drawbacks compared to other Cricut devices, but it has features that some machines do not provide. We are going to look at all of these:

Cricut Joy is simplistic. It does not have any keys, and when you connect it in, it is turned on.

Compared to 11.5'' on Cricut Maker and Cricut Explore, the cutting width is 4.5'' broad. It has a single tip, a blade with a fine edge—no fancy tools or specialized blades for scoring. A pen may also be used in the housing, so you have to take turns between the pen and blade.

But Cricut Joy's characteristics as never before seen are also featured. The Cricut Joy's Card Mat is my favorite, making it extremely simple to create cards.

Mattless cutting is also available for smart iron-on and smart vinyl (yes, cut without a mat!). These "smart" products have a thicker supporting material that acts as a mat, ensuring you don't need a real mat to score them.

Chapter 2: Unboxing of Cricut Joy

Circuits' packaging is indeed top-notch, and they did an outstanding job with the Cricut Joy.

It'll arrive in a standard brown package based on where you ordered the unit, and when you open it, you'll see the fancy packaging.

What's in the Box?

You'll find in the box:

- Cricut Joy with the blade and housing
- Electrical Cable
- Welcome envelope
- Pen in black 0.4 millimeters.

You'll notice the blade inside the Cricut Joy, and the housing is already mounted. And you'll see some smart sticky vinyl and a little sheet of paper for a practice project inside a welcome envelope.

The Cricut Joy comes with over 50 + Free Designs, but not inside the package.

Specifications and Set-up

While small, the Cricut Joy provides amazing stuff that some larger machines can't even do.

Are you willing to find out all the characteristics that this little device has?

- Weight: 3.9 pounds
- Measurements (In the box). 8.4 x 5.4 x 4.2 inches
- Cuts more than 50 materials
- Bluetooth Built-In (You will require a device with Bluetooth to work it)
- Cuts the "Smart" material without the Cricut Mat
- Draws on numerous material types, like "Smart writing vinyl."
- Cut a singular image up to a length of 4.5 x 4 ft. or repetitive cuts up to 20 ft.
- Offline use on a laptop or iOS device.
- Compact and highly portable. You may carry it to the home of a buddy and craft it with ease.
- The cards can quickly be produced in minutes.

- With the ability to upload your photos in the free app Design Space
- Purple Gel Pen already installed on the Cricut Joy.

One of the aspects I like about Cricut as a company the most is that they provide a first practice project for your machine.

This project of practice is a little bit distinct from the previous ones I saw. They used two different materials, some cardstock and a sheet of smart vinyl.

There was only one choice for cutting the smart vinyl in the instructions, however.

You need to link your device to your desktop, laptop, or mobile through Bluetooth and install Cricut Design Space to do the first practice project.

I was so pleased by how, without the mat, the Cricut Joy cut! The process of cutting was extremely smooth.

What Can Be Done with Cricut Joy?

About 50+ materials can be cut with the Cricut Joy. Most of them are various forms of paper and vinyl.

Still, given the scale of this unit, 50 is a substantial number.

Here's a compilation of several materials that can be cut by Cricut Joy.

- Flat Cardboard

- Foil Posterboard

- Glitter Mesh Iron-On

- Corrugated Cardboard

- Glitter Cardstock

- Smart Iron-On

- Insert Card (a Cricut Joy product)

- Holographic Iron-On

- Medium Cardstock

- Everyday Iron-On

- Cricut Infusible Ink

- Smart Iron-On Glitter

- Faux Leather (Paper-thin)

- Pearl Paper

- Sport Flex Iron-On

- Adhesive Deluxe Paper

- Adhesive Vinyl

- Foiled Embossed Paper

- Dry Erase Vinyl

- Smart Label Writable Paper

- Chalkboard Vinyl

- Sparkle Paper

- Premium Vinyl (frosted, holographic, etc.)

- Shimmer Paper

- Window Cling

- Party Foil

These are only a few implementations of this small device, and here's a collection of the other projects you might create for it.

- Organizing solutions for use in the kitchen and other parts of the household.

- Vinyl cutting for large horizontal stickers

- Stickers for your mobile, vehicle, etc.

- Cards for every occasion in even less than five minutes

- Personalize classroom chairs, educational equipment, backpacks, etc.

- Iron-On and Infusible Ink T-shirts.

Cricut Accessory Options

A Cricut Joy comes with some nice gadgets that make it much more superior. These accompaniments are essential, and so you will need them indefinitely.

The Joy Blade

The only blade on the Cricut Joy is a single "Fine Pointed Blade."

This latest cutting housing and blade is distinct from other Cricut's items and is very small.

If you're new to the world of the Cricut, you ought to learn that there are two pieces to the whole blade.

One is housing, and the other is the blade.

The housing protects the blade and its position, and the accessory you apply to your kit. The Cricut blade is positioned at the housings bottom side.

If your Cricut blade is not working as it once was, you can buy a new blade. There is no necessity to acquire a new Cricut blade housing.

The blade housing is accessible separately, but you will not want it unless you lose it or you break it.

To switch the blade, click the little pivot at the base of its housing and detach it. Then gently put the fresh blade into the socket.

The Joy Mats

Cricut Joy mats have an adhesive surface that you use on a cutting machine to hold the material in position as you cut it.

As per the Cricut Joy, there is no need for a Cricut Joy mat for materials labeling the term 'smart.' Cardstock and other products like them need a mat for cutting.

Three various kinds of mats are required for the Cricut Joy.

- Blue-Light Grip Mat: Used for copy paper, iron-on, and sticky vinyl, with thin materials

- Green-Standard Grip Mat: Used for glitter cardstock, iron-on glitter, Infusible Ink, corrugated cardboard, which are medium-weight materials

- Card Mat: Used for card inserts. Your paper could also be used and trimmed to the same scale as the card inserts.

The Standard grip and the Light Grip mats are available in two (2) sizes, 4.5 by 6.5" or 4.5 by 12".

Note: The design should not be bigger than 4.25 by 6.25/11.75 inches while you are cutting with a (blue or green) mat. And the design can't be bigger than 4.25 by 6 in when utilizing the Card Mat.

The Joy Pens

The Cricut Joy Pen is designed solely to suit and work inside the Cricut joy; thus, it cannot work with other Cricut units.

- They have a range of styles and colors, including:

- Infusible Ink Pens & Markers

- Metallic Markers

- Gel Pens

- Pink and Purple Cricut Joy Pens

- Glitter Pens

- Pink gel pen installed on Cricut Joy.

- Cricut Joy Pens assorted colors

Each of the above pens will work on "Smart Vinyl" to create tags for labeling your spice cabinet, pantry, children's toys, etc. (other than infusible ink).

The Cricut Starter Tool Package

I strongly recommend taking a beginner's tool kit to support your weed and raise your ventures off your mat if this is your first Cricut.

This kit comprises three tools;

- **Spatula:** Ideal for extracting fragile cuts, mainly while with the Card Mat.

- **Weeder:** Important for weeding ventures with vinyl (removing opposing sides).

- **Scraper:** a very flexible device that can support you smooth and clean surfaces on the Cricut Joy mat. It is a valuable instrument for conducting tape transfers.

There are several collections of more sophisticated weeding instruments. When you are going to work a ton with Vinyl, you can try them out.

The Joy Storage Bag

You should invest in their carrying case if you decide for your Cricut to craft for friends and relatives on the go.

When you intend on keeping your device at home, it is not important at all.

Cricut Joy of Raw Materials

I identify Cricut materials as the "basic materials" to build different projects with any Cricut accomplishments I have already described.

Insert Cards by Cricut Joy

Card Insert is one of our favorite Cricut items!

Together with the Joy Card Mat, the insert cards add a whole new knowledge to card making.

They have several sets of insert cards with lots of choices and are very cheap, considering it can be 4-6 dollars for a single greeting card from the shop.

This item's concept is to engrave and take-out pieces from the Card's face and put the "card insert" so that your card can pop up!

Smart Materials by Cricut Joy

Cricut also launched "Smart materials" along with the Cricut Joy. These items are connected to a thick transporter sheet that holds them in position throughout the cutting procedure.

Whenever you read the term "Smart," it indicates that you can work on the design without a mat, so that is a lovely feeling, my friend!

- **Smart Vinyl:** It is a kind of substance that clings to an extensive range of surfaces, such as metal, wood, glass, ceramic, and more.

    o The two primary vinyl forms, "Heat Transfer Vinyl" (HTV) and "Adhesive," both of which have a wide variety of possibilities.

    o Adhesive (glue) vinyl has an adhesive surface, which can also be transferred on multiple surfaces, like paper, metal, mugs, acrylic, windows, etc. It comes up to 20 feet in length! The packaging is clear, and the product can be identified.

- **Transfer tape**: You require transfer tape for transferring Adhesive Vinyl. While you could use standard transfer tape, The Cricut has also produced a transferring tape that works perfectly with "Smart Vinyl."

- **Important:** Get the High Grip transfer tape for using frosted or glitter vinyl.

- **Smart Writeable Vinyl:** The Smart Writable Vinyl has been a pretty innovative product!

People are asking me how to compose on vinyl all the time. Ok, since pens operate on brittle materials such as cardstock, paper, etc., standard vinyl is not intended to be written. While, Writable Vinyl is glossy, and the quality is very smooth. And this vinyl would stay permanent on the surface on which you place it.

Deluxe Paper with Adhesive-Backed

See the deluxe paper like a sticker page with patterns on top of it. This is an ideal paper for applying add-ons to your designs without the need to use an adhesive.

You could also consider it for party labels, scrapbooking, gift tags since you can also mark on it!

Using your machine to cut it, strip it out, and apply it wherever you like!

How to Get Started with Cricut Joy?

Note, you must be frustrated by the multitude of materials and supplies we covered today. You only need a handful of basics if you're just starting up. Only by this, and you're all done.

- Cricut Joy

- Joy Card Mat

- Joy Light Grasp Mat

- Joy Standard Grip Mat

- Cricut Pens (Pick two assortments of colors you prefer, including gold and silver pens so that you can paint on dark items)

- Insert Cards Selection Pack (Choose your preferences)

- Smart Vinyl: Choose a few shades that you need; remember to have a transfer tape for them and a good grip transferring tape when you have frosted or glitter vinyl.

- Smart Iron on Select your choice shades to select a few pieces.

- Smart Writable Vinyl: When you want to customize items in your house.

You'll feel excited when you receive your machine. Be willing to step up to the experiment; you will be able to do this; you'll work hard at it; you'll do it!

Joy's Smart Vinyl Directions

The Smart Vinyl adhesive comes in a variety of lengths, including a pretty long 20' roll in some shades. Single cuts can be created up to 4' in length, and whether you cut shapes smaller than that (like pantry tags or window decals), you can easily cut that whole 20' of vinyl adhesive in one go. Given its limited size, the matless design often allows for an increased amount of images to be cut at once. Plus, there is no need to purchase new mats!

For cutting and adding Joy's Smart Vinyl, follow the directions below.

1. Designing, cutting, and weed out
2. Applying Transfer Tape
3. Applying to the project surface

Materials and supplies:

- Cricut Joy
- Design Space software or Cricut Joy app on a computer, laptop, or a mobile
- Joy's Housing and Blade.
- Joy's Smart Vinyl
- Cricut Transfer Tape*
- Weeder
- Scraper

*The Transfer Tape is used for almost all vinyl varieties. For textured finish vinyl-like Glitter and Shimmer, use a StrongGrip Transferring Tape.

For other types of vinyl, the Strong Grip Transfer Tape is pretty strong.

1. Designing, cutting, and weeding

Create a custom template with the Design Room software or Joy app, then pick Make It. Pick your style of material loading (Without Mat) with your unique type of material.

Note: Cricut Joy requires one inch of room at the uppermost of the template for the rollers to grasp and prepare the material, and half an inch at the end. To guarantee that you have adequate Smart vinyl Materials for the project, wait until the cutting is done then trim.

Insert the material under the guides, using both hands. Constantly feed into the unit until rollers grasp the material. Make sure the material is in a horizontal line for optimum performance.

When the device detects the materials underneath the rollers; the material is measured to ensure that it is adequate for the project

The room behind the unit should be at least 10 inches because the vinyl has to feed out when it is delivered out the machine's back.

When loading, smart materials can bend in the center. If the content is not lying flat at the finish of the measurement process, pick Unload icon in the program, then reload.

Click Go and see the magic taking place!

Click Unload when the cut is done.

Using a weeder tool, strip extra vinyl from and around the template, keeping the design cut on the lining.

Suggestion: Smart Materials should be at least four inches in length to be used minus a cutting mat. By positioning them on the StandardGrip Mat, you can also use shorter ones.

2. Applying the transfer tape

Realize: Most vinyl forms use transfer Tape. Using StrongGrip Transferring Tape for vinyl with a rough coating, such as Gloss and Glitter. StrongGrip Transferring Tape is too effective for most vinyl forms.

Peel the liner from the Transfer Tape.

Carefully observe these measures to put the Transfer Tape on the design:

Apply a tiny Transfer Tape region to your layout. It may either be in the middle or at the end of the design.

Using the Scraper, burnish the Transfer Tape on the template, working out from the place you applied the tiny section.

Flip the design and then burnish the design.

3. Apply to the surface of the project

Important: Consideration and preparation are necessary for the implementation of lengthy designs. Take the time to prepare the approach.

Making sure the surface of the project is dry and clean. Peel the vinyl liner from the Transferring Tape and the design.

If the vinyl does not detach off the liner, quickly burnish the liner back on the vinyl then strip it away again. Peel the Transfer Tape at an extreme angle for better performance.

FAQ for Cricut Joy

1. Do I purchase Cricut Joy or some other Cricut machine?

   I adore Cricut Joy, it's so compact, and I see that I use a lot of it. But If I had one option because of the budget, I might choose either the Explore Air 2 or the Maker.

Nevertheless, if you like easy and feel that what you see here is exactly what you need, then have at it!

2. Will I print and then cut with the Joy?

Sorry, you cannot do that.

If you need to print and clip your layouts, you're best off with the Cricut Explore Air 2 or Maker.

3. Can the Joy materials be used with other Cricut devices?

The thickness of the items that the Cricut Joy will cut is consistent with the depth that can also be cut by the Builder and the Explore.

Therefore, all of the latest items Cricut introduced with the Joy can be worked on (with a mat) by your bigger machines. E.g., if you choose to draw and cut a writable vinyl, just pick a product that compares in thickness, in your experience.

Note: You cannot use the Cricut Joy's Pens, Mats, and Blade on any other Cricut machines.

4. Do I need to have a computer to make use of Cricut Joy?

No, not at all.

You will use the Software on your iOS device or Android. Bear

in mind that the mobile app will not be as versatile as the computer version.

5. Should I have a connection to the Internet to use the Joy?

No, not needed.

You may use Cricut Design Room on a laptop or iOS device without an Internet link (iPad, iPhone).

Remember that you will need an initial link to your device or to download the program first.

6. Can we cut fabric with Cricut Joy?

Currently, cloth materials are not classified as a material for the Cricut Joy to cut.

7. Do we need a pen connector for the Cricut Joy?

No, you don't. The Joy pens fit the unit perfectly.

8. How will I know if products can be cut without a mat?

Any material labeled with the term "Smart" is to be cut without applying any mat.

Chapter 3: Cricut Joy Set-up

It's just as easy as setting up any other Cricut machine!

If you have never installed a Cricut machine before, you will be really shocked at how simple it can be.

Connecting Bluetooth

Cricut Joy connects wirelessly to your compatible iOS, Android, or computer using Bluetooth technology. To connect Cricut Joy to your computer, follow the steps below:

Installation on Windows/Mac

1. Ensure the computer and the Cricut Joy are turned on and are within 10 to 15 feet of each other.

2. The majority of PCs are Bluetooth-enabled. However, right-click the Start button to determine if your system is Bluetooth-enabled or choose Device Manager.

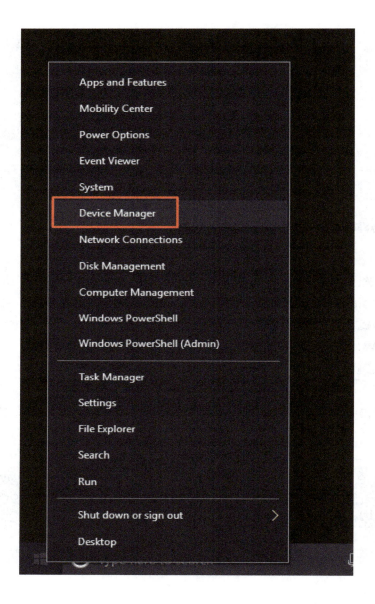

3. Your system is Bluetooth-enabled if Bluetooth is mentioned. If not, in order to enable your machine to connect to other Bluetooth devices, you would need to buy a USB gadget called a Bluetooth Dongle.

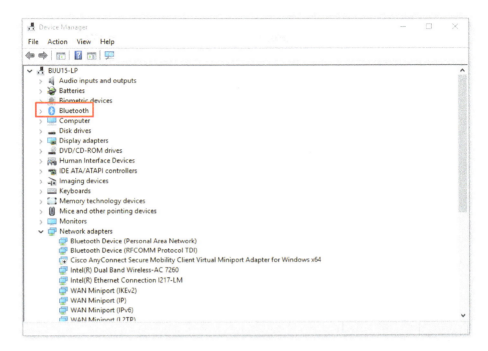

Note: We have discovered that Bluetooth dongles from (Cambridge Silicon Radio) CSR do not operate with machines from Cricut. If you require a Bluetooth adapter for your device, we recommend purchasing one that allows audio devices. We do not ensure that all dongles can match with Cricut machines, but they can always pair effectively with those that help audio equipment.

4. Exit Device Manager.

5. Click the Start menu, then pick Settings.

6. Choose Bluetooth & Other Gadgets.

7. Make sure Bluetooth is ON, then select Add Bluetooth or some other device.

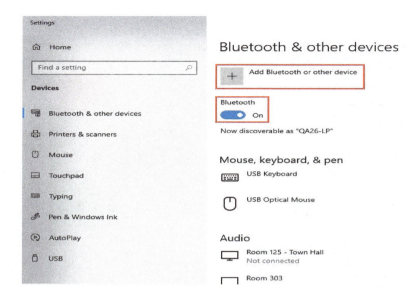

8. Pick Bluetooth and wait for the Cricut machine to be detected on your device. To start pairing, pick your Joy Bluetooth device name from the index. The Bluetooth module of your Cricut has been written on the bottom of the Joy.

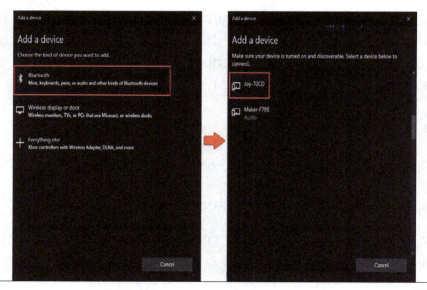

9. Your Cricut Joy is paired with your computer now!

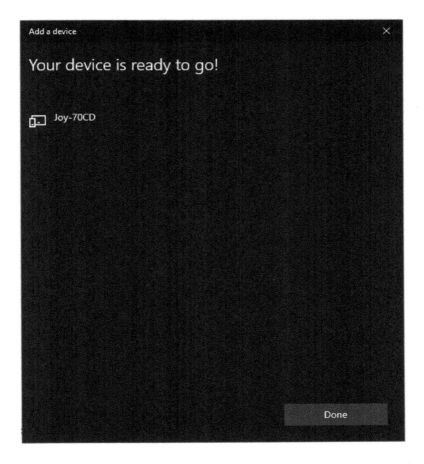

Note: These measures and screenshots refer to Windows 10 only. Please consult Member Care if you have a particular Windows OS and need support.

Tip: It is common for the Cricut Joy devices to appear in the list as Audio. You will find the one you want to combine using its system code if you have several Cricut machines. It can be seen on the machine's rim.

Installation on Your Desktop

1. Using Bluetooth, pair with the Cricut Joy.

2. In order to use the launcher, open your web browser, and then go to design.Cricut.com/setup

3. Follow the on-screen guidance for generating the Cricut ID.

4. As asked, download the plugin and install the Design Space plugin.

5. When this configuration is done, you will be required to make your first task using Cricut Joy.

6. Check and follow the on-screen directions to cut the first practice project.

7. Your latest Cricut Joy immediately registers with the computer setup.

If the configuration wasn't done, you could register by heading to Design Space's Account menu and selecting New System Setup.

Installation on Your Mobile Phone

1. The latest Cricut, Joy, saves so much room for crafters.

2. Using Bluetooth, connect the Cricut Joy device to your mobile phone.

3. Find and download the Design Space app.

4. Once completed, open the application on your iOS/Android smartphone.

5. Generate your Cricut ID or sign-in if you by now have an established account.

6. Select the Machine Setup and App Overview tab on the menu list.

7. Select the New Machine setup and, when asked, follow the directions.

Follow all the instructions coming up. I'd tell you what they're going to be, but if there's an upgrade or you are not a Cricut app member, you may have to swipe through several different screens! However, you would be on a similar page once you select 'Register Your Device' after agreeing to the terms and conditions.

When the configuration is done, you will be required to build the first project using the latest cutting machine. A menu shows up to let you chose what cut you would like to begin with. There are a variety of super cute choices. You will be using the smart vinyl included in the box.

Load your Smart Vinyl in. A detector on the unit automatically starts the tiny rollers and loads the vinyl onto them. Mind that you don't have to place it on your mat! Simply load it straight in!

On your smartphone or your screen, press 'Go' and experience it do the magic! Follow the directions on-screen to cut.

Your latest Cricut Joy is immediately registered with the mobile setup. If the configuration is not done, you can register it by heading to Design Space's Account menu and selecting New System Setup.

Cricut's Design Space

The Cricut Design Space is web-based software and a companion app and now beta computer software that helps you make, upload and maintain files to run the Cricut machines. Design Space is going to become your best mate. It guides you to every step and shows you exactly whether something isn't going to fit. It is perfect as you're not going to waste materials.

This software can be accessed wirelessly on certain machines, through your desktop, an iPad, and even your mobile device.

Cricut's Design Space also helps you browse a library of designs and files that you can import.

Many projects and files are accessible; some are to be purchased. But when you buy them, they're in your library forever.

You can also import your own data in the Design space and use the app editor to develop and edit files.

What is Cricut Access?

One more benefit of Design Space is Cricut Access—it is a membership they provide. With this membership, you can download 100,000 exclusive images, thousands of fonts and access, especially licensed designs, special discounts in the Cricut shop, and other non-included content.

You may choose a weekly or annual membership and save still more.

Is the Design Space Free of Charge?

There appears to be a misunderstanding between Cricut Design and Cricut membership Service named Cricut Access.

The software, the web-based edition, and application enables you to modify, import, and buy craft files named Cricut Design Space; these are fully FREE to use. The only other thing you need to pay for is whether you choose to purchase designs or files.

The paying service is named Cricut Access, which is a weekly or annual subscription with lots of perks and data that you can have access to.

How to Use Cricut Joy to Upload Your Own Designs

Cricut machines are the Joy of a crafter, cutting through precision forms of diverse fabrics that you may use for a range of projects. Design Space, Cricut's app, has thousands of hundreds of pictures you could use for your projects with Cricut. But then you can also take images of your own or use pictures you have seen on the internet. To use the images for your Cricut, you'll have to export them to the Design Room. Let's get going without further delay!

Everything You're Needing:

- Cricut's easiest machine: Cricut Joy
- Cricut apps: Design Space

We'll concentrate on the Joy in this part. However, these instructions will apply to any Cricut machine. Please remember that you can use.jpg, .jmp, .png, .bmp, .dxf or .svg, files, but I will concentrate on .svg files since they are the simplest to deal with.

1. Create or search the .svg file that you would like to use.

2. Go to the Design Space by Cricut. You may use it on-site or follow the instructions on your computer to download the software. You can still use the iOS software on your iPhone if you choose, but I find the greater screen size on your computer simpler to use.

3. Pick "New Project."

4. Select "Upload."

5. Either click and drag your file in the Design Space or select "Browse" to locate the image on the computer.

6. Name the file and apply tags, if needed.

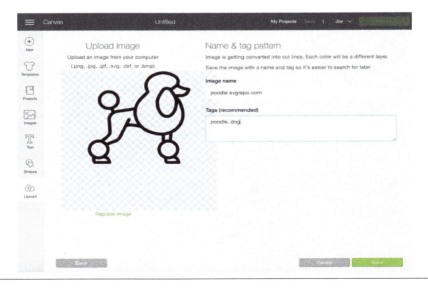

7. Select "Save." and that's it! You are ready to use your file.

Now the internet is available as a design to cut using your Cricut machine. You may use several other forms of files, as I described above. If you pick a png, .bmp .gif, or. jmp, file, but you will have some cleaning to do in the Design Room, you may have to define cut lines and delete the background items.

You may still use a .dxf format, but only on the computer desktop, not the iOS app. If you start, you bet off searching for.svg data. They're the simplest to use for Cricut.

Tips & Tricks of Cricut

Design Space You Would Really Like to Explore

No question using a Cricut system has a steep training curve. And though one issue is the device itself (not to forget all the material it can cut!), by far, the most queries we get from beginners are linked to the design tools of the Cricut Design Space App.

The app itself is not difficult. It's not challenging for Cricut Design Space itself, but certain aspects are surely not as simple as we would want them to be. And it may also seem like even the simplest methods are unnecessarily complex if you are just getting started.

However, you may soon find that Cricut Design Space really contains everything you need to build awesome projects once you get started in the first several projects, and there are tons of great techniques that make it not just simple to create, but really efficient too!

Sharing 20 tips from Cricut Design Space today that you might not have known before.

These tips and hacks are found after spending HOURS within the software and will surely save you loads of time and frustration so that with ultimate ease and belief, you can build whatever your heart wishes!

We ARE going to divide these tips and tricks for Cricut Design Space into two categories:

- In Design Canvas – where you develop your projects and modify or manipulate your designs
- In Cut Screen – the sequence of screens that enable you to configure your cutting settings when clicking the "Make It" green icon.

In Design Canvas Strategies:

1. Using Slice, Weld, and Contour to customize the designs. Using the three key editing features: Weld, Contour, and Slice, every file, whether it's one by the Design Space Photo Library or if you upload one yourself, can be modified, personalized, and customized endlessly. These tools are situated in the bottom right-hand toolbar and would only be illuminated when the features are available for a particular design. These tools, at first sight, might not look like they are doing much. However, they are amazingly strong, and the keys to configure your projects.

2. Experiment with the keywords. We've found that the search feature in the Design Space Picture Library can be a bit specific. A fairly common word that can produce all kinds of photos sometimes doesn't. But if I alter a single word, or maybe even a mere letter, all of a sudden more photos populate. As such, messing around with some search words to figure out just what you're searching for.

Leave the "s" off. If we enter the word "Dots" in the search bar, there would be around 115 photos. But if I enter in the term "Dot," it generates more than 200 pictures. As a law, we noticed that leaving the "s" off our search produces much more results!

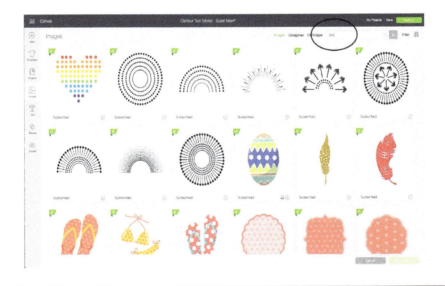

Look synonymously. Another smart strategy is to look for various synonyms as each picture is marked with different search words. E.g., while trying to cut labels, always check for tags, labels, squares, circles, and rectangles to ensure that all the potential photos are shown! Similarly, look for a plant, flower, spring, garden | love, affection, Valentine, etc.

3. See more on the same cartridge. You can locate one picture you love in the core of a whole range of other photos that you don't, then you're using this search feature. If you want to find more pictures like the one you want, what should you do? The best spot to start with is the cartridge (set) from which it came.

To easily and accurately access the cartridge, just press the tiny information circle at the bottom right corner of each picture in the Design Space photo Library (below left).

Open the picture info with the clickable (green) link, which will take you to the complete range of photos (below right)! It is the best way to locate a coordinating/matching picture to the one I've found in a search!

4. Using Free Photos & Text. If you're a regular craftsman, then Cricut access membership is for you. However, many people, particularly newbies, do not want to invest money to practice a cut in their machines, particularly at the start.

Be sure to use the FREE resources inside Cricut Design Space whether you are just working your way around, wanting to see your Cricut in action, and/or would really like to keep your craft costs to a minimum.

Use the filter in the Design Space Picture Library to locate FREE images. Simply pick the "Free" button to see an assortment of photos that you can apply to your projects at no extra cost!

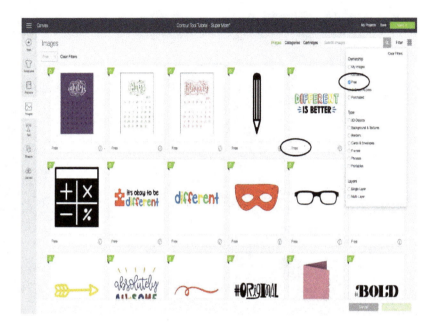

To access free fonts, your Cricut will cut any font that you have downloaded on your desktop. This not only indicates that you can cut every font that has been pre-installed on your desktop, but even any cool font that you can locate and import from any free pages, such as DaFont or Font Squirrel.

To locate the fonts that you will use without incurring extra costs, simply select "My Fonts" from the text selection filter.

It will display all the texts loaded on your computer and any Cricut fonts you might have bought (either separately or with a Cricut Access Pass).
It is a perfect way to make sure you select fonts that you won't be paying for!

5. Recreate patterns. Now you can adjust how the picture is filled using the latest Fill feature at the toolbar's top. You may switch out colors or apply a design to the inside of the picture with a specific layer chosen.

Filling photos using any of the previously filled designs is a nice way to bring enjoyment to your designs without depending on paper or cardboard patterns.

In addition to several designs accessible, one could even control the layout's size and alignment by pressing "Edit Pattern" in the Pattern toolbar.

Remember: The design choice may only be used with the Print-then-Cut technique.

In Cut Screen Strategies

If you've done developing the project and submitting the photos to be cut through the "Make It" green tab, you may assume your potential to control the task is over.
Even then, there is much stuff you can do on the cutting screen to retain not just some time but also Cricut joy material.

The below tricks for Design Space are selected finest stuff to understand about the Design Space; let us get through it!

1. Shift things across the mat. Have you realized that you can transfer things across the cut mat on your own cut screen? Although the Cricut Design Space application auto-populates the photos on mats depending on their pigment and direction, it might not be precisely where you were liking them to be.

Merely drag and drop the photos. You can shift a cut anyplace on the cut mat and also adjust it by using the top right corner controls.

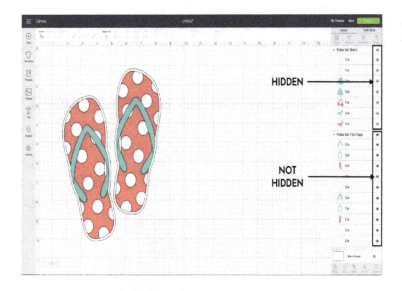

Not only does this enable you to chuck items up closer than the program initially proposed, then it also guarantees that the cut is exactly where you want design to be (like when you are attempting to use an oddly-shaped or scrap piece of material). Only ensure that users duplicate the line segments on the panel to the line segments on their mat to guarantee that the template suits the fabric everywhere you get it!

2. Repeat and Skip Mats. A few of the friendliest aspects of how the Design Space functions are that you don't have to focus a lot when you submit the project to cut.

If you supply the correct color and scale of the sheet to your system, as seen on the left-hand part of your cut panel, your work can look as you planned it!

That being said, you might feel that you need to forgo which mat will be next cut, cut the mat again, or ignore the mat entirely. Luckily, it's quite simple, and you don't need to leave the cutting screen. Until you load the Cricut mat into the device, you can physically pick which mat to be cut after choosing it on the left part of the mat. The device can skip to whichever mat you physically pick.

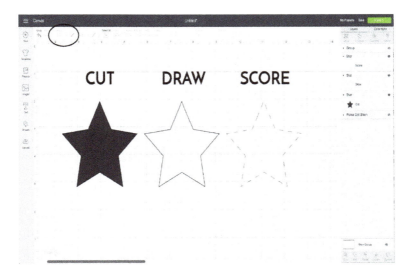

You may even use the exact thing to cut a sheet again, even though you see a green tick next to the cut mat (which shows it has been cut beforehand). It is a perfect technique to cut significant amounts of the exact pattern without replicating them on the design canvas.

3. Change the Cut Pressure effortlessly. Although it's nice to change every material's settings, you often need a bit extra or slightly less pressure to cut past cleanly. To achieve the latter after you have picked your stuff on the actual cut screen, adjust the compression to the Standard, Less, or More through the drop-down toolbar: immediately

That is a perfect method to get the cutting deepness correct quickly and conveniently without thinking about customized settings!

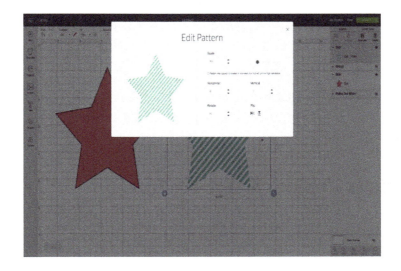

4. Adjust Mirroring. There would be occasions, particularly when you deal with the Iron-On models when you need to slice the project in reverse (also known as Mirror). While you may horizontally turn the pattern on the design canvas screen, there is also a possibility to replicate the patterns on the cut screen also:

Not only does this help you to copy the mat you need to turn over, but it also helps you to build and adjust the un-clipped template on the designing panel (which is easier to see and change according to your needs)

5. Foolproof directives. The great aspect of having the instance to pick your personalized stuff on the cutting screen is that the Design Space can send you useful updates to make sure your plans work perfectly. For instance, when you pick the "Iron-On," you would be notified to reverse your work and put the sparkling part of your fabric down on the mat.

Once you pick anything, such as chipboard, you'll be prompted to inspect your cutter, secure your fabric or paper to the mat.

The secret here is to not ignore these discreet guidelines since they will really spare you a lot of precious time and items!

A Cricut Project Start-to-Finish

So, you have purchased your first Cricut machine. You've had it all prepped, and (hopefully!) you've made the demo projects included with the pack. But now, you can create your own project.

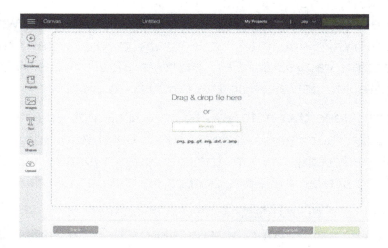

From the start! Use this accompanying step-by-step guide to feel how the Cricut project works together from beginning to end!

Begin a New Project

Select the plus sign (+) on your home screen of Design Space or the canvas's left toolbar. Ensure that the proper machine is chosen in the top right panel drop-down display.

Design the Project

Add pictures to your board from either the Image File, the Shapes Menu, or the Uploads Library, and/or add some text to the project using the Text Tool. Using the different Design Space resources on your images and texts till you have what you want.

Send the Template to Cut

To submit your template to be cut with the Cricut unit, click the green button "Make It" in the upper right corner. You will be sent to a set of cut screens in which you will make final changes and requirements.

Making Modifications to the Mat Layouts

Make sure that every design is cut in the right color on the first screen. You may easily transfer images across the mat (or to another mat by tapping the dots at the top right corner of each picture) to adjust colors, save materials, or position designs in a particular mat spot.

Cut the Template/Design

On the last screen, make sure you have chosen the right material(s) for your project.
Then, merely obey the on-screen instructions to load/unload the mat, equipment, pens, etc., till your work is complete!

Chapter 4: Projects

Cricut Joy Smart Vinyl Planner Stickers

Requirements:

- Cricut Joy
- Cricut Removable Smart Vinyl
- Designing Space
- Weeder

Instructions:

1. Create Your Stickers in the design space

Use the left-hand toolbar to pick images and browse for images. The sheets created here are themed for summer, so searching for ice cream, beach, summer, and also cars and bikes will yield you the images you require. If you want to build a summer beach look, search for all the summer stuff.

Single images do well, like the one shown when picking your images. Check that the picture is also completely connected such that it peels off in one piece.

Decide on the color for the mat images. Before submitting a cut, all pictures must be in the same color to be correctly cut on the same vinyl panel.

2. Making of Cricut Joy Vinyl Stickers

You have two choices when you pick a sticker graphic that has several layers. You may ungroup it and delete sections you don't need; you can see that on the right-hand side. Or you may weld it, but this would render it a solid picture. We ungrouped and disposed of the glass to clear the black glass.

3. Removing layers to make Vinyl Stickers for Cricut Joy

If you choose to carve shapes into a single picture for stickers, just layer the object you want to slice. Click and hold with the cursor to pick slice with the bottom right-hand corner illuminated.

4. Using slice in Cricut design space

To create your pictures for the Joy Vinyl Stickers and also to make sure you have the correct size, create on a mat about 4.5'' x 11" (Or more if you have a longer vinyl). It will offer you an indication of how much bigger space you need.

5. Cut the Joy Vinyl Stickers

Understanding how the stickers would be cut, clicking on MAKE IT in the upper right corner will give you an idea. To reduce space and prevent waste, Design Space may shuffle, but this does not always play out. Before you would see the cut mat image, you will need to select your material. Then you can see the layout of the final cut. The Joy would now pull the smart vinyl through to verify if it is sufficient for the cut.

6. Prevent Unused Space on the Cricut Cutting Mat.

There are gaps on the cutting mat view, you can insert a few new pictures to cut to prevent wastage, but you have to drag the images over on the mat to create room.

Drag a picture simply by tapping on it and moving it; this is a perfect way to stop getting negative spaces and wasting vinyl. Until your mat is loaded, you should keep doing this. The lines represent the mat's corners, and it will not allow you to go beyond those lines.

We could have dragged the images even more together before cutting the stickers, thereby making several more stickers.

DIY Labels with Cricut Joy

Requirements:

- Transferring Tape
- Smart Vinyl
- Weeder
- Cricut Joy

Instructions:

Begin with a blank file in the Design Space on your computer or smartphone, and then select the text tool on the left sidebar to access a text entry window.

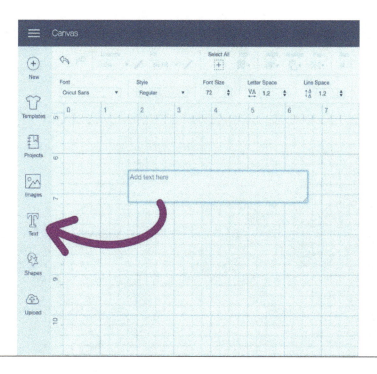

1. Write the text on the label. You can alter the font if you prefer, even as the text is still chosen. For most of my work, I prefer Cricut Sans as it's a clean and easy to read choice. You may also adjust the label's scale when you change the font size or drag the corners of the text window.

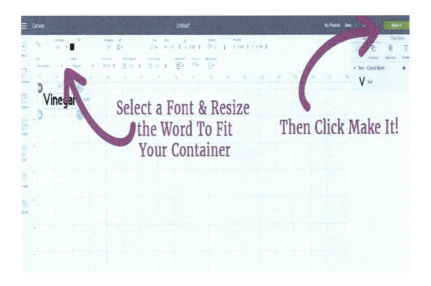

2. Select make it!

3. When the screen alerts you to load the vinyl into the unit, you only have to put it underneath the guides on either side of the tray (without any mat). It's going to "see" that you inserted it and then start moving it in place. You just need to let go.

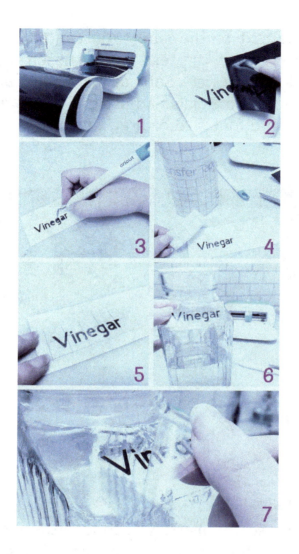

Now that you have assembled the label and mounted the vinyl, here's a visual guided by written steps about how to complete cutting and attaching the label.

1. As the vinyl is mounted, the Design Space will trigger the Go button that is on the bottom right side of the panel. Click it, and let the Cricut Joy do its magic!

When the cut is completed, the joy can unload by itself; you do not have to perform anything.

2. Using the scissors to take off the fresh label from the vinyl roll. Then strip the excess vinyl from the corner and pull it back to show your word.

3. To clear any leftover excess vinyl, such as the inside of e's, g's, a's, etc., use the Cricut Weeder.

4. Cut a slightly bigger portion of the transfer tape than the phrase. You will be using this to get the label all as a word to your bottle.

5. Peel off and discard the backing of the transfer tape, leaving the sticky transparent grid. Apply the transfer tape on your word/label, then rub it to ensure the letters hold onto the tape.

6. Pull up the transfer tape, which is meant to carry the letters on with it, and remove the white behind.

7. Press the fresh label on your bottle, wipe over the letters, and then finally peel the transfer tape away to leave just the letters.

Now you've got a perfectly labeled bottle ready to use!

Cricut Joy Organization Labels

Requirements:

- Paper
- Smart Vinyl
- Weeder
- Cricut Joy

Instructions:

1. Prepare labels in the Cricut Design Room

You may either select pre-designed labels or create your own! I created these with the form of a hexagon, duplicated it, then decreased the scale by 1/4'' of one of the forms, modified it to a line, and finally, then centered them all.

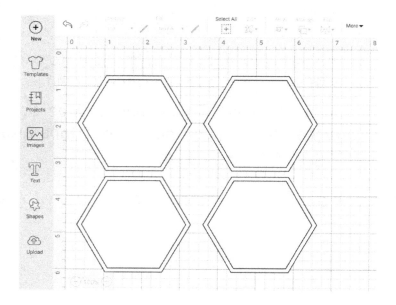

2. Add unique organizational objects to the labels

I added different labels for my bin with a writing font. After I scale them correctly, I chose all three layers (Trim line hex, create link hex, and Sticker name) and pressed the attach button. Do it with all the labels.

3. Making it

Select make it, choose JOY Machine, and then pick Material.

The machine would blink, and you will click load on CDS to load the vinyl. There's no mat required.

4. Insert the Joy's Pen & Compose

Release the clamp, lower the pen in, and shut the clamp. Now your joy can create the boundaries of the hex and the names of the labels.

5. Change Pen to Blade

The same procedure as before, open the clamp, detach the pen, insert the blade, and shut the clip. Click Go on CDS, and the machine is going to cut the external hexagon layer.

6. Click the Unload button and Complete

Press Unload on CDS to unload your vinyl label from the unit. Press Finish, and you're ready for the labeling!

7. Adding labels

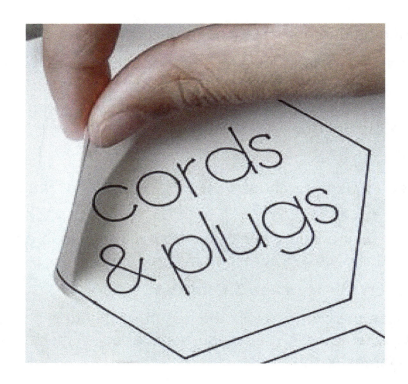

Smart Vinyl Labels do not need a transfer tape. Just peel and stick as normal stickers!

Notebook Design 'Somewhere over the Rainbow"

Requirements:

- Cricut's Joy Machine
- The Joy Transfer Tape
- The Joy Starting Tools
- 1 notebook

Instructions:

1. Open the "Somewhere over the Rainbow" design in the Cricut Design Room. Simply use the "Anytime" font to build the custom text.

You can effortlessly build your own script using different fonts to customize your notebook. Continue to cut—no mat needed with the Smart Vinyl!

2. After the text has been cut, start with weeding.

3. Use the transferring tape to put the text on the book. Using the Cricut Scraper eliminate bubbling and help smooth and clean transfer.

4. Use the "Rainbow" illustration from the Sweetie Shapes sequence—for the cute rainbow layout. Cut it down to about 3' by 2.' Steps were repeated above to cut and shift the image to the register.

And you're done just like that. Isn't it adorable!

Spring Flower Mug

Requirements:

- Cricut's Joy
- 1 mug
- The Cricut Transfer Tape
- The Joy Starting Tools
- The Joy smart Vinyl

Instructions:

1. Open my "Spring Flower" template in the Cricut Design Space. Change the sizes of the photos to the scale of your mug.

Continue to cut—no mat needed with the Smart Vinyl! Choose the colors you like to use and execute the Cricut Design Space prompts to cut each layer.

Likewise, you may make a flower print of your own. Launch a new project in the Cricut Design Room to do this. To select the flowers and leaf patterns that you like to use, click on the images. Adapt them to the scale and size of the mug and continue with the cutting. Follow the instructions in the Cricut Design Space to cut each layer.

2. After all the pictures have been cut, switch off the Cricut Joy and continue to weeding. Using the Cricut Weeder to properly weed your pictures and make them ready to be transferred.

3. You're nearly there! Take the transfer tape pieces that are slightly bigger than the pictures. If you use the same image of a flower as shown, it would involve layering. Place the first layer of the picture on the transfer tape and, after that, the second part. Using the Cricut Scraper removes bubbles to have a clean and smooth transition.

4. It's time for the picture to be transferred to the mug. Position every flower and every leaf where you like on your mug. Again, use the Scraper to get a smooth and quick transfer. Voila! It's just that simple.

Card for Mother's Day

This project is a ready-made idea accessible in the Cricut Design Space that you cannot stop attempting to do! You wouldn't believe how fast and simple it is to create such a handmade, beautiful card.

Requirements:

- Cricut Joy 4.5'' by 6.25'' Card Mat
- Starter Toolset
- Cricut Joy Insert Cards
- Cricut Joy

Instructions:

1. Enter "Happy Mother's Day Card" in the Cricut Design Space browser.

2. Set the stock card on the design mat. To cut, follow the given steps in the Cricut Design Space.

3. Use the Cricut Weeder to weed out the layout and dispose of the cutouts. Move the card stock gently from the mat.

4. Insert the colorful insert, and you're all done. What a lovely Mother's Day card!

Pretty Monogrammed Ring Dish

Requirements:

- Starter Tools
- Cricut Joy
- Transfer Tape
- Ring Plate
- Smart Vinyl by Cricut Joy

Instructions:

1. In the Cricut Design Space photos, search your monogram. In the search bar, type "monogram," and lots of choices come up. That tropical H is the one we liked and chose to use.

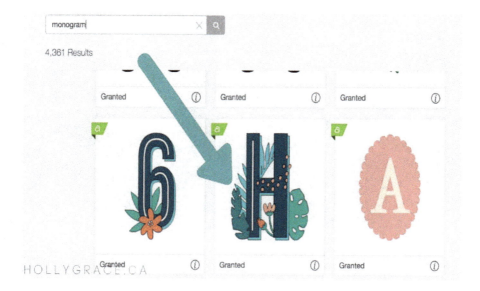

2. Turn on the Cricut Joy and link it to the Design Space. Follow the cut screen instructions to see what colors you want to load in the Cricut Joy. Use the Cricut Joys Smart Vinyl to cut the surface without a mat.

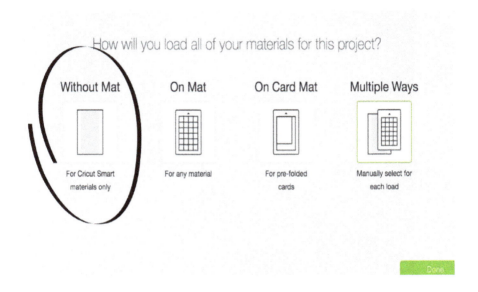

3. Continue loading in Smart Vinyl colors by observing the Design Space project.

Don't think about not cutting with a mat. This Cricut Machen always checks first to ensure if you have sufficient material to cut.

4. Using a weeder, weed all of the cut design pieces when your design has done cutting.

5. Layer the template in the right order utilizing the transfer tape. To smooth out each layering of vinyl and remove any air bubbles, you should use the scraper.

This project was completed in less than 10 minutes with the Cricut Joy. It is so easy!

Perfect Wine Tumbler

Requirements:

- Smart Vinyl by Cricut Joy
- Starter Tools
- Cricut' Joy
- Transfer Tape
- Wine Tumbler

Instructions:

1. Found these two illustrations in the Cricut Design Space and sourced them for my project.

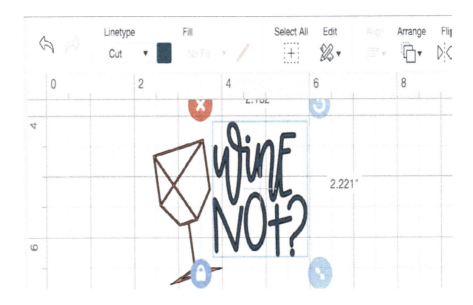

2. Then adjusted the scale of both pictures to work into the size of the wine tumbler. Then I adjusted the shade of both pictures to be cut out of 2 distinct Smart Vinyl colors.

3. When my design was completed, I have used Transferring Tape to attach it to my project.

It took me five minutes to prepare this wine tumbler. And it's super-fast and quick, and isn't it so cute, too?

Customized Tote with Zipper

Requirements:

- Cricut's Joy
- Zipper Tote
- Smart Iron-On
- Starter Tools

Instructions:

This project is a super easy one. If you need a small zipper bag to hold your tablet in or to carry your stationery, you can personalize this blank canvas.

1. It was super quick. I built the layout in Design Space and equipped the Cricut Joy machine with the Smart vinyl Iron-On.

2. Again, with the Cricut smart products, no mat was required. These smart fabrics save you energy and cost! No extra supplies are required, like a mat.

3. Make sure the project is mirrored since this Iron-On performs exactly like every other Iron-On brand from Cricut.

4. After my Cricut Joy had finished cutting the pattern, I weeded it and added it to my tote, using the Cricut Mini Quick Press

Bathroom Decal "Show U Care, Spare A Square."

With the toilet paper in low supply, this is one of the decals to put over the toilet paper holder on the roll to encourage family members to be conscious of their toilet paper use.

Requirements:

- Smart Vinyl or Cricut Vinyl (in your favorite colors)
- Weeder
- Standard Grip Mat (Optional—if you are not using Smart Vinyl)
- Transfer Tape
- Scrapers
- Cricut's joy

Instructions:

1. Access the "Show U Care" file. Select the "Make It" tab.

2. Obey the instructions on your display, put each colored vinyl on your cut mat with the colored side facing up, load the mat into your joy, and click "Go" to cut. As each mat is done, unload it from the Cricut Joy and again load its next mat as instructed.

3. Weed the vinyl, strip the excess vinyl from each template, leaving only the design on the back of the white paper.

4. Use the transferring tape to shift the vinyl decal to the clean wall. Scraper tool over the template to ensure sure it is securely stuck to the wall.

Now! You have a beautiful wall decal that will alert people of how much paper they're using!

Pantry Organization with Smart Label

Quarantine is the best opportunity to organize the pantry! The transparent mason jars are airtight, and you can immediately tell what's inside with the stickers

Requirements:

- Joy Pen's
- Cricut Smart Labels
- food containers or Mason jars
- Cricut's joy

Instructions:

1. Open the file with Cricut Joy Pantry Names. Select Customize and pick the labels that you want to create. Adjust them to the scale you like for your containers. Select the "Make It" tab.

2. Obey the instructions on your screen, load the Cricut Joy pen, and also the Cricut Smart Labels roll. First, the Cricut Joy would write the words then draw the template. Then it will instruct you to mount your cutting blade in the machine such that the labels can be cut. Once your labels have finished cutting, unload your unit.

3. Weed out your smart labels, strip the extra stuff from your labels, and leave the labels on the back of the paper. Peel off the paperback of your labels and transfer them to the food storage containers you desire.

Now! Arrange your pantry with your Smart Labels in minutes!

A Greeting Card, "You Are Cute and I Ain't a Lion."

This card is great for a birthday party, but equally nice to use as a regular greeting card!

Requirements:

- Cricut Card Inserts
- Joy's Pen
- Cricut Joy Card Mat
- Cricut's joy

Instructions:

1. Open a file named "You're Cute and I Ain't Lion." Select the "Make It" tab.

2. Obey the instructions on display. Load the card onto the card cutting pad so that the inside of the card is within the pocket and the back of the card is against the sticky portion of the mat.

Load your Cricut Joy with the card mat. You will be instructed to load your Cricut pen first; then, after printing, you will be instructed to load the Joys cutting blade back into the Cricut.

Note: I found this pattern to be very intricate to cut. Until unloading your mat, keep checking and see if your card is being cut thoroughly; if it doesn't, click the "try again" switch, and the Cricut Joy should allow a second pass to cut your card. I kept the blade/pen grabber empty for the first step of the second movement where it was printing and then mounted the blade once it was ready to cut.

3. Unload the mat and peel your card carefully. Discard the cut bits of paper that did not come out of it. Slide the card insert into the card.

And you have a lovely lion's card, suited for the Lion King himself!

Coffee Please

Making Cricut Joy projects is as simple as 1-2-3! Just pick a project or a picture from the Cricut Design Room. I figured the style of "More Coffee Please" would be ideal for my mug!

Instructions:

1. Choose an image and put it onto the Design Space canvas. Scale the picture to suit the project (for a 16 ounce. mug, my version was 2.7'' by 3.25'') and press the green button "Make it" on the upper right side of the screen.

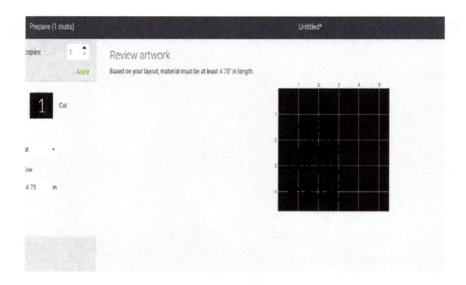

2. On this window, choose whether you might be cutting either the latest Smart Materials or whether you would use a Cricut Joy mat. I used Smart Vinyl (Permanent) for my mug; therefore, I chose "no mat from the drop-down list."

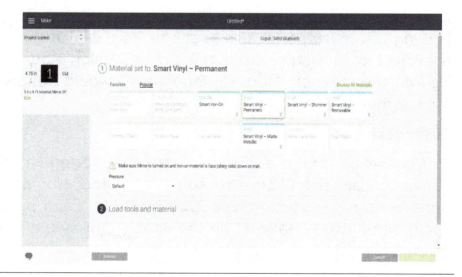

3. Pick the material from the list (hint: if you do not see the material mentioned, select "Browse All Materials" that's in the top right corner of the screen) and then select the desired level of pressure (I like to select "more" pressure mostly on all materials).

4. Then, Design Space will instruct you to install the materials to Cricut Joy. Just feed the joys Smart Vinyl (or any other stuff) between both the rollers, so the device will automatically draw it in and adjust the vinyl for you.

5. To start cutting, press "Go" in the Design Room.

6. When the machine has completed cutting, you will be prompted to unload the product in the Design Room.

7. By using a weeder, eliminate any excess vinyl.

8. Take a piece of Cricut Transferring Tape that's only slightly bigger than the design. Attach the transfer tape to the design and, using the scraper, gently burnish the paper. Cautiously remove the back of the transfer tape.

9. Attach the template to the mug, then use the scraper tool to burnish before gently removing the transferring tape.

Chapter 5: Troubleshooting

1. Material is not staying on the mat

It is strongly advised that you utilize a scraper to build a firm contact between the material and the adhesive mat.

2. Machine tears into the material

Making sure that the material is stable on the mat for cutting. Using a scraper to establish a firm contact between the material and the adhesive mat.

Making sure that the blade's housing is correctly placed in the clamp. Release the clamp and place the housing in the holder. The tip of the housing is expected to sit properly with the clamp. Lock the clamp, then.

If these problems are not solved, please notify Member Care for more assistance.

3. The machine could not cut through the material

Be sure that you use the right cut setting for the particular content. Ensure that the blade's housing is correctly placed in the clamp.

Release the clamp and again place the housing in the holder. The tip of the housing is expected to lie flat with the clamp. Lock the clamp, then.

4. How to Forget/Remove/Unpair Bluetooth Devices

This will help to forget/remove Bluetooth (Bluetooth

Connector or Cricut Explore or Maker) from your Mac/Windows computer or Android/iOS system for troubleshooting purposes.

1. Click the Start menu and pick Settings.

2. Then, you can open the Devices choice.

3. Pick the machine you wish to uninstall and press Remove Device to validate the action.

Note: The procedure can differ noticeably depending on the version of your operating system. Once you forget/remove the Bluetooth unit, you may have to restart the pairing procedure if you decide to use it once again.

5. How do I locate my serial number for Cricut Joy?

The serial number of Your Cricut Joy is written at the bottom of your unit. It is composed of 12 letters, starting with the letter V.

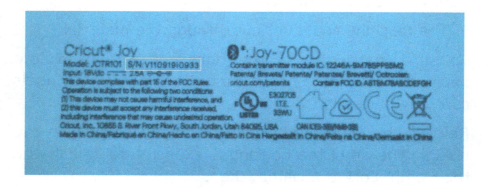

6. Firmware Upgrade for Cricut Joy

Firmware is necessary for any of your Cricut machines to function properly and connect with your mobile device or computer. When you are setting up your Cricut Joy machine for the first time, you will be directed to upgrade your firmware whenever an update is required.

After initial configuration, you may periodically upgrade the firmware when new functionality and performance updates are introduced.

1. Ensure your machine is turned on and combined with your computer

2. You will be notified when a firmware upgrade is required, if it is during the latest system configuration or when you are continuing to cut your latest project.

3. The firmware upgrade will start, and the progress bar will show on the computer.

4. During the update, the Cricut Joy machine must reboot, and you will get a message that the upgrade has been successful. Pick Move ahead with a new system configuration or just proceed with the cut.

Conclusion

Cricut Joy is a remarkably small and versatile machine with a lot of innovative and functional applications! It's dynamic creativity that fits into the palms of your hand.

Since you already possess a Cricut cutting unit, it is bound to become your fave sidekick—the best partner for your larger Cricut machines.

Keep your full-size devices for bigger designs and thicker materials, yet start a relationship with this latest mini machine that can easily transform you into a super crafter by creating easy cards, decals, labels, and more.

Cricut Maker

A Beginner's Guide to Cricut Maker + Tips, Tricks and Amazing DIY Project Ideas

Anita Wood

Introduction

If you do not know about the Cricut machine, allow me to introduce you. In simple words, this is the system that cuts the designs or patterns you make in the Cricut Design Space app and draws them on paper or even leather, through wood to material to many more; you can use all kinds of materials to make anything you can think up.

It is the cutting machines' workhorse; just about everything you want to do will do it. With the Cricut Maker, you can make any crafting material with various blades for different purposes. You can also upload the design and font of your own choice in the Design space via Bluetooth technology.

Enjoy Crafting!!

Chapter 1: Cricut Machine

Cricut machines are cutting machines controlled by computers. They are used for cutting fabrics, leather, wood, papers, and vinyl, etc. It helps you to explore your DIY passion. It enhances your craft 's abilities.

You can wirelessly attach a Cricut to your device, build or import designs to your computer, and upload them for cutting to your Cricut.

Cricut has applications called Design Room that helps you to build and import machine-cut designs. Blades are installed within the Cricut. You will attach your preferred material to a 12-inch-wide cutting mat until you have a design prepared to break in Design Space, submit your design to your Cricut wirelessly from your phone, and then insert your materials into your system.

You will begin cutting your project with the click of a button. It is very easy now to make the design of your choice with your own hands.

Moreover, it has many models, which are discussed below.

Cricut Explore One

It is a machine for DIY projects. It makes the work easier. It can cut many materials. We can also write through it. It is an innovative machine that makes it easier to accomplish your artistic vision.

It can personalize many things like t-shirts, mugs, cards, etc.; it makes it easier for us to make our designs and use them where we want. It also has its designs, fonts, and ready-to-make projects.

Cricut Explore Air

For the past several years, the demand for this machine is increasing. Besides its cutting blade, you can insert a scoring tool and you can insert the pen tool. It offers us a deep cutting blade, which is very helpful in cutting heavier materials. It has its software called Design Space.

In this software, they offer us a broad variety of designs. In the folder of the projects, you can also download your Cricut cartridges.

Cricut Explore Air 2

Cricut explore is an artistic instrument that can help you make your project more comfortable by providing you a range of materials.

The notable feature of this Cricut is wireless. This machine is cloud-based, which means you can design your project from anywhere.

Cricut Maker

It is the newest addition to the Cricut family. The maker's worth mentioning feature is the broad variety of blades available, which helps cut thick materials, fabrics, and papers. Like explore, it also has the design space software.

Cricut Joy

Joy Cricut is targeted at the small crafters market. It cuts many materials in any form with precision. It has smart materials and specialty accessories, which makes it more advanced than others.

You can cut cardstocks, vinyl, iron-on, and also construction papers, but with the Cricut joy, you cannot print or cut to make stickers.

Cricut Maker 2

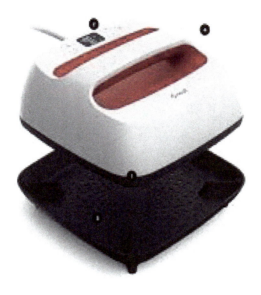

This device has a surface of the square size, which is used to transfer the heat and infusible ink materials. It provides continuous pressure and heat over the materials for different projects.

On the top of this device is the start button, the power button, the timer button, and the increase button and decrease button.

Easy Press Mini

It has a length of 4 inches and it is 2.5 inches wide. It has three heat settings: low, medium, and high. Low heat is used for sensitive bases. Medium heat is used for more basic materials and high heat for infusible ink.

Chapter 2: How to Use Cricut Machine

You must know how to use the cricut machine. The chapter will provide step by step information for you to understand this process.

Go through the steps carefully, and your machine will be ready to produce amazing products.

Machine Setup

1. In the bottom of your Cricut machine, there is a port where you can place the square end of the USB cable.

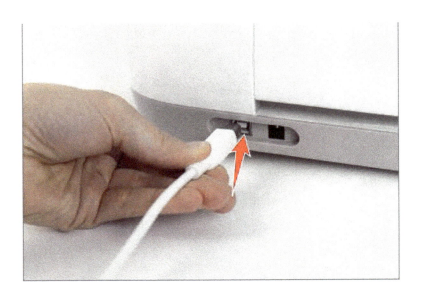

2. In your computer, place the rectangular end of the USB cable.

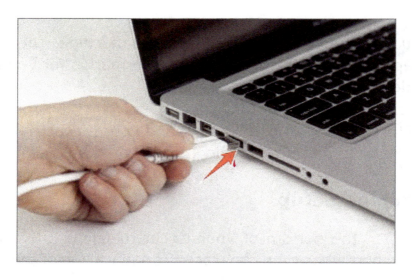

3. Next, switch on the power outlet.

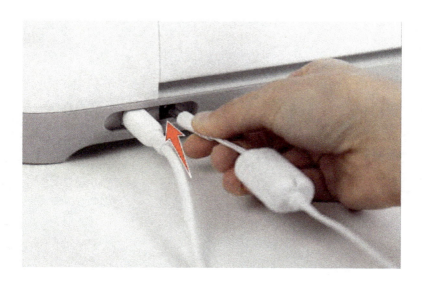

4. Now, hit the start button.

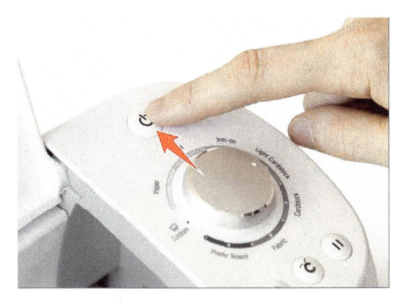

5. To open your machine, click on the open button.

Mat setup

1. First, remove the cover from the mat.

2. Now, in the top left corner of the grip, place the material on the mat.

3. Now, place the mat in the cricut machine.

4. Press the load or unload button by holding the mat tight against rollers.

5. Now, make sure that there should be enough space for the mat to run smoothly in the Cricut machine.

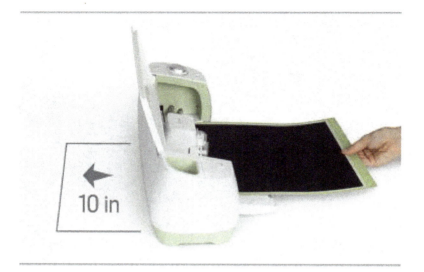

6. Unload the mat when your task is completed.

7. Now, bend the mat from the end to avoid large cuts and waste materials.

8. Now, hold the mat on the flat surface until all material is released.

9. Bend the mat to release the edges of the mat and gently peel cuts pieces of the mat.

Mat Care

- Now covers the mat again.

- Do not store a mat if it still has material on it.

- Evenly use the surface of the mat modifying, which end you place in the machine.

The Loading and Unloading of the Pen

1. First, Open clamp A.

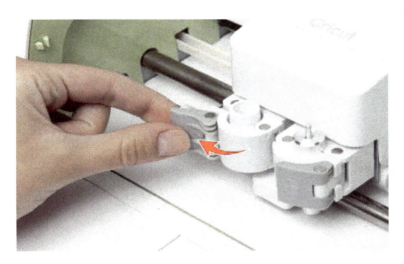

2. Second, remove the cap of the pen.

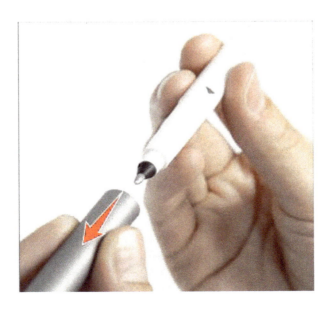

3. Now, tightly grip the pen until the arrow on it disappears.

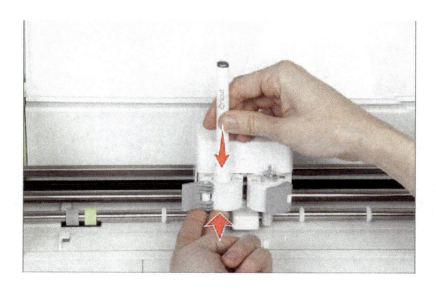

4. Now you will close the clamp

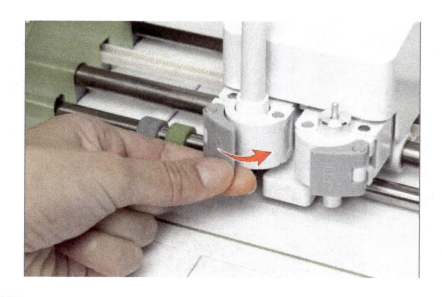

5. When your task has been completed, pull the pen upward.

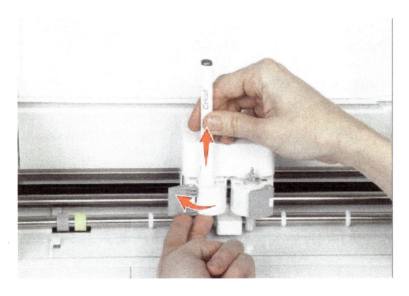

6. Now again, place the cap to stop it from drying.

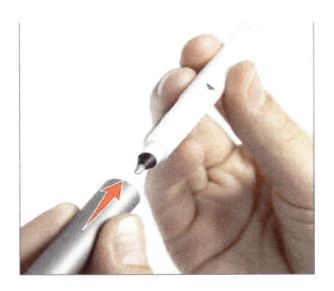

Accessing setup

Safari, Internet Explorer, Mozilla Firefox, Google Chrome can be used in accessing setup.

Google Chrome Guide

Following are the steps used to access the setup website using google chrome.

1. Open the Google chrome app on your desktop.

2. Now click on the search bar at the top of the browser.

3. Put the web address **www.cricut.com/setup**. Also, make sure to search with the right spelling.

4. The screen will appear, which welcomes you to the Cricut. To begin the setup process, click on the get started button.

Safari

Following are the steps used to access the setup website using google chrome.

1. Double click on the safari icon on your computer.

2. Now, click on the search bar at the top of the chrome.

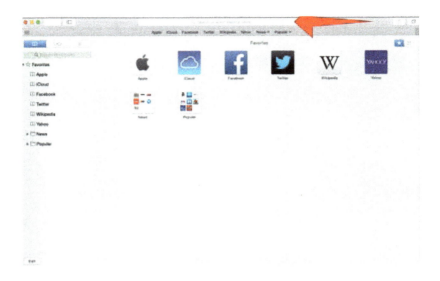

3. Put the web address **www.cricut.com/setup**.

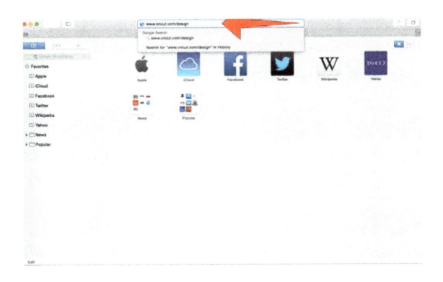

4. The screen will appear, which welcomes you to the Cricut.

Adobe Flash

To use the Cricut design space, adobe flash is necessary. Adobe Flash is the software from adobe system. If you face some problem, kindly visit

http://helpx.adobe.com/flash-player.html

Cricut Plugin (PC)

If you want to access all the innovative Cricut design space's innovative features, you must download the plugin's design space.

The plugin stores on your computer and runs by your browser. Moreover, the picture below may not reflect the recent version on the PC.

1. First, click on the "Download Plugin."

2. Open your Documents folder.

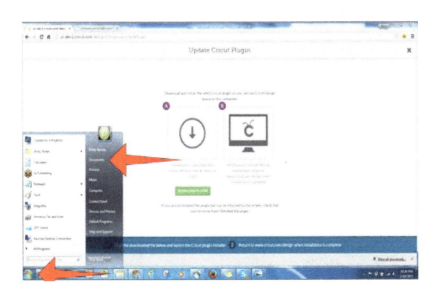

3. Open the "Downloads" folder and then double click the Cricut Design Space file. Open the Cricut design space folder.

4. It will open the Cricut design space. Click next to continue.

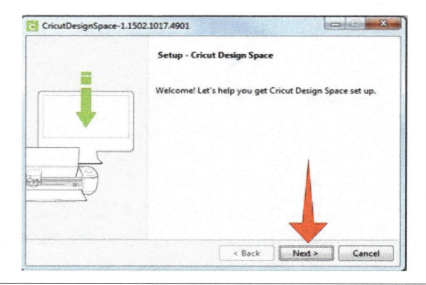

5. Now, the screen will appear. Press the next button.

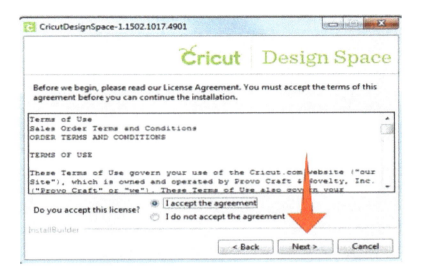

6. Now, the next screen will appear; you have to click "Quit and continue."

7. The unsaved work may be lost, be sure to save it, now click "YES."

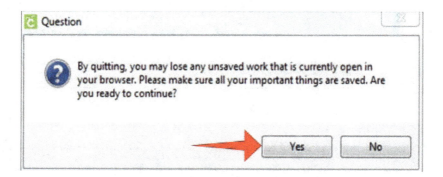

8. The next screen will appear in which you have to decide whether you want to create a shortcut of that file or not. Now click on the "NEXT" button.

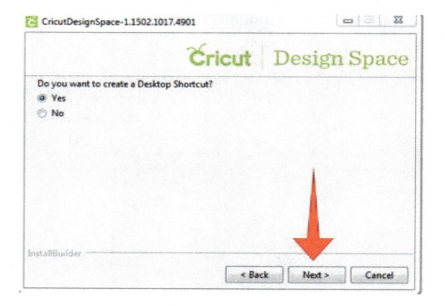

9. Now click on "next "to install the plugin.

10. Questions may appear according to the computer setting. Now press on the next button.

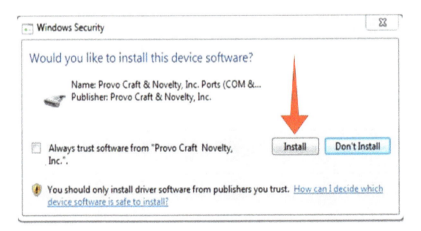

11. Now, it will successfully be installed. Click on the finished bar.

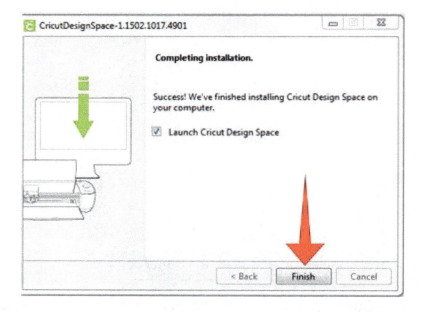

Cricut Plugin (Mac)

If you want to access all the innovative Cricut design space features, you must download the design space plugin.

It will run on your computer and run by your browser. Moreover, the picture below may not reflect the recent version on the PC.

1. First, click on "Download Plugin."

2. Plugin the "Finder" at the bottom of your screen

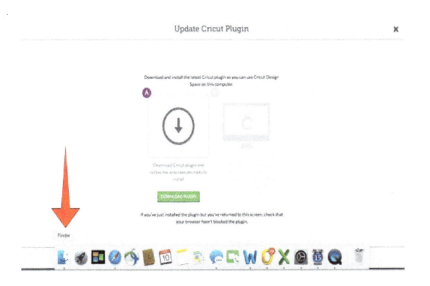

3. Third, click the "Downloads" folder and then double click the Cricut Design Space zip file.

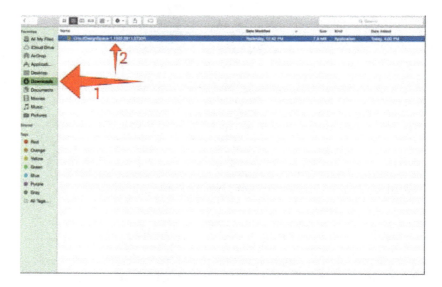

4. According to your computer setting, the downloaded application may appear. Click on the 'Open" to continue.

5. Add administrator 's name and password and click on the "OK" button.

6. Click "Next" to continue.

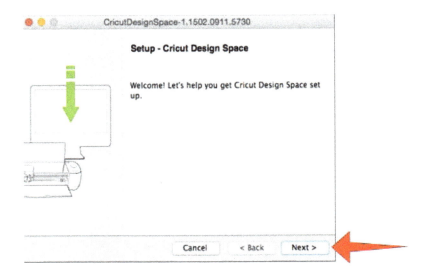

7. Accept the terms of use. Click "Next"

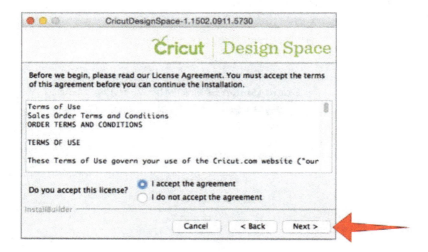

8. Now, close all browsers and click "Quit and Continue." The unsaved work may be lost. Be sure to save it and click on "yes. "

9. Click "Next" to start the procedure.

10. It will automatically be installed. Leave the box unchecked if you automatically want to launch it in your browser.

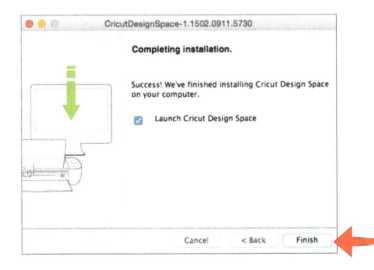

Updating the Cricut

Updating the plugin process.

- **Phase 1 – Delete history.**

1. Click on Google chrome.

2. From the menu, select "History."

3. Delete all the history.

4. A "Clear browsing data" window will open next to the selection menu with the words "Obliterate the following items from." Select "the beginning of time." Don't worry; this process won't harm your machine; it merely lets Chrome work from a clean slate. Make sure that there are at least the following boxes checked:

5. Download history Cookies and other information about the Website and plugin data. Click the 'Simple browsing details' button.

6. Now, exit chrome.

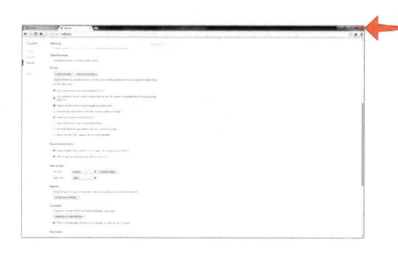

- **Phase 2 – Update Google chrome.**

1. Now reopen Google chrome.

2. Pick "About Google Chrome" from the menu.

3. Check Google Chrome for your version. a. Continue to phase 4 if it is version 42.0.2311.90 or above. b. If your version is below 42.0.2311.90, your browser will be modified automatically. Wait until the update is complete, and then press 'Relaunch' to complete the update.

4. Once your Chrome version is up to date, enter this URL into your browser's address bar:

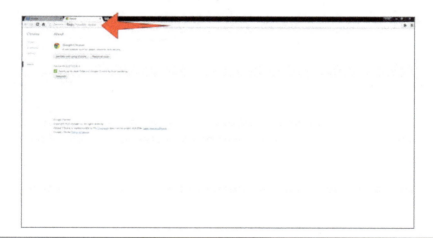

5. Several links are found in the resulting tab. Locate "Enable NPAPI" with the highlighted text. Press "Enable."

- **Phase 3 - Download the Cricut plugin**

1. Click plugins connection or input this URL into your browser's address bar:

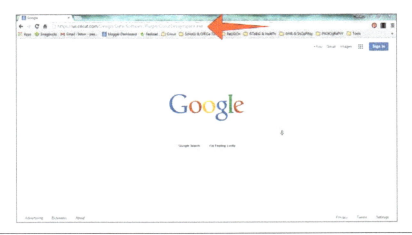

2. At the bottom of the window, the downloaded file will appear. Double-click on the file to begin the process of installing the Cricut plugin.

3. To proceed, press 'Next.'

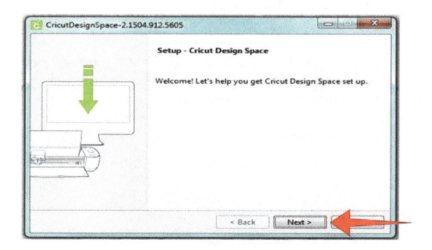

4. Check the Terms of Use and approve them. To proceed, press 'Next.'

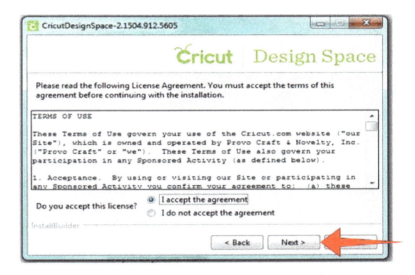

5. Now again, click next.

6. You have preselected the components that you want to install. To proceed, press 'Next.'

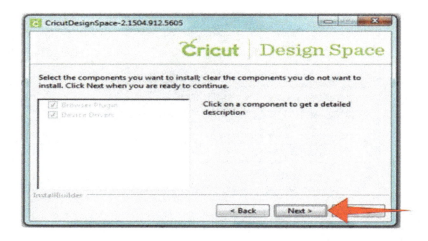

7. You will need to shut down all the browsers. It will prompt you to do so. However, you will always have to do this manually if you are not asked. Tap the toolbar (3 stacked lines in the upper right-hand corner of the browser) and click 'Exit.'

8. To begin the procedure, click on 'Next.'

9. A security question can appear, depending on your computer settings, asking if you would like to install the Provo Craft & Novelty, Inc. system program. To proceed, press 'Install.'

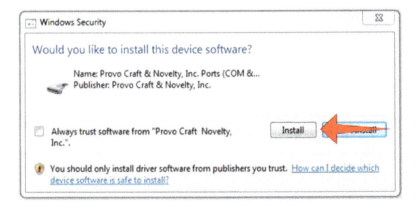

10. The phase of installation will then automatically begin.

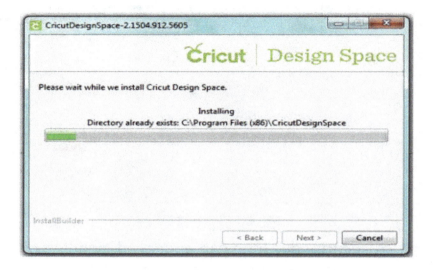

11. The Cricut Concept Space plugin is successfully installed.

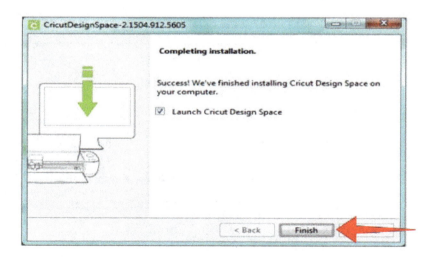

12. If you've checked the Launch Cricut Design Space box, you will be taken to Cricut Design space when your browser reopens. Also, you can open your browser and enter this URL in the address bar to go to Cricut Design Space:

Enable Google Chrome's Cricut plugin

1. Open a new browsing window in Google Chrome by clicking on a tab at the top of the page.

2. Input this URL into your browser's address bar: chrome:/plugins

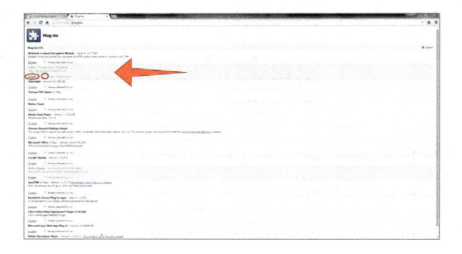

3. In the setting If the Cricut plugin bar is highlighted in grey, click on the word 'Activate' and check the 'Running is still allowed.' If the Cricut plugin bar is "Disable," ensure that the box is checked for "Always allowed to run" and proceed to step 4.

4. Your Cricut plugin is ready to go. Tab on the browser.

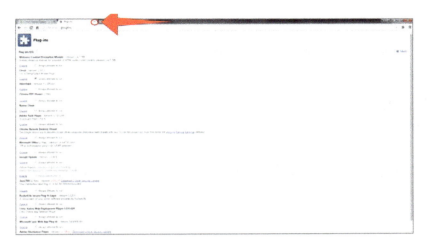

5. You have completed the process of setting up the plugin.

   Enter this URL in your browser's address bar if you need to return to Cricut Design SpaceTM: **www.cricut.com/design**.

Have fun designing!

Cricut Plugin Update Mozilla Firefox

You'll need to install the Design Space plugin to access all the innovative Cricut Design Space. When new features become usable, you'll be prompted to update the plugin from time to time. It's installed on your computer and executed by your browser, so you'll need to install it on each system if you use Design Space on more than one computer. However, to use the Cricut Design Space software on the iPad, installing the plugin is unnecessary.

- **Phase 1** – delete history.
- **Phase 2** – installing Cricut plugin.
- **Phase 3** – activate Cricut plugin.

Phase 1—Delete the History

1. Open the browser and click the menu.

2. Select' History' from the menu.

3. We'll show your browsing history. Select "The Recent History Clear..."

4. A popup window for "Clear All History" will open. Choose "Everything in the "Time range to clear" drop-down menu.

Don't worry; this process won't harm your machine; it just lets Firefox® function from a clean slate. Make sure that there are at least the following boxes checked:

- History of Browsing & Downloading
- Cookie
- Cache

5. Click the button for "Clear Now."

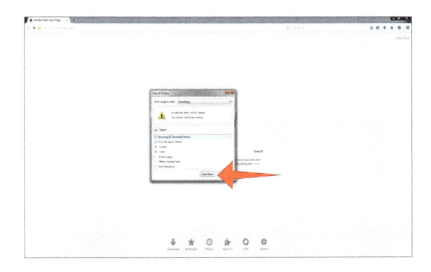

6. The pop-up window will dismiss the browsing data until it has been cleared. Click 'X' in the upper right-hand corner to exit Mozilla, Firefox.

Phase 2 – Download the Cricut Plugin

1. Type this URL into your browser's address bar.

2. To save the file, you will be asked. Tap "File Save."

3. You can open the file by clicking on the arrow in the upper right corner of your screen and then clicking on the file.

4. If you would like to allow Cricut Design Space to be downloaded from the internet, you may be asked. "Tap "Yes" if so.

5. To configure Cricut Template SpaceTM, proceed by clicking "Next."

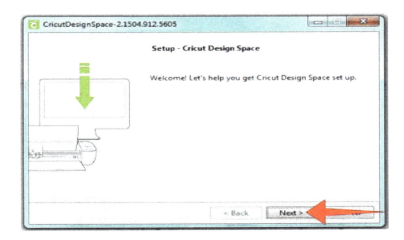

6. Check the Terms of Use and approve them. To proceed, press 'Next.'

7. Click next.

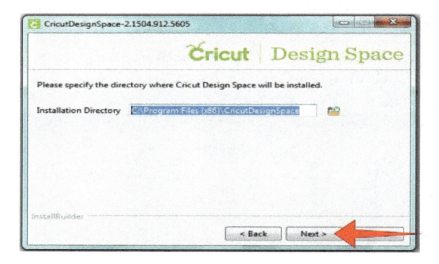

8. You have preselected the components that you want to install. To proceed, press 'Next.'

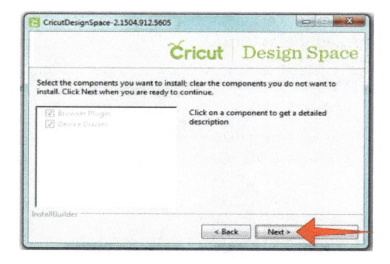

9. You will need to shut down all the browsers. It will prompt you to do so. However, you will always have to do this manually if you are not asked. Click "X" in the upper right-hand corner to exit all open browsers.

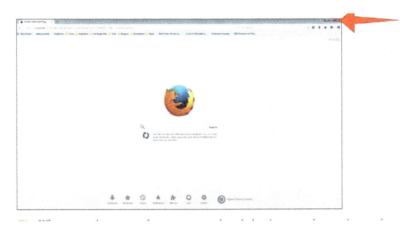

10. To begin the procedure, click on 'Next.'

11. To begin the procedure, click on 'Next.'

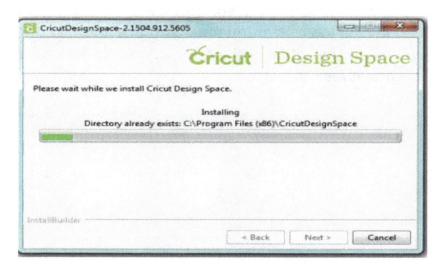

12. A security question can appear, depending on your computer settings, asking if you would like to install the Provo Craft & Novelty, Inc. system program. To proceed, press 'Install.'

13. The plugin for Design Space has been successfully mounted. If you want to open Cricut Design Space automatically on your default browser, leave the box checked and press "Finish."

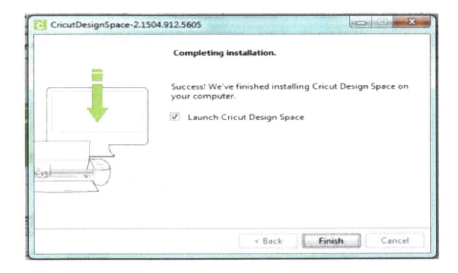

14. Your Cricut plugin has been enabled. You will then be brought to Cricut Design SpaceTM when your browser reopens. You can also enter this URL in your browser's address bar to go to Cricut Design SpaceTM: **www.cricut.com/design**.

Cricut Plugin Update on Mac

You'll need to install the Design Space plugin to access all the innovative Cricut Design Space. When new features become usable, you'll be prompted to update the plugin from time to time. It's installed on your computer and executed by your browser, so you'll need to install it on each system if you use Design Space® on more than one computer. However, to use the Cricut Design Space software on the iPad®, it is not mandatory to install the plugin.

- **Phase 1** – deleting history
- **Phase 2** – installing circuit plugin
- **Phase 3** – activating Circuit plugin in the plugin

Phase 1- Deleting history

1. Open Safari, and from the top menu bar, press History. Then, press Simple History and Data from the Website

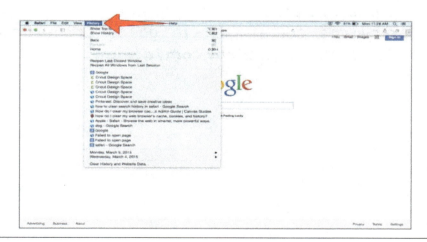

2. It will open a new pop-up window. Select "all history" in the "Clear" drop-down menu. Don't worry; this process won't harm your machine; it merely makes Firefox® work from a clean slate.

3. Click the button for "Clear History."

4. The pop-up window will dismiss the browsing data until it has been cleared. Click "Safari" in the upper left-hand corner to leave Safari. Then from the menu, press 'Quit Safari.'

Phase 2 – Installing Cricut Plugin

1. Plugins URL into the address bar of your browser: **https://us.cricut.com/Design/Data/Software/Plugin/CricutDesignSpace-2.0.0.2R.zip**

2. Click on the Downloads folder on your desktop machine.

3. Click the Cricut Design Space file that you want to access.

4. **Tip:** You will be asked if you are sure that you want to open this application, depending on your device settings. Select 'Open' if so.

5. Enter your password if prompted.

Enter your password if prompted.

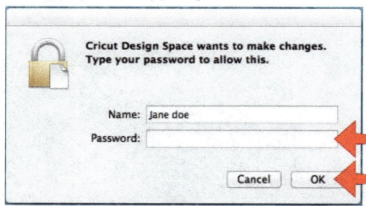

6. It will open the plugin in the plugin. To configure Cricut Template SpaceTM, proceed by clicking "Next."

7. Check the Terms of Use and approve them. To proceed, press 'Next.'

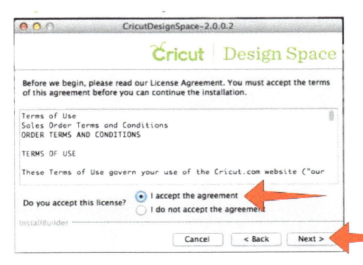

8.   Now click next.

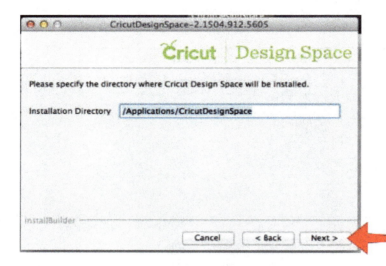

9. To confirm that you want to install the browser plugin for plugins Design Room, click "Next."

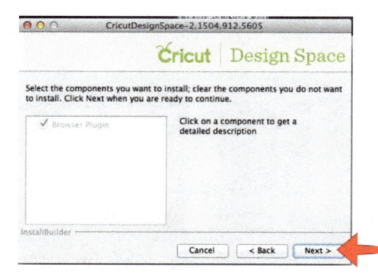

10. Browsers would need to be powered down. Select 'Next' to continue.

11. **Tip:** When you leave, unless it is saved at this stage, you will lose any unsaved work that is currently open in your browser. Click Yes," when you are ready to proceed.

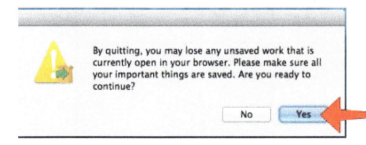

12. The phase of installation will then automatically begin.

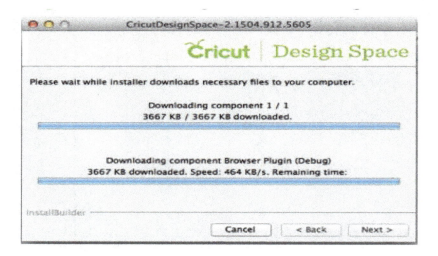

13. The plugin for Design Space has been successfully mounted. If you want to open Cricut Design Space automatically on your default browser, leave the box checked and press "Finish."

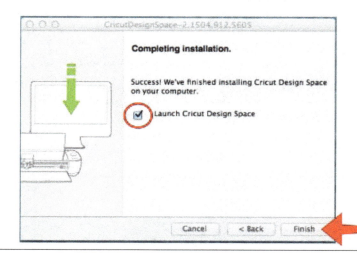

Phase 3 – Activating Cricut Plugin

1. Click on the preference in the menu bar of safari.

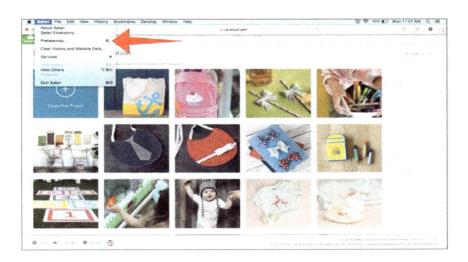

2. Now, click on the security button.

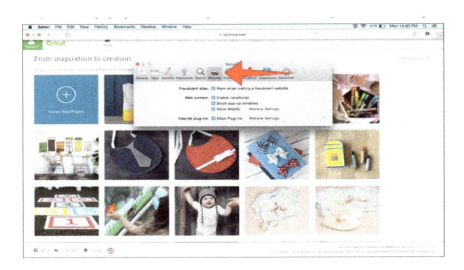

3. Click on the website settings, and the Allow plug-ins options must be ticked.

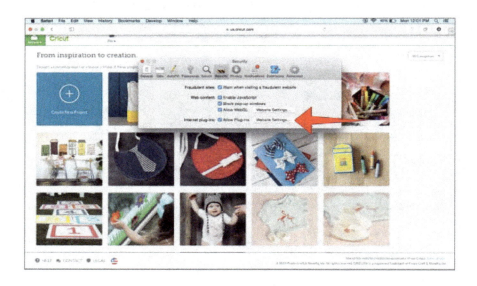

4. Click on "Cricut" and "always allow."

5. Now, click on the 'done' button.

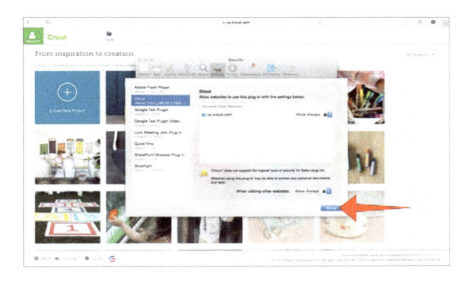

6. Click on the X button to close the window.

7. Now, the process is completed. You can go back to the Cricut design space and enjoy crafting.

Cricut ID

Making Cricut ID

1. You have to create a Cricut id if you are logging in for the first time. Your first name, last name, and the country in which you are living is required.

2. Click on sign in under the account menu.

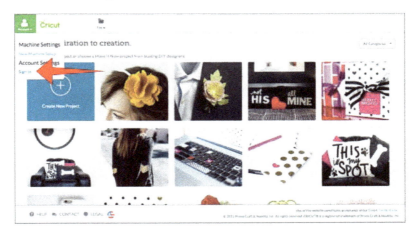

3. The sign-in page will be led to you. In the blue box in the center of the page, press "Create Cricut ID."

4. Use your first name, last name, country, email address, and password to fill in the details. You also will need to check and approve the Cricut Terms of Use to proceed. Click on "Create Cricut ID" in the green box once you have finished filling in the necessary details.

5. Your account will be established, and Cricut Design Space will now be logged into your account. Simply pick 'sign in' under the account menu when you return and then sign in with your email address and password.

6. **Tip:** You can view all of your bought, subscribed, and free photos on all devices with your Cricut ID. You can also access your saved projects from any compatible device or through the Cricut Design Space iPad app.

Signing in With Your Cricut ID

1. If you have done anything before like this, then you have created your id.

2. Access all the pictures that you have ordered, subscribed to, or got for free.

3. Open projects that you have developed and saved on the computer or the iPad app using Cricut Design Room.

4. Save projects while you plan.

5. You can also access the feature under the menu.

Cricut ID Signup

1. Click on the sign-in bar in the account menu.

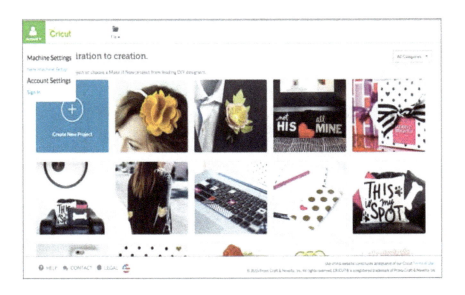

2. The sign-in page will be led to you. Complete your email address and password and then press the green box in the center of the page, 'sign in.'

3. Your name will appear on the account menu, signaling that you are now signed in to your account.

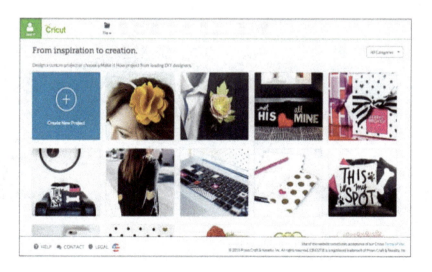

Editing Your Account Details

1. Via Cricut Design Space for PC and Mac, you can update your Cricut ID account details.

2. Click on the signup button on the account menu.

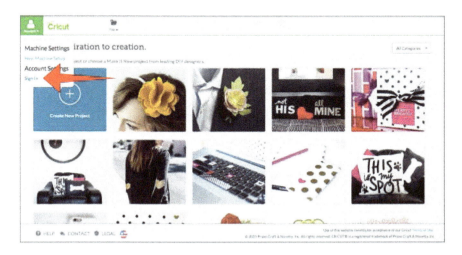

3. The sign-in page will be led to you. Please enter your email address and password

4. Then press 'Sign in' on the green box in the center of the screen.

5. You are returned to the screen from which you began (in this case, the project screen). Tap "Account Details" in the top left corner of the screen under the Account menu.

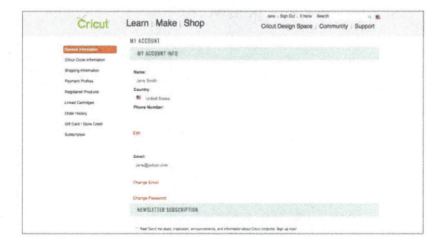

6. To change your account information or update/add your billing information, press 'Edit account.'

7. You can close the tab when you've finished editing your Cricut ID account information. Close the Account Information screen in Design Space by pressing X.

Chapter 3: Maintenance of the Cricut Machine

Cleaning the Cricut Machines

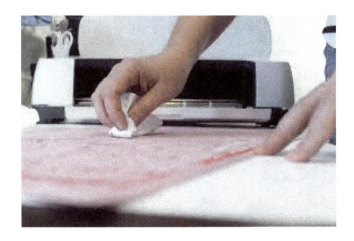

- Wipe the exterior panels gently with a damp rag.

- Dry any surplus moisture instantly with a chamois or other soft fabric.

- Do not use the machine with chemicals or alcohol-based cleaners (including but not limited to acetone, benzene, and tetrachloride carbon). It would help if you also avoided scratchy cleaners and cleaning equipment. Do not dip the machine in water or any part of it.

- Try not to eat and drink when using the unit, but stay away from food and liquids.

- Keep it in a dry, dust-free spot

- Don't put the machine where there is too much dust.
- Do not expose to direct sunlight for long.

Caring for the Cutting Mat

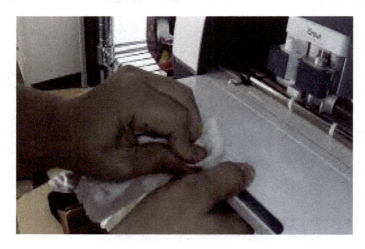

- You should expect the Cricut Cutting Mat to be used anywhere from 25-40 full mat cuts before replacement is needed.
- Depending on the settings you use and the papers you cut, the actual cutting mat life can vary.
- It's time to replace the mat when the paper no longer sticks to the cutting mat.
- It is often recommended that only real Cricut replacements be used.
- You can get replacement parts for Cricut machines from Cricut itself, and you can also get parts online from several other locations.

- We suggest that you only use original parts that would not only void your warranty, but these parts are 100% compatible.

Applying Grease to Circuit Machine

- Switch off a Cricut Explore machine

- Shift the carriage of the Cut Smart by moving it to the left slowly.

- Shift the Cut Smart carriage by turning it slowly towards the right.

- Repeat the entire process in the bar.

- Slowly move the Cut Smart carriage towards the center of the unit.

- Open the lubrication packet and squeeze the end of the cotton swab with a tiny amount of grease.

- Apply the grease equally on the counter and then patiently apply to the right and left.
- Clean the grease at the end.

Chapter 4: Materials That Can Be Worked on Using a Cricut Machine

Cricut Machine works with the help of some materials. All of them are explained briefly in this chapter

Mats for Cutting

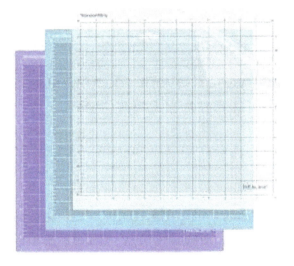

The mats have a layer of plastic sheeting, which exposes a sticky surface when removed. During the cut, this will keep the materials in place. Several brands sell varying stick levels, but an essential mat will work well for this book's projects.

Frosted Text-Weight Paper

It is one of everyone's favorite documents to use with the cutting machine for many reasons.

Firstly, this paper can be sliced effortlessly and cleanly by most blades.

Second, for paper projects that are flat or curved, or otherwise shaped, the frosted finish adds a gorgeous dimension.

Finally, because of the illusion of added color, the frosted finish provides the material of choice for most paper flowers and plants.

Text-Weight Paper

For flowers, leaves, and other elements that do not need card stock's stiffness, the follow-up option is always a colored text-weight paper when we cannot find a color in the frosted paper.

Vellum Paper

We love to add a touch of this translucent paper for lantern windows, bug wings, and even leaves. While windows and wings look best in white vellum, you can choose colored or frosted vellum for other projects.

Glitter Paper

Some projects need glitter quite clearly! We find that those made by the cutting machine manufacturers or papers with a tiny glitter that does not rub off are the best glitter papers for the cutting machine.

Paper cannot cut too well with big pieces of glitter and sometimes dulls the razor.

Card Stock Paper

With the stiffness of card stock paper, many projects perform best. We have found that some brands perform best on the cutting machines and when being separated from the mat, mostly mass-market brands break and peel. Make sure your blade is set correctly (you might want to test a scrap) for the paper's weight and use a cutting mat with plenty of grips so that the paper does not move during the cut.

Art Paper

We find a great variety at the art supplies store when we need extra-large paper for jumbo tropical leaves or cactus plants. Similar weight to card stock is Canson or similar brands and will need to be trimmed to match the 12X12 or 12X24-inch mat.

Vinyl

You can buy so many vinyl types and shades, and new options debut every year: matte, polished, silver, frosted, glitter, and to name a few brushed metals. With your machine-branded vinyl; you can have better performance, as it is high quality and created to fit well with the machine.

Iron-On Vinyl

Also known as heat-transfer vinyl, iron-on vinyl comes in several colors and finishes, similar to standard vinyl. Again, different brands will give you different results, so be sure to test a small cut with your material if you buy one for the color. We have found a few varieties that offer us too.

Materials from Paper Art

There are many issues, but we prefer to stick to the three iron-on vinyl cutting machine brands.

Paper Craft Materials

Foam Balls and Wreaths

For wreaths and topiaries, we prefer smooth-surface foam because it is more potent than Styrofoam. Before inserting cut paper leaves and flowers, you will always have to camouflage the foam by covering it with ribbon or crepe paper.

Floral Wire

For crafting solid flower stems with a clean finish, we prefer an 18-gauge paper-covered floral wire. Remember that you prefer the wire version without the paper covering if you are making paper flowers to mix into a vase of fresh greens or flowers so that your paper blooms remain dry.

Grapevine Wreaths

For the fall-themed models, WE love the grapevine look. At your nearest craft shop, find these pre-made wreaths. For an easy-to-assemble decoration, they make a perfect foundation.

Brown Paper-Covered Wire

Use this wire to form shapes; your paper cut shapes look good peeking through it.

Gold Metal Hoop

At fabric stores or online, you can find these hoops. For small wreaths, they make a pretty foundation.

Wood Embroidery Hoops

For a tablet, an embroidery frame's internal hoop is the right size and can also be used as a simple type of wreath.

Yarn

For the Easter brunch, we use yarn for our unicorn tail and mane (this page), as well as the carrot tops and bunny tails (this page). Instead of twine or ribbon, you can also use thread.

Twine and Thread

Our picks for adding garlands, flags, and paper leis are cotton and baker's twine. For ornaments and holiday garlands, we use gold embroidery thread when we need a metallic look. For the jumbo flower backdrop, the cotton rope makes a solid stem (this page) and a flexible base for the fall leaf garland (this page).

Ribbons

Pretty ribbons add the final touches to a mini wreath or glitter flower wand (this page). We often have a stash on hand to wrap presents or tie festive jars around the lids.

Wood Toothpicks, Skewers, Dowels, and Beads

Wood toothpicks or skewers are convenient for the cupcake toppers to put the paper decorations in the frosting (this page).

For a selection of bamboo skewers, visit the cooking section of your local kitchen supply store and the craft store for various thicknesses and lengths of wood dowels and wood bead sizes.

The long thick dowels for making flower backdrops can be found at your local hardware store.

Pan Pastel Pigments

These beautiful pastels have become a favorite in the studio, particularly when paper flower petals and leaves are given a soft ombré effect. Online or at your nearest art supplies shop, you will find them.

Markers or Colored Pencils

Markers or colored pencils based on water or alcohol add detail to some paper craft projects in this book (this page). At your nearest art supplies shop, find an extensive range of colors.

Papercraft Adhesives

Low-temp Hot Glue Gun

We have concluded that a low-temp model not only gives me the sticking power we need when using hot glue with paper, but keeps blisters off the tips of fingers. For this friendlier edition, we highly recommend you trade in your high-temp glue gun.

Foam Adhesive Squares

Loved by scrapbookers and card makers, these small foam risers provide the gap between the layers to add dimension to paper-cut artwork.

Glue Dots

These dots are a perfect solution when your project needs only a touch of a stick.

Double-sided Adhesive Roller

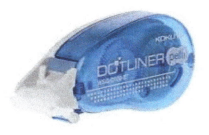

We keep this tape stored in our studio for paper projects that need a smooth, slim adhesive. For the best performance, we suggest you pick a permanent stick.

Iron-On Tools of Vinyl

Weeding Tool

While this tool looks like you picked it up from your dentist's office, it is a must to extract quickly the cut bits from within your design information.

Iron and Ironing Surface

For iron-on vinyl, a regular iron and ironing board will fit.

With its wide surface, even temperature, and a built-in timer, Cricut provides an iron called the Easy Press, which has become a favorite in our studio. For a larger ironing surface than what your ironing board offers, you can buy a table-top ironing pad (or look up instructions online to make one).

Ironing Cloth

We still have an ironing cloth nearby while making projects with iron-on vinyl. Some top plastic layers work well with the iron directly heating the surface, whereas other brands do not. In that scenario, the ironing cloth would cover the rubber. You can make an ironing cloth from a recycled 100 percent cotton sheet or a piece of white quilting fabric made from cotton.

Tools from Vinyl

Vinyl Transfer Material

This material is necessary for the efficient transfer of vinyl to different smooth surfaces (such as glass and plastic), so in our studio, we keep many rolls on hand.

- **Burnishing tool:** While you can use the edge of other flat tools, we prefer the plastic burnishing tool.

Weeding Tool

We discussed this tool in an earlier paragraph, but it is a vital instrument for your craft room because it simplifies removing tiny bits inside your detailed design.

Sometimes you are left with vacant spaces, bigger walls, or new rooms asking for something, well different!

Since art seems costly, and you can never be sure that it will work from home to home; whenever possible, you can add your own DIY. Everyone is not an artist, though, so you can turn to the Cricut sometimes to support.

We have come up with a process that is not just foolproof but also very simple and highly flexible, having made a lot of art for our walls over the years. We want to break down the easiest way of creating art with a Cricut so that you can also have amazing DIY designs on your walls!

Scissors

A good pair of crafting scissors is required for each maker. We love the 8" and the smaller 5" smaller types of crafting scissors. Scissors must be used precisely.

Chapter 5: What Projects Can You Make on a Cricut Machine and How to Use Them?

Decals on Vinyl

Our first hobby is to cut vinyl stickers and decals, and naturally, with the Cricut, you can do so.

It is easy to slice through every vinyl—you need the template in Cricut's design room; the machine can be instructed to begin cutting, weed, and move it to the desired surface.

Cutting Cloth

The assumption that it came with the new brand Rotary Blade is the key selling point of the Manufacturer.

It means the machine can cut practically any material thanks to a single gliding and rolling action, along with the massive 4 kg strength of the Cricut Builder. That's right. That's correct. Denim? Denim? Check out.

We had to use a special cutter until we could only handle heavier fabrics on desktop cutting machines. We love the fact that the Maker is a total computer.

It's also ready fitted with a fabric mat that can be cut without any assistance from hundreds of different fabrics. Outstanding! Excellent!

Patterns in Sewing

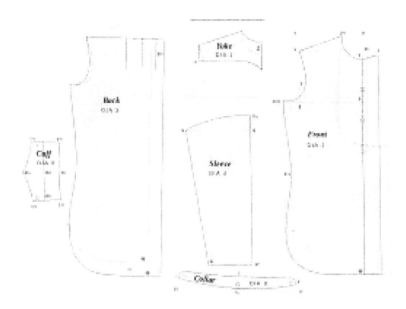

Another significant pro of both the Manufacturer is the vast knitting pattern collection, which you can access after the machine has been purchased.

It includes hundreds of patterns—some of them are from Convenience and Riley Blake, and you can pick the pattern you like, and the Maker will cut it for you. No more manually cutting off the patterns (but no more errors of operator error)!

A reusable fabric design that shows where the design parts should fit along has been included.

Cuts in Balsa Wood

The Cricut maker can cut objects up to 2.4 mm deep with a massive force of kg and a separately sold Knife Blade.

It means that we now have dense textiles that had been beyond the limits of the Cricut and Silhouette presses. We can't wait for it to begin cutting wood!

Thick Cutting of Leather

Thick leather can be trimmed with the Maker in a similar vein as point #4!

Household Cards

Both paper artisans and the maker are not left out. Owing to the computer's strength and accuracy, page and board cuts are more straightforward and faster than before. You only went a step up your homemade items.

Puzzles Jigsaw

We know from the Knife Blade that the Cricut Machine can cut materials much denser than ever.

Do we want to do the first thing? Create a puzzle. Make our own. We're going to keep you up-to-date!

Ornaments of Christmas Tree

The Rotary Blade, which promises to cut all the textiles, is the perfect instrument for decorating.

Scour the Christmas themed design library (we have an eye on the man's gingerbread ornament!). Scour the pattern with the felt or anything that you like.

Quilts

The cricut has collaborated with Hayden Casey Designs in the stitching design library to display a collection of needlework patterns.

Dolls and Soft Toys by Felt

The 'Felt Doll and Clothing' pattern is one of the Simplicity designs we have our hands-on in the stitching pattern library. You know many little girls and boys who would love to add to their collection a homemade doll.

Pick, cut, and stitch the pattern. Yeah, Easy Strategic options!

T-Shirt Transfers

Of course, the Cricut Maker would be a whizz at cutting out your heat transfer vinyl for you to transfer your designs to fabric.

All you need to do is plan your Design Space transfer, load the maker with your vinyl heat transfer (or even HTV glitter if you feel adventurous), tell the machine to start cutting, and then iron your T-shirt with your transfer.

Baby Wears

Unfortunately, the Cricut Maker's mat scale is just 12" x 24", so you won't be able to cut patterns of adult size clothing on this unit. But the size should be just large enough to cut the patterns of baby clothes.

Clothes for Dolls

For doll clothes, too! Take a look at these American Baby Doll trends in action.

Appliques of Cloth

The bonded fabric blade in the housing is also available for purchase separately, which will allow you to cut more complex fabric designs, such as appliques.

The bonded fabric blade needs bonded backing on the cloth, unlike the rotary blade, to cut effectively.

Signs from Calligraphy

The primary selling point of the Cricut maker is its adaptive tool system.

It is the function that will ensure that you stay forever with your maker. It's a tool system that not only works with all the Explore family's tools and blades, but will also work with all Cricut's future tools and blades.

The calligraphy pen is one of these devices. Ideal for designing cards and making signs!

The Making of Jewelry

You can probably try to merge the two at some point if you want to dabble in jeweler making alongside your craft cutting.

The Cricut Maker intensity means that thicker materials can be cut than before, which are well suited to the complex jeweler designs.

While you're not likely to be cutting gold, silver, or diamond on it anytime soon, a lovely pair of leather earrings is certainly within reach.

Invitations for weddings and Save the Dates

We all know how 'small' costs like invitations and STDs will add to a wedding's mega cost.

But as designers, by making stuff like that ourselves, we also know how to cover some of those costs.

Not only can you cut out intricate paper designs, the Cricut Maker is great for making beautiful invitations, but the calligraphy pen will again be useful.

Menus for Weddings, Location Cards, and Favor Tags

Of course, before the wedding, you're certainly not only limited to crafts; you can even use your Maker to decorate for the big day itself.

The sky is the limit here, but certainly start with menus, place cards, and favor tags for crafting. To keep the theme front and center, try to make sure that you use a similar style for all your stationery.

Book of Coloring

Do you know those 'mindful coloring' books right now that are all the rage? Well, if you don't want to splash the cash for one thing, why not make your own with the Cricut Maker?

All you need is paper, a card, and a template that cracks and then just commands the maker using the Fine-Point Pen tool to create your very own, completely original, coloring book.

Coasters

Coasters are another thing we can't wait to build with our new maker brand.

As far as materials go, the world is your oyster-everything from leather to quilt, to metallic sheets and anything in between.

There are also some nice coaster designs in the sewing library to try out too.

Key Rings Fabric

Something else that caught our attention in the sewing pattern library was a few basic designs for fabric key rings.

The Maker makes it simple again; just cut the pattern out and then sews it together.

Headbands and Decorations for Hair

Cricut has launched a machine that can cut through thick leather; you have a great idea for intricate hair decorations influenced by steampunk and even headbands. For amazing fashion statements, who knew the maker could be so useful?

Christmas Tree Cut Out

You know everyone during the holiday season needs a real Christmas tree.

But just in case you don't have space in your living room for a towering tree, or, heaven forbid, you're allergic to pine, you may want to make a tree of your own.

Assume that an interlocking wooden tree is a perfect project to play with this year, as the Cricut maker can cut thick materials such as wood. When the manufacturer is at your beck and call, no laser is needed!

Toppers for Cake

Remember when Cricut pulled out the cutter machine for the 'Cake?' It was for making forms made from fondant, the paste of gum, and the like.

Yeah, the Maker isn't a professional cake machine like the Cake, but we think it's just the machine we would use to decorate our cakes to produce tiny and intricate paper crafts.

Magnets for Fridge

The Builder can cut out magnetic stuff, much like the Cricut Explore units. Good news for magnet collectors and anyone who would like to spice up their fridge!

Coats with Craft Foam

The Cricut machines have always said that craft foam can be cut, but we've found that the outcome is never as perfect as we want. Not so with the Cricut Maker: the force of 4 kg means this machine can cut through craft foam such as butter, leaving the machines behind in the dust to explore.

Stencils

With the Maker, if your goal is to create things that can help you create other beautiful things, and then you're in luck. It is the perfect stencil making machine, especially now that you can use thicker materials, including wood, to create the stencils on it.

Temporary Tattoos

Would you like a tattoo, but are you not so keen on lifelong commitment?

Washy Tape

The wash tape is the decoration of the year for scrap bookers, but if you buy a lot of it at craft shops, it can be shockingly pricey.

Why not make your own then? The Cricut Maker will cut out sheets of wash, enabling you to print and cut your designs on them.

Envelopes Discussed

Perhaps you should move on to the envelopes when you've done those personalized wedding invitations we were discussing earlier.

But when you have the producer, there's no need to waste time and energy addressing them yourself. Since both a Fine-Point and a Calligraphy pen are fitted, you will be able to address automatically the envelopes, using whatever elegant font you want. Only make sure it's plain enough to be read by the postman.

Decoration

You will be able to build it with the Cricut Maker, whether it is stunning signage in your closets, adorable cut-outs in your living room, or 3D wall hangings.

Transfers of Cushion

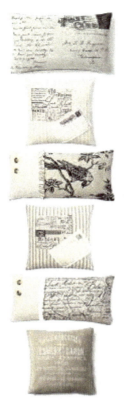

Adding one of your homemade designs to it is the easiest way to brighten up a dull pillow or cushion.

To do just that, several individuals would use heat transfer vinyl on their brand-new Maker unit. The flocked iron-on vinyl that gives the beautifully textured feel is our favorite type of vinyl for cushions.

3D Bouquet

That's right; we're back on the subject of weddings again!

It is a perfect way to add a touch of home crafting to your wedding or, even better, without thinking about their imminent demise, to add some flowers to your home. In no time, you will have a lovely, immortal bouquet for yourself!

Tags for a gift

Gift tags, particularly during the holiday season, are another of those irritating expenses that easily add up over time.

Bags

It is where the purchase of a knife blade to slice through thick leather is likely to come in handy.

Collars from Peter Pan

So, we mentioned earlier that the variety of the clothing patterns you're going to be able to cut on the Cricut Maker is about baby and doll clothes.

Ok, that was a lie (sorry!)—you can certainly cut patterns for accessories for adult clothes here.
We've spotted more than one simple collar styles that fashionistas would love.

Cricut Maker Covers

You can also use the Maker to produce stuff for the Maker. For the egg, a dust cover, we love that the Maker can cut canvas!

Cushions of Pin

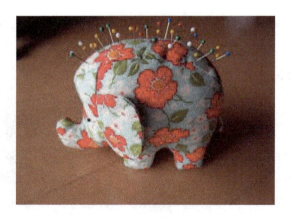

For the sewers, this is one.

Cushions and Pillows

With the Maker, you will also be able to cut patterns for little pillows and cushions. These would be small since the overall cut size is just 12 "x 24 ", but for the living room and children's bedrooms, that's plenty of decorative scatter cushions.

Clothes for Dogs

If you have a toy or a small dog, with the Maker you'll also be able to create some fun things for them.

It is currently limited to only apparel, specifically dog hats.

We know our canine friends won't last two seconds with top hats on their heads, but if your dog loves a good photoshoot, it could work for you!

Socks

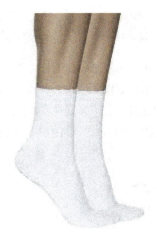

Make sure your tootsies don't skip the crafting action by cutting the Cricut Maker with some woolly sock designs. They look like they're going to be a doddle for sewing together too!

Stockings for Christmas

Have you cottoned on yet that we're extremely excited to use our new Christmas celebration Maker?!

Anyway, there's a particularly interesting template in the sewing pattern library for a Christmas stocking that we will certainly be playing with next December.

The only question is which material should be used? We're not sure it would be suitable for thick leather here.

Merry Christmas! #50ShadesOfChristmas

Wall Art

We've spoken a lot about the paper crafts you can do with the Maker, but we believe it's worth noting that wall art is also a possibility for you.

The accuracy level provided by the Maker is so advanced that with ease, you will be able to build something beautiful and flawless.

Corkboard Hanging

You can cut your cook board, and there will be a lot of opportunities for you.

How about a heart-shaped corkboard that hangs behind your craft table on the wall?

Keepers of Cupcakes

You could use the Cricut Maker to make cake toppers, but what about the bottom of what brings the cake together?

Chapter 6: Where to Find Materials for Ideas about Projects

- You can find the material ideas from internet explorer, interest, and many websites by just typing the name of the cricut project you want.

- If you want to see the projects' list, type the cricut projects in any browser, and you will get many project ideas.

- Here we are providing you a great website where you can easily find elegant project ideas for your cricut maker.

Cricut Community

It is easily available in the design space. Be sure to be more descriptive while searching.

Type urn in the search box.

https://help.cricut.com/hc/en-us/articles/360027251034-How-do-I-search-for-projects-in-the-Cricut-Community-

Guidelines

1. Sign in with your Cricut id.

Sign in with your Cricut ID

Email / Cricut ID

Password

Enter your password

Forgot?

☑ Remember me

Don't have an account yet?

Create A Cricut ID

2. Click on the ribbon button to enable the project list.

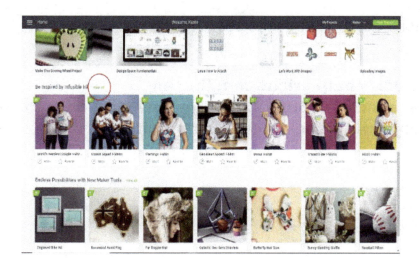

3. Click on Cricut community.

4. In the search section, search for the content.

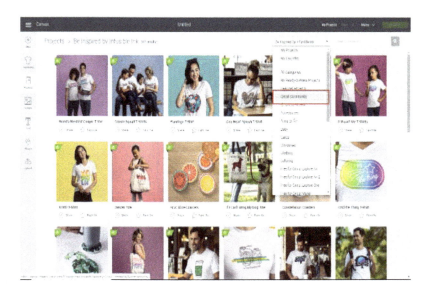

5. The more clearly you search, the better. You can get many ideas from this website. Enjoy making or downloading designs!!

Chapter 7: Cricut Project for Beginners

Spinner Card with Cricut Template

Customize the top sheet. Now add words, shapes, etc. It will be easier to get before the card's rest is layered. Remember that you don't want to close the track with something with dimension since it could mess with the portion you're going to spin later.

Next, fold the base of the card in a quarter and adhere to the grey layer downwards. Then glue the two foam bits of the rectangle to the bottom of the white cardboard. Hold them up to the sides, not near to the cut-out track.

Layer the form that is going to spin on top of that.

Glue the whole mixture of white cardstock/craft foam to the front of the card and practice spinning the card when it is dry.

Simple Flowers of Paper

We love paper, blossoms! There is a beautiful thing about a flower that never stops flowering. In the Cricut Design Space, we found the perfect flower shape (for what we needed), and we wanted to show you how to personalize it and make it your own.

1. **Type 'Crop' into the Design Space search bar:** There are several choices for flowering; most will work as long as it has an intense center. The choice is up to you!

2. **Insert your choice of the flower into the project:** We have chosen a flower with five points and the concrete core we need.

3. Five Times copy and paste flower:

4. Be sure to make each one smaller than the one before when you paste each flower. For your final product, this will generate different sizes for depth and texture.

5. **According to layout/mat, line paper:** The light map was used.

6. Cut the project now.

7. Take freshly cut flowers out of the mat.

8. Take your time and lift them gently off the Light Grip mat and away from it.

9. **Line up cut flowers from largest to smallest in order:** Put in an order for your flowers so they will be ready for stacking.

10. From the middle, bend petals up.

11. Start with your most giant paper flower and repeat with the other four, each time bending a little more.

12. Join flowers with glue.

13. Take your adhesive and layer the flowers on top of each other, beginning with your base flower (the largest) to the smallest.

14. Your project is finalized! Any room or even event will brighten up these flowers. Choose to use them or appreciate the flexibility of a single bloom in a grouping of multiples.

How to Do Glass Etching with Your Cricut's Machine

To cut out a graphic on a stencil, use Cricut. As it makes it easier to stencil, make sure to leave enough space around the graphic (you don't have to worry about being too close to the edge).

Weed the graphic—instead of the usual taking away all except the graphic, you will do the reverse.

"Be careful of the fine swirly font specifics & the insides of letters such as "o," "b," "e," etc.

Wash with rubbing alcohol to prepare the bottle. It eliminates fingerprints from any mark and any sticky residue.

Use transfer tape to pass the stencil onto the bottle, including the insides of the letters. The Cricut brand is too sticky for certain people, but in this situation, it's a good thing because you want to make sure you don't skip the inside of your letters or the dots on top of your letters, such as the letter 'I.' Right on top of the stencil film, put the transfer tape. Pull up both layers of the backing paper and add them to the bottle. Remove the transfer tape once it is on the bottle.

For burnishing use the scraping tool. You want to pay careful attention to the actual graphic. It doesn't need to be flawless; you need to be specific around the cut-outs so that there is no leakage. Bubbles (away from the graphic) around the outside are perfect. Since the glass is curved, it will be challenging to get it perfect (if not impossible)-so think about the actual stencil.

Wait for the etching cream for 20 minutes to work its magic. Set a timer easily and do something else.

TIP: Regularly inspect the glass and pass the etching cream around. This method allows you to get an even coating. There are also tiny air bubbles that are stuck, and you can't see them, so you're going to get an even etching. You should re-use the cream for etching!

Peel the stencil off. Unfortunately, the stencil is not reusable with the Oramask; it may rip when you take it off. You're going to have to scrape the little bits from within the letters.

Rinse with water. Wash the glass at the same time, too. Make sure all the cream for etching is gone. Let it sit down to dry. On the stove, turn stuff upside down.

With the Cricut Simple Glass Engraving

Stage 1: What You're Going to Need Here

- It is essential to have protection goggles. The etchant that we will use is based on hydrofluoric acid, and if you get it in your eyes, it will mess you up. Nitrile gloves may also be considered. It is not a Kid's Project. Keep the etchant out of reach well.

- Choose a beer mug that has smooth sides. We're going to stick your name on the vinyl side, so you can imagine how hard it would be with a dimpled mug. If you screw them up, the local dollar store makes lovely mugs you can afford to trash. (Although you will be pleased to say that your first attempt was just fantastic).

Stage 2: Build a Stencil

- We're going to cut the vinyl out of your name and stick the remaining vinyl hole in the mug to reveal the glass you want to etch. Therefore, power up your Cricut; you can cut your name straight from the Cricut's keyboard if you are familiar with it.

- Cut a piece of vinyl that will fit on your Mat (with the backing still in place). In the center of your article, place the text roughly.

Stage 3: The Stencil Is Added

- Put the stencil on very carefully and then smooth it over. You don't want any creases in vinyl, at least not anywhere near the letters' edges.

- Place spare vinyl cuts all over the edges after you've applied the stencil so that the mug is well covered—just in case any etchant drips on to the mug or elsewhere.

- If you have a letter with a hole in it, such as 'O' or A,' the only tricky part here is that you will need to place carefully the tiny vinyl cut-out that reflects the hole into the gap belongs in the vinyl.

- Before we continue to etch it, it may be worth cleaning the glass where the letters are with a clean lens cloth.

Stage 4: Etch!

- Put your protection goggles and nitrile gloves on now and take the mug and your etchant to work outside. This material is sticky and doesn't spill much, but you don't want to take the risk of a pet knocking it on your carpet—make sure there are no pets around, and for the next ten minutes while the etchant is exposed, have someone else look after any children.

- Paint the Armor Etch on the letters' edges very thick and even, particularly around them. The bottle says to wait for 5 minutes but a better etch will be provided for 7 minutes.

- All the Etchant's Hose Off

- Done!

- Dry the mug clean, and you're able to drink it out!

Chapter 8: Cricut Project for Intermediate

Pumpkin Pillow

- A season pillow was one thing that was lacking at home. We picked up a bunch and made a bunch of holiday-themed pillows because Cricut came out with pillowcases as another choice for Infusible Ink Cricut Gaps.

- For the fall-inspired pillow, we had a lot of ideas, but until we saw the black and white gingham Infusible Ink pads, it sealed the deal. In this layout, we figured a pumpkin might appear pretty adorable and it does!

Get Template Tips

Phase 1—Your Designs Are Created

For the most part, when making projects with other Cricut devices, this move is identical. The key difference is to make sure that you have the correct machine selected from the drop-down menu once you open the Design Room.

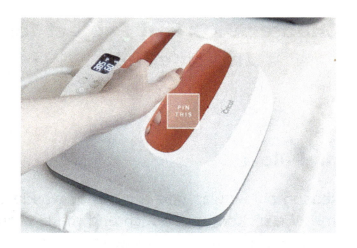

Using the Cricut Room, build your design. The cricut has free tones of fonts, images, and read-made designs. Via Cricut Entry, there are loads more available too. You can also upload your templates in any of the following formats if you are graphic design savvy: jpg, gif, pang, and .bmp.

Making a Notebook with DIY Leather

Did you know that you can use Cricut Maker to make your DIY?

To Add the Iron-On

- Now you can start making your custom notebook. Begin to add the iron-on to your piece of the leather outside. A couple of tips here:

  1. You can use Easy Press to achieve optimum performance.

  2. With the carrier sheet still attached, placed the snuffed piece of iron-on directly onto the leather. To protect the ground, cover a whole thing with parchment paper.

  3. For time and temperature, follow the official Cricut Easy Press guidelines.

  4. Remove the carrier sheet while it is still hot.

Your Bits Folding

- You can now divide all of your paper bits on those score lines you built in the Cricut Builder. The scoring wheel helps you to create folds that are flawless and effortless.

Your stock of white cards should be put in three of the three stacks. On two of the score lines, fold the foil poster board as it will line your leather piece.

Designing the Notebook Leather

- Then, as shown below, use a quick dry adhesive to position the foil poster board inside your notebook. With the wide slits in the leather, line up the folds.

- Once dry, use a craft knife to transfer those cut slits to the foil piece.

- You will also want to mark each card stock piece along the fold exactly where the slits will end up once assembled. Then use a needle to poke a hole in these locations. It will make sewing a bit easier later.

- Then use a needle and thread to sew up your journal. Start with your knot on the inside; go through the three card stock sheets, then through the foil and leather.

- You will then go up through the next slot in the leather and foil, then through the next set of holes in the card stock. Repeat for all four slit locations.

- Continue through each of the three sets of three until all of your paper has been sewn into the leather notebook.

- Knot off your thread and you have completed your project! But how do you keep your new leather journal closed? Well, that is easy!

- Just pull up on the loop you created in the leather and then pulled it through the rectangular hole. Add a pen, and this is one cute DIY leather journal!

- You can write all of your deep thoughts or jot down some notes!

Cricut Maker—Cutting Basswood with Knife Blade

- With the Cricut Maker and the knife blade, trim the basswood. When using your knife blade to cut timber, there are a few things to mind.

- Be sure to use your right grip pad and use masking tape to tape the wood down along all edges.

- Cut with the required basswood setting and carefully monitor your unit. Start testing the cut at about halfway through the cut to see if it is complete. When the bits are cut all the way through, remove the material from your machine.

- The knife blade fits well with this starfish template, but very complicated designs won't cut well.

- You would want to use a glue gun to stack them up until your pieces are removed. On each of the coasters, apply two circular arcs and one circle with a starfish picture frame. On top of your wood bits, set something heavy, and let them dry completely.

- You're ready to paint once you dry up. Paint the coasters well with blue paint on all sides, including the inside. Could you enable them to dry absolutely?

- The contrasting resin can then be applied to the inlay. In compliance with the product instructions, blend a small quantity of the resin. Using the pigment to tint whatever color you like with it. Then pour in the formed hole with this resin. You would need to be able to cure this overnight. Ensure that any bubbles that rise to the surface pop and allow them to heal on a flat surface.

- Again, weigh and combine the 2-part substance according to the instructions for the box. Pour over the top, then. Once again, make sure that any bubbles pop and recover on a flat surface. Enable to cure before touching, overnight.

Cut the Burlap

- Cut the rotational blades and the pink textile mat out from the vinyl.

- Cut out the bunnies next. You can use various Hematite Vinyl colors or only one color. Another fascinating substance will be felt. Just put some "Heat n Bond" back on it and use that rotational cutter to cut it off.

- But you do need to make sure you put the Iron-On down on your mat on the right side. To secure the picture on to the burlap, use your Easy Press or your Iron. Use it at 385°F for 25–30 seconds on the foil level.

- Before wicking out certain moisture that may linger there, be sure to turn your burlap. Dampness and the application of vinyl should not go easy. Now thread your banner in between our letters.

T-Shirts Personalized

- Focus on cutting your pieces of vinyl. Click here for Design Space access.

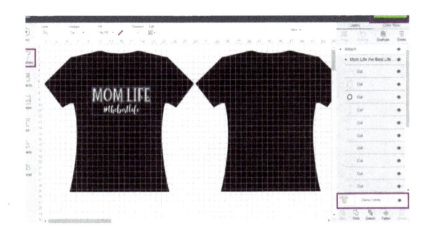

- Using your fine point blade to cut your iron-on vinyl terms.
- Don't forget to mirror the iron-on vinyl cuts and put them on your mat shiny side.

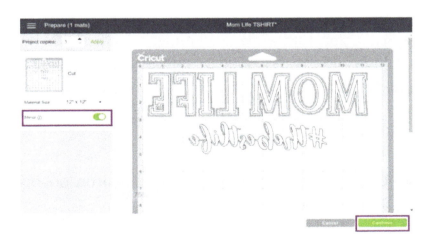

- Break the sleeve out of the felt.
- Use the weeding software.

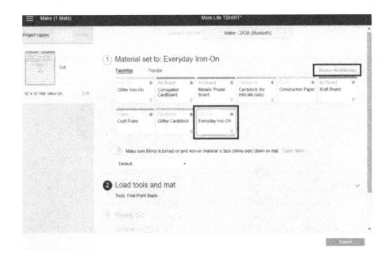

- Attach your coffee sleeve with vinyl.

- Break the Velcro out to complete this project. Cut a section to match your sleeve and apply to the overlap with fabric-designed glue. Could you enable it to dry entirely before use?

- Download the above SVG file. Then follow the instructions in Cricut Design Space for upload.

- To send your Cricut unit, press "makes it."

- Switch your mat's mirror on.

- Tap on "Continue."

- Choose from the list the type of iron-on or heat transfer vinyl that you use.

- Add the face of the material to your mat. Typically, this is light or "right side down.

- Feed your computer into the mat and press the "C" to cut your template.

- Then, all the excess of your Cricut t-shirt style must be washed out. It means getting rid of everything around and the letter centers. Here you can get the top wedding tips.

- Use an Easy Press or Iron to put your design on your shirt. Here you can see how your iron-on is applied.

Chapter 9: Advanced Cricut Project

Cricut Maker—Knife Blade Basswood Cutting

What Is the Size of the Cuts?

- Overall cut size: 10.5 inches' x 11.5"- or 10.5-inches x 23.5"

- Minimum cutting size: 0.75" x 075" (includes interior and exterior cuts).

- The cuts should not be less than the pencil diameter.

- Ensure that all cuts are at least 1/4" away from the basswood edge (if the blade crosses the edge of the basswood, there is a high probability that the blade will be damaged).

What Is the Mat That You Want to Use?

Mat Strong Grip

How Can You Make the Materials?

- Carefully treat the Wood as it can be very delicate.
- Preserve the surface of your work. Use a craft knife and safety control to cut the material to the project's size.
- Make several passes as required using a craft knife.
- Ensure that the wood piece is not larger than 11."
- Erase all wood labels or packaging.
- Remove substance with cloth or towel cloth or sprinkle with compressed air for dust removal and stray particles.
- Build Room mirror images.
- Position it so that the curves go to the mat if the Wood has a bow or warp (the concave side facing down).

Wood shouldn't be larger than 11." If the Cricut 12" x 6" basswood is used, placing it on the mat so that the length is not up, but down (vertically) (horizontally). Turn the concept on the preview screen for the project to fit with the Wood on the mat. Use a brayer to make a firm bond between the material and the system mat's adhesive surface. Place the project materials on the mat and roll the brayer gently over the whole floor.

Make sure that the edge of the Wood is at least 1/4" away from all cuts. If the Knife Blade crosses the Wood's edge, the risk is high. Shift the white star wheels to the right on Cricut Market (Learn More). Star wheels will leave an impression on the project material when left in place. Test a cut before cutting the main project, if possible. If the edges are rough, replace the blade before the final cut.

How Long Are the Cuts Going to Take?

Thicker materials require many cutting passes with increasing pressure gradually. It means that cutting of Knife Blade takes much longer than cutting thinner materials with other knives. Production Space tells you about the time a Knife Blade is going to take.

- When you pick a cutting setting and load your mat for a Knife Blade project, you will be informed with an alarm that you expect a longer than average cutting period.

- After completing the first pass, Design Space determines the estimated cut-up time, based on the duration of the first pass and the number of passes pre-programmed for the content. It also indicates the execution of the machine and the estimated total number of passes.

What Should You Do During the Cutting of the Machine?

- Check the cutting of the machine also to check the cuts.

- You will notice the finishing of small pieces and no longer hold down on the mat until all passes are done. Stop the computer and, if necessary, delete bits.

- Some images can appear complete before all passes are completed. Enable the computer to complete all passes for better performance.

Once the Cut Is Over, What Do You Do Next?

- Check the cut before removing the mat from the unit, press Cricut "C" to add a new cutting pass if it is still attached to the material.

- Remove the tape carefully.

- Bend the edge of the mat back carefully in front of the straw.

- Run your fingertips slowly between wood and mat, one inch at a time until the whole piece of wood is free from the mat.

- Prepare to see impressions of the Knife Blade or wounds on the mat.

- For better results, position the picture on different sections of your cutting mat if you cut many of the same images.

- Verify that all sections were entirely cut.

- Do not attempt to pop it out if a piece is not fully cut. Pushing the piece could break it.

Trouble Resolution

- Your mat can not be sticky enough if your material moves when it is cut.

- It might be necessary to repair your blade if your material is not fully cut.

- The machine can sometimes stop while cutting, but additional passes are still possible. If this occurs, follow Design Space® on-screen prompts. Repeat the process when the computer starts to stop in the same place. It can take many attempts.

- If the system cannot step beyond this point, the material might be imperfect. Remove your machine material, discard, and start cutting again with a new material component.

Stage 1—Inserting and Editing Text

- Click the "Text" button in the left panel and type "Happy Birthday."

- Your text will initially be Cricut Sans, but because we're focusing on party decoration, let's change the font.

- Pick the text and press "Font," and select your favorite text. We chose "A Child's Year" for this tutorial because it has a nice (party) atmosphere. Once your font is updated, keep your text specified, go to the top of the canvas, click "Advanced," and select the "Ungroup to Letters" option. Each letter can be edited separately by ungrouping into layers.

- Select and rotate each letter, increase the size and release proportions from each angle of selection to edit each letter.

Stage 2—Weld and Overlap Text

- It's time for the cake topper to be molded, and we have to arrange every message.

- Then all your letters are overlaid, all your items on the canvas are selected, and "Weld" (located on the bottom panel) is clicked to create one sheet.

Stage 3—Design of Copies and Flips

- Typically, most cake toppers have a sweet paper on their front and nothing white on their back. It will help if you put this thing in a certain place to cover the "dark side."

- Not only would your cake topper look better if you have another (or the same front paper) paper on your back, it will also bring additional power to the final project.

- It's a win-win, in other words.

- To add another color on the back of the Topper, click on "Flip" and pick the option "Flip Horizontal" to replicate it (top of the layer panel).

Stage 4—Resize, Color Shift and Render

- You may change the colors of the cake topper at this point.

- **Note:** Change colors by clicking on the next line type color box (you need to select the latter first).

- Check your project's scale until you cut the template; if you need to raise or decrease the project size, ensure that the top and front are the same.

- As a guide, the mine was 7 X 4.6 in.

- When your design is fulfilled, go ahead and press the green "Make it" button.

- **Note:** Pick the machine type (Explorer or Maker) you own before the cutting process begins.

Stage 5—Process Cutting

- It is the view you should have when you submit your project. Every material consists of two mats. If you pick the same color for both the front and back, you're only going to have one mat.

- Click on the Continue button if anything looks fine. It is time to pick your materials.

- Instructions for Cricut Explore: switch the intelligent set dial of your Cricut to Cardstock Plus if you have one of the family explorer machines.

- **Cricut Maker Instruction:** if you have a Cricut maker, click on the button "Browse All Materials" to pick your Cricut Design Space materials.

- For both types of devices, the following instructions apply.

- You must mount the Fine Point Blade and prepare your mat for the tools. Now let's switch to some real pictures to see the next thing you can do. We use a regular green mat for this project, but you can also use a purple mat and put your cardstock down. Place the cardstock on the top of the mat with your fingertips, Scraper, or our favorite tool, brayer on the planet! If you don't have one, make today the small investment.

- Load the paper to your Cricut and press the Flashing Go button to start the cut.

- If your Cricut finishes cutting, unload the insane material and remove it.

- The best way to remove the cake topper is to tighten the mat and allow most of the work to be done. There was a mistake (Check the photo right above). Clean the mat now with the Scraper and repeat for the second mat the same operation. We used a different material for the second cut, so we had to change the material again.

- If you have another material, don't forget to change things, such as moving the Smart Set Division (Explorer) or changing the Design Space material if you own a Maker.

- It's time to assemble your Birthday Topper once you have both cuts.

- We still tell something that glue is to keep away from the child's glue. It is not intended for these projects; they won't look fine because the paper gets bubbly and wet.

Cake Toppers with Cricut Images

- You can use Cricut Photos if you search for something faster or even more elaborate (located on the left panel of the canvas). Cricut's library is full (over 100k) of designs and can be sorted by groups, keywords, etc., for any occasion. If you are looking for a specific occasion, you can type the word that best describes it. We sorted by "wedding," for example, and we have a variety of choices. It is the thing; not all pictures are for cake toppers! If you want to cut with a minimal edit instantly, you need to find a picture that overlaps all letters (just as we overlapped the birthday topper).

- Although the choice is great to make cake toppers, there will come a time when you want a picture that's not ready.

- Like the photo, in the screenshot above, as you can see, it's all divided. But don't worry, if you like this, let's see how to turn a simple picture of the design room into a cake top.

Phase 1: Insert the Picture into the Region of the Canvas

Phase 2: Repeat (Copy/Paste) Until Three Copies Are Available

- **Note:** you need more copies if you have more text lines or elements that are scattered.

Phase 3: Use the Contour Tool (Below the Layer Panel) to View Only the Pattern's First Line

- You don't need to contour the about part, but remove or cover the pink underneath the sheet.

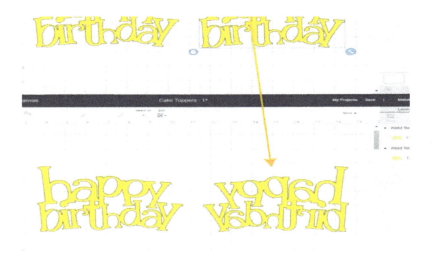

Phase 4: Make the Various Things into a Cake Top by Overlapping Each Line (Wild, About, U)

Phase 5: Pick and Click "Weld" to Have All Things in One Sheet

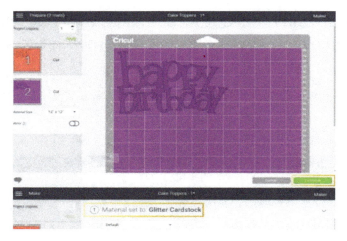

- With glitter, you should add another bit of imagination!

- Look how fine and elegant this Topper Love Cake looks.

How to Grave the Critter Acrylic

- The first thing about acrylic blanks is that they probably have a protective coating on both sides. For graving it, this protective film needs to be removed from one side. The protective film can be left behind. Then find the blank on your mat. Locate where you know where it is, so you can switch it around when we're in Cricut Design Space. We put the circle in both directions on the three-inch side.

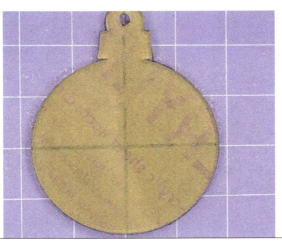

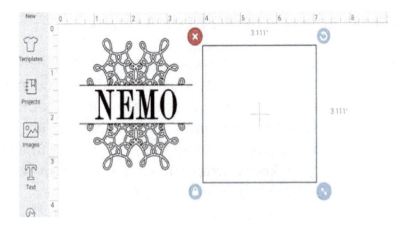

- Tap it down and then execute the brayer to make sure it's stuck.

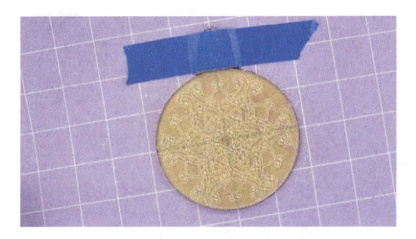

- Put masking tape on the edges. Make sure that you do not apply the tape in any of the places that you are graving. For example, the gravure is a little over three inches, so you must tape the quadruple circle's edge. We like the extra protection of walking with the tape.

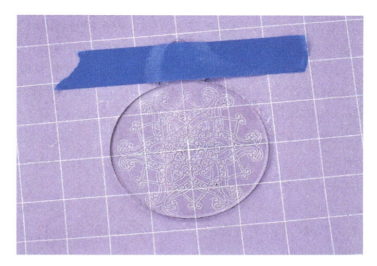

- Open the design space for Cricut and choose your design. The designs that best fit with your graving tool can draw files. If you look for designs, just select the art form and draw your results by drawing files. These will increase the gravure.

- Place the pattern on the mat. We are making a gift tag for the idea. We went through a circle with flowers and then some email. So, what you can do is insert a circle and make it four centimeters, just for example. Give the circle back and grey. It will help you see what is happening:

1. When you're done with the design, remove the circle from your canvas.
2. Do the same thing with email. Go to fonts and filter to write. Type your text and make sure it's now ready to draw.
3. When you are satisfied with the template, select the picture and the text and connect them. Adjust your line style to "engrave" with the chosen two.
4. **Note:** Make sure that your form of machine is on the manufacturer. This option will not appear otherwise.
5. In the Design Space, locate your design exactly where your blank is on your mat. In this case, this is in both directions at the 3" mark.
6. Set the material foundation. There are two choices for acrylic, two mm thick, and one mm thick. There are two mm thick. The blanks used are very small, so we are going to choose one millimeter. But if you use a thicker blank, choose only the two mm.
7. Load the Clamp B gravure tip and load the mat to start. Ensure the star wheels pass through the bar to the right, so they do not damage the acrylic mask. Click the load arrow button and start the C button.

Upon completion, unload the mat and remove the blank.

- Find some ornaments for a better appearance.

How to Grave Aluminum with the Maker

- Add aluminum blanks to the hot grip mat.

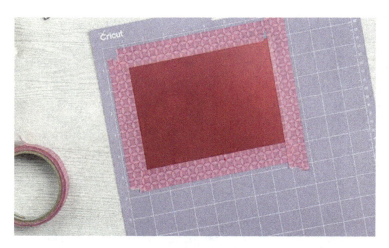

- Second, you must add your blank aluminum to your solid grip mat. Although the aluminum blanks used have been pre-painted, you should spray the blanks with a plain aluminum blank or a marker after graving, so the graving itself stands out a little more.

- Ensure that any protective coating is removed from the front and back of your piece, then add your blank aluminum to the solid grip mat and make sure you put a 1" x 1" mark at the corner or the middle at the 1-inch mark. You have to know where the blank is on the mat to locate your design in Cricut Design Space. You would then place the masking tape around your blank's outer edge to prevent it from shifting while graving. Your mat is ready for your computer now.

Your Gravure Template

- Start by designing a cut file to grave into your aluminum. You can either cut the file used or build your own. Then press in Cricut Template Space to render it. You will note that we have drawn the white color and the template we want to graze on the file.

- You need the square or circular shape of your blank to put the graving on the mat.

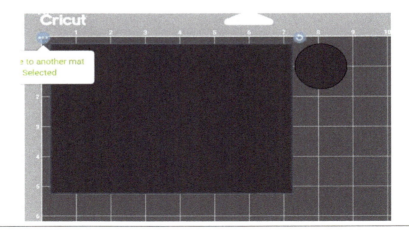

- Remove the excess gravure from the first mat. Tap on the three points to pull up the menu and cover the one you don't want to grave.

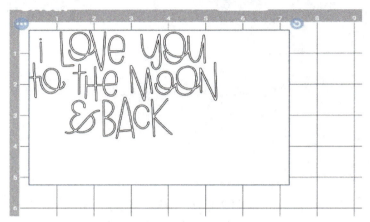

- You just want the one left on the computer that you are using. Then transfer the blank on the second mat to the first mat so that both the blank and the gravure are on the same mat. To do this, click on three points and move to a different mat.

- The style you want to grave and the blank you want to place on the same mat should be left to you.

- Just align the blank with the 1-inch mark as you align it with the mat itself. Then move the graving to the position exactly as you want it to appear on the blank.

- Then hide the blank itself with the selected hide feature, so you just have to grave the mat.

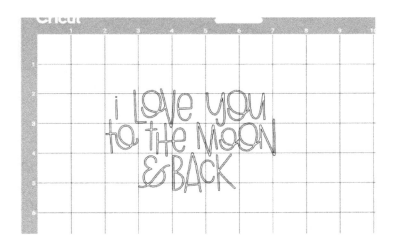

Use the Aluminum Gravure Tip

- You are now ready to grave your aluminum. Add the gravure tip to the box and put it in your Cricut machine. Note that only the Cricut Maker deals with the graving tip itself.

- Then load the mat into your computer with the blank in place and press to grave your aluminum. Select the aluminum configuration for cutting. Please bear in mind to move the white wheels to the right, not to mark your floor.

- This method is the same for small aluminum sheets as for jewelry blanks.

Your Graving Completion

- You may want to run a masking tape or a lint roller over the aluminum portion to remove any debris when you're finished. Please be careful as aluminum cuts will penetrate your skin. Then remove the blank from the sheet, remove all the masking tape, and peel the mat from the blank aluminum.

- Be sure to use the marker on it for gravure on plain aluminum, wait a few minutes, and remove any excess. It helps to discern the gravure on these pieces.

- You don't have to do anything more to apply a graving to a painted object. It's just awesome right outside the Cricut Maker.

- Now you've been able to graze aluminum with the Cricut Manufacturer. Make sure you buy plenty of blanks because you will always want to do this. It's very easy to do, but once it's over, it just looks great.

Cricut Infusible Ink Adorable Baby Onsite

Phase 1: Select Your Style and Size for the Blank You Put on

- Click on the "make it" button.

- On the screen below, make sure you click the mirror slider and then continue scrolling.

- Choose your Cricut cutting machine and pick your cutting material Infusible Tin Transfer Sheet.

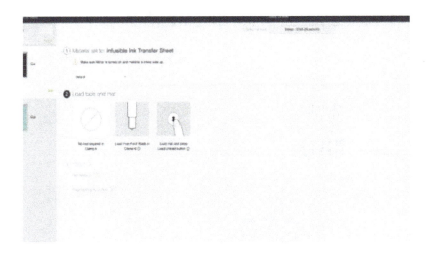

- Load your transfer sheet with the pattern facing up and down on your mat. We preferred using the brayer tool to transfer the transmission sheet onto a mat.

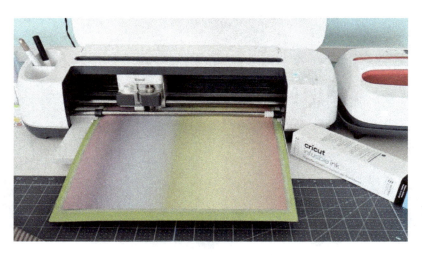

Phase 2: Erase Your Cutting Mat Designs

- Cut the design and save the extra transfer layer. We remove the excess sheet that leaves your template on the clear plastic backrest. Notice that the material on the transfer sheet is lighter than when it is pressed.

Phase 3: Heat Your Easy Press Cricut to 385°F

- Place your slip on the top of your Cricut Easy Press Mat and inside your slip to avoid the infusible tint bleeding to the back of your slip. Using your lint roller to remove any lint, hair, or dust particles.

- Place a piece of butcher paper and heat for 15 seconds. Don't miss the move. Heating the cup removes any moisture from your cup and helps the infused incense to infuse the cup and works its magic correctly!

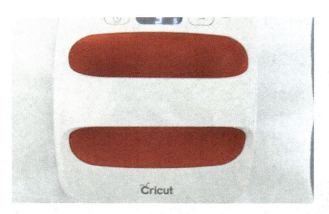

- Remove the butcher paper and put your template on your skewer. Since the template was cut from two transfer sheets, we cut the plastic back near the words to put all three parts on it so that no plastic overlap. To keep the concept in place, we used heat-safe tape.

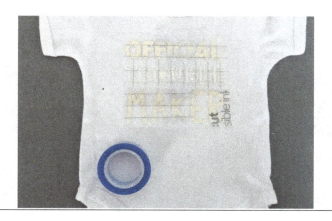

- Remove the one-see with your butcher paper and then click your Easy Press for 40 seconds. Be careful not to slip or move your hands when the Easy Press is pressed. You want to keep your Easy Press quiet. At the end of the 40 seconds, raise the Easy Press carefully, and leave your hobbies cool with the butcher's paper.

- Just raise the butcher paper and peel up the plastic liner that exposes your template once you have cooled it! (Note if the sheet does not have a plastic backer that uses a pair of tweezers to lift them carefully.)

- Clean the unit in cold water with mild detergent inside. Dry low tumble or dry line. Do not use fluffy, dryer, or bleach fabric.

Are you excited to try the new Infusible Ink from Cricut?

Chapter 10: Techniques for Cricut Cartridges

1. **Cutting iron-on vinyl:** Look at your design before cutting vinyl. Often the design looks perfect in either direction, but reading is crucial when letters or words are involved!

2. **Removing iron-on vinyl from the plastic layer**: After the excess vinyl is removed from the design, you are left with an adhesive plastic. It is suitable to put your iron-on cut on your fabric. When the substance is hot enough to peel the plastic coating back, peel it sharply. If you see spots that did not infuse the fabric, substitute the plastic layer and heat again.

3. **Infuse iron-on material:** Cover the iron-on design with the smooth cloth after pressing the heated iron to protect the design and then peeling the plastic layer off the design. It secures the pattern into the fabric and ensures it lasts through many washing cycles.

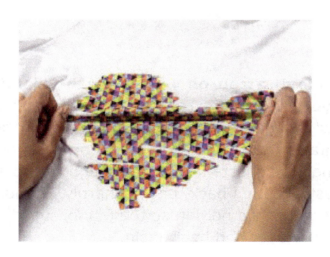

4. Washing iron-on vinyl: Wash iron-on t-shirts and other fabrics in cold water for the best performance, and then dry in the breeze. To prevent iron-on from melting, cover the vinyl region with a smooth cotton ironing cloth.

5. Removal of black vinyl paper: Peel it gently at a sharp angle to the vinyl style.

6. **Vinyl washing:** While vinyl is not permanent, we have been lucky enough to wash smooth ceramic or glass dishes with regular vinyl designs. Some of our pieces are many years old and were washed regularly in the dishwasher, but we suggest you wash your pieces by hand. Only apply oil to the surface to release the glue to remove the vinyl permanently.

7. **Reset the blade's depth:** Before cutting a new project, remember to reset the depth of the blade. By cutting them, few mats will be wasted. Keep the mats clean: Before they are stored, the easiest way to keep your mats clean is to cover them with their plastic cover. We did not find a suitable way to restore the mat's stickiness, and it is our best option to keep them between uses.

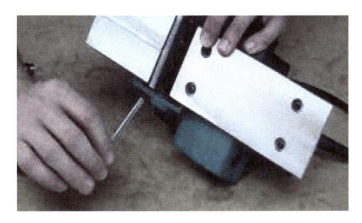

8. **Material removal rolling pad:** The simple trick to remove almost any cuts from your mats, particularly when fresh and at the peaks of your stick, is to roll the mat instead of peeling it off. It prevents the paper from curling, as the adhesive mat is quickly popped off.

9. **Usage of battery-operated candles:** Note to keep flames away. To keep the paper free of flame, use battery-operated candles.

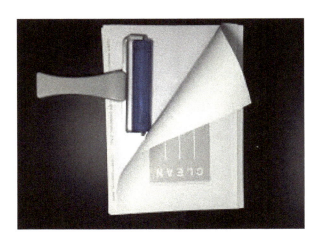

Chapter 11: Cricut Maker Troubleshooting

Computer Machine

Cricut Doesn't Cut the Stuff

- Check the stickiness of your mat.

- Check if the material you are cutting has the right color mat.

- Clean the blade; make sure any debris is stuck around the tip of the blade.

- Use a foil ball to sharpen the blade, stabbing the blade many times. If that doesn't fit, a new blade would have to be considered.

- Check that the material you are cutting is set correctly. Switch your computer to custom and select from a wider variety of materials if you are a Cricut Explorer user.

- Enhance blade pressure by the change of material setting.

- Enhance the image size; the image may be too small and bulky.

- For intricate cuts on the card, use the click.

- In card setting; try the wash sheets setting for complex vinyl cuts.

The Machine's Power Button Is Red

Red Light Flashing

- Check the settings of a firmware update. If the issue persists, contact customer support of Cricut.

Solid Red Light

- Turn off the unit, and then switch it on for a few minutes before plugging in.

- Check the computer for debris and dust.

- Check and adjust the power source.

- Call Cricut if the issue continues.

Printing and Cutting

- **The system does not register the written and cut marks:** Ensure that the computer is in the shade and bright sunlight will prevent the sensor from collecting the lines; if that does not work, your room may be too dark! Try to shine a spotlight on the sensor. The explorer aircraft can only register white cardstock, the manufacturer, but you can spot colored print lines and cut lines and Kraft card. Go with black sharpie over black lines to help your computer pick up line.

- **Printing and cutting are not exactly:** re-calibrating your unit, you can have to do this many times to produce the best results. Check if the bleed is allowed. Switch on Machine Dialog (underneath the print screen blood). This gives you more printing options.

Mats

The Sleeves Are No Longer Sticky

- Wash with liquid washing, rub softly into the mat surface and rinse in warm water and allow drying up.

- Designate mats for certain materials.

- Buy a new mat!

- When we remove it from the mat, the material is rippling.

- Turn over the mat and peel the mat off the material.
- Check that you have the right colored mat for the right type of material.
- On first use, tune the mat against a piece of clothing to get rid of stickiness!

Quick Press

- Check that the surface is strong and so use your Easy Press Temperature.
- Check the correct temperature and time for your materials and vinyl on the on-line Easy Press Guide.
- Https:/cricut.com/heat guide.
- Check the vinyl peeling temperatures you are using; if it is cold, wait until it cools completely before peeling a vinyl.

Tools

Blade of the Knife

- **The image does not cut with the Knife Blade:** Check the image dimension; the interior of the image must not be less than 3/4 of an inch. Check the lines; they should at least be as thick as the ends of the regular pencil. Use the knife blade only while the computer is linked via the cable USB, not Bluetooth.

- **Cutting the chipboard is difficult for me:** Keep the chipboard out of the packaging for at least 24 hours.

- **The knife blade takes so many steps and cuts the mat:** Pause project and verify that after a few steps, the knife blade sometimes fully cuts the material before it has been cut. If so, pause and throw your project away. Adjust the number of passes.

- **The knife blade doesn't cut the stuff:** Check material settings. Further passes are added.

Resources for Scoring

- **The computer automatically selects the marking wheel to mark, but you have the marking type:** clicking on the editing tools to pick the marking style.

- **How can we change the scoring tip on the score wheel?** Click the button to release the tip on top of the scoring wheel.

Design Space

- **'Smart' design Space:** Verify software updates and download accordingly. Verify that you don't run too much software on your device and have enough storage space. If this happens on the app, complete the app, and reopen it. Check link internet—how can we communicate with Bluetooth?

Enables Bluetooth on Your Computer

- Pick your machine and enter 0000.

- Explore and Explore air machines need a Bluetooth adapter for connecting to an activated Bluetooth unit.

- You can charge design space for pictures that have already picked up access and is Cricut subscribed and paid for photos to access.

- Log out and register in your account; the design space often signs out without you understanding that.

Chapter 12: What Can You Make and Sell with Cricut?

Wall Art Canvas

Find famous quotes and use your Cricut machine to make and sell canvas wall art from stencils.

Jewelry Leather

You can make beautiful leather jewelry with tooling leather.

Customized Tools

You can make and sell customized equipment and gadgets with vinyl lettering. This will be a perfect gift for the Day of Dad!

Custom Cutting Boards

Create vinyl stickers and mount them to a slicing board for a perfectly peculiar, warming donation for family and friends.

DIY Towels Kitchen

Lanyards Personalized

Build a selection of personalized lanyards for sporting events and other heavy traffic occasions.

Doormats Seasonal

Model Cricut builder with your stencils for making seasonal doormats!

Signs Rustic

Create and build home decoration sets with rustic signs. This is a brilliant idea to make and sell for cash with your Cricut.

Cofee Mugs

Although those lovely taps are hand-colored, you can use stencils from your Cricut Machine to recreate a similar style

Custom Holiday Buckets

It would be a brilliant idea to create and customize buckets for children during seasonal holidays!

Team Sports Cuffs

Develop cuffs for school, sports, or family events and sell for fast cash

Key Shells

Key chains are small items that you can easily sell to those who want to personalize their keys, book bags, and bags.

Hand-Lettered Signs of Wood

Create and sell handwritten vinyl and your Cricut machine wooden signs.

Dish of the Monogrammed Ring

Develop a monogrammed ring and jewels that can be manufactured and sold at crafts and trade shows.

Chapter 13: Can You Create Your Designs on Cricut?

There are numerous ways to import and cut your images using Cricut Design Space. Such instances are as follows, using adobe illustrator would be beneficial for you.

1. **Drawing, hand letter, or a paper template:** Scan the photo, or take a picture and save it to your machine with your phone.

2. **Use the template of someone else:** You can buy pictures on Etsy (search for 'cut images' or 'SVG').

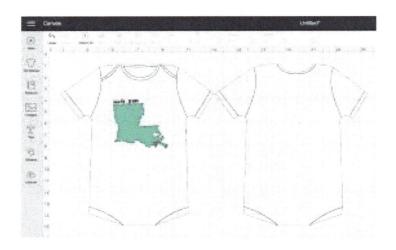

3. **Free SVG files:** Love SVG is a great place we recommend. There are so many fantastic designs free of charge with a commercial license (if you are making products to sell, you will need it).

4. Facebook groups: Cricut users have various large groups, and people exchange projects and files there. Many people in the community can point you in the right direction for a certain picture or customize anything for a small fee.

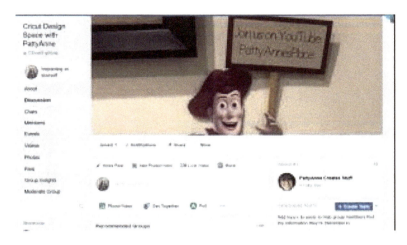

5. Blogs: So many wonderful files are available free of charge. Check for Pinterest and Google.

Chapter 14: Cricut Business Ideas and Opportunity

Knitting

It's all about making exquisite and exclusive hand-knitted items, from sweaters to an assortment of stuffed animals. Notice that your chances are endless; you need a creative spirit, knitting needles, yarn, and company.

For the professional entrepreneur, create a website featuring knit clothing and a tailor-made service, in which visitors to the site can fill out a form for the size and type of knit items they like.

Vests of Sportsmen

With a Cricut, you can design and manufacture custom sports jackets to hunt, fish, and boat. This is a great home-based company to have

For a genuinely informed business person, create a website with knit clothing items for sale and personalized service. Visitors to the website will complete the form for ordering the size and design of the knit products they wish to order.

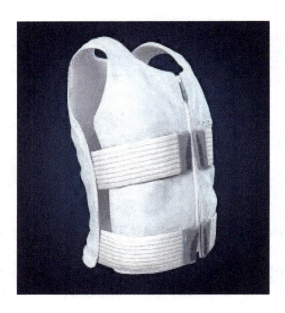

In this type of specialty apparel manufacturing company, the secret to success is to ensure the jackets perform several roles relevant to their operations and ensure the materials are of the highest quality.

When finished, such items may be distributed to national sport products retailers for wholesale or via mail-order catalogs, leisure trade shows, and the Internet. The sportsmen's vest may be sold directly to customers.

Modification of Fabrics

Using a Cricut, you can harness your sewing skills by offering clothing and fabric modification services directly from the workstation and earning a bundle of money. Dry cleaners, fashion stores, suit retailers, bridal shops, drapery studios, and clothing shops are potential clients.

Please note that all companies that rent or sell clothing of any sort are potential customers for this company. Place a comfortable pair of shoes calmly and start calling those companies in person, offering your modification services. Offer free pickup and delivery, quick processing times, outstanding service, and high-quality production at reasonable prices.

Company of Car Wrap and Graphics

If you intend to start your wrap and graphics business, you're in a profitable enterprise. This form of company is entirely scalable. It takes only basic equipment and training, some talent, and a strong and consistent plan to start a vehicle wrap company.

Development and Manufacture of Handbags

The design and manufacture of handbags is a great company to start with the aid of a Cricut. Not only can the company operate part-time, but there are also virtually no business overheads to gain monthly income.

Be aware that innovative designs and the use of unusual handbag fabrics can be your competitive advantage, and finished goods can be wholesaled to fashion retailers or distributed to local retail outlets. The handbags can also be sold directly to customers by showcasing or selling items online at fashion shows and craft shows.

Accessory Business Customizable

Notice that there are endless opportunities for this form of company. Whether they are pet collars, telephone cases, glass frames, frames, people like custom items, you name them. This kind of business has huge growth potential, as long as you discover your niche.

You can start your business with customizable telephone cases. You can consider offering cases with customized inscriptions. Later, you can extend your bid by using custom 3D graphics in your phone cases.

Artisan Exhibits

It is very easy to host craft shows, and this business model is quite straightforward. You only secure 100 craft suppliers per craft and charge per supplier $100 for table rental. Keeping the spring, summer, and autumn shows will produce cumulative revenues of 50,000 dollars (five shows x 100 suppliers display each x 100 dollars per table stand = 50,000 dollars).

Weaving of Basket

You may also start a company making and selling custom-made baskets. This is an amazing start because people from all walks of life still look for the right piece of practical home decoration.

You are making baskets and producing a diversified and interesting product line using a wide range of raw materials and with the aid of your cricut machine.

Don't worry if you don't know how to weave baskets; you can always take a few instruction courses or find other weaver basketball and sell your finished goods.

Designs of Paper Art

The critter may also be used to produce other products. These involve paper and plastic forms. Therefore, this method is a treasure for people interested in papermaking because it can provide ideas and solutions to current dilemmas.

Sometimes you are left with vacant spaces, bigger walls, or new rooms asking for something different! Since art seems to be costly and you can never be sure that it will work from home to home, whenever possible, so you can add your own DIY.

Everyone is not an artist, though, so you can turn on your Cricut sometimes to support it; it is a process that is not just foolproof but also very simple and highly flexible, having made a lot of art for our walls over the years. If you want to break down the easiest way of creating art with a Cricut today so that you can also have amazing DIY designs on your walls!

Models in Depth

While several companies have moved to make models in the digital space as long as possible, they still have to build a working model at some stage. A cricut may be used to manufacture these models for different companies.

Sticking Service

Recent technological advances have made it very easy for a novice to start a brothering service in the multibillion-dollar brokering industry. Cricut and other stickers will allow the operator to create more products simultaneously.

These modern devices are also computer-aided, so designs can be produced using special software and a computer and then automatically transferred to the sticker to complete the design portion. The company can be run from a home location easily.

Decorative Phone and Laptop Coverage

These are vinyl decals that are highly common for the two electronics. These decorative parts are typically sold with an adhesive back that very easily sticks to the piece.

Instruction on Arts and Crafts

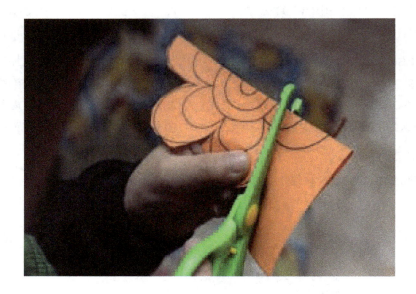

Days, nights, or weekends, you can teach arts and crafts from a home studio, rent a shopping room, partner with a trade vendor who uses the space, together with the community center or school, or even in a park where the weather allows.

Promote the classes in art and craft retailers, running newspaper announces, networking in business and social events, publishing notices on group newsletters and showcasing arts and crafts exhibits. Through this, you can earn a good amount of money. It just required your hard work and luck.

Conclusion

This book discusses all the relevant information about the Cricut machine. It includes the different important topics, the projects that can be made, beginner 's guide to use the Cricut machine, and the materials used in the Cricut machine.

It covers the topic of different techniques on the Cricut machine and solves some troubleshooting problems.

It includes different projects with pictures for different levels. It also provides you the information on business opportunities that Cricut machine can provide you.

Cricut Design Space

A Beginner's Guide to Getting Started with Cricut Design Space + Tips, Tricks and Amazing DIY Project Ideas

Anita Wood

Introduction

As a novice or an expert, Cricut has impressive capabilities that will boost your productivity. As a matter of truth, even though you are not so creative in everyday life, this machine will make you come across as a master craftsman.

A perfect way to be a skilled crafter is to find a platform or companion that offers you the opportunity to pursue your passion.

Thankfully, Cricut has created an awesome machine with advanced cutting technologies for anybody who wants to go into crafting, which will help you cut, draw, and put all your beautiful craft ideas into existence. Knowing what equipment and tools to use for your Cricut is imperative to minimize your training time and save time.

The Cricut machine is very flexible and can be used with many sorts of products to construct any time of project you can dream up. For almost any reason you might think of, Cricut machines provide a broad selection of cartridges. The cost varies from $25 to around $60 each for these cartridges.

There are fonts and pictures in these cartridges that can be customized for all designs you have. For your designs utilizing the same cartridge, you can even change the textures and shades of the components and achieve various looks.

Whether you have friends or relatives who also use Cricut machines, to save money, you can share or lend cartridges.

Cricut machines may be bought at a craft shop or online. The price would rely, of course, on the model you chose. Their prices will vary from an average of $100 to $350.

Chapter 1: Understanding the Cricut Design Space

A Cricut is a cutting and crafting machine that helps you to cut using materials that you didn't even realize existed to make exquisite and glorious crafts.

You can also sketch, emboss and make folding lines based on the model you have and make 3D designs, greeting cards, boxes, etc.

The Cricut is a perfect machine for people who enjoy crafting, and for people who need to cut a ton of stuff and various types of materials. You can install and uninstall the design space on any device.

What Is the Cricut Design Space?

Cricut Design Space is a web-based software that lets you access pre-designed project websites and pages, as well as design your own laptop, desktop, tablet, and phone designs. Approximately 75,000 pictures, 400 fonts, and even more than 800 pre-designed Make-it-Now projects are housed by Cricut Design Space.

You already have the Make It Now projects ready, and all you have to do is select "Go." Cricut Design Space also helps you to import your private jpeg and svg files and use your own fonts. It is like a workhorse.

How to Install and Uninstall Design Space Software?

You may install Design Space on the Android or computer or IOS smartphone or device.

Installing for Windows PC

To download, mount and activate Cricut setup for Windows for your Desktop pc:

1. Open a browser on the internet and load the website www.design.cricut.com.

2. Choose Download. While downloading, the screen may shift. This function would be a bit different in each browser.

3. Once the downloading is finished, open the setup file in the tab or in the Downloaded folder.

4. If a new window emerges and queries if you rely on the application, choose the answer to trust and verify the application.

5. A configuration window shows installation progress.

Beta v4.2.4

6. Log in with the Email identification and password for Cricut.

7. The Cricut Desktop icon inevitably gets connected to the screen of the desktop.

8. Right mouse click on the symbol and move the icon/symbol to the Taskbar to tack the option into easy reach.

9. Enjoy having Cricut Design Space.

Points to Know
- Your log-in is remembered by the app. Every time you start, you would not have to log in until you have logged out from the previous session.

- There is no auto-save in the app. Save the tasks recurrently as you layout the project and until you exit.

Uninstallation

1. If you would like to delete Design Space permanently or for security reasons from your computer system or mobile device, please follow these steps:

2. Ensure that the Desktop Design Space is closed. It would not uninstall properly if the program is not closed.

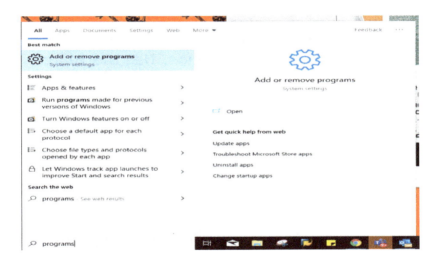

3. In the lower-left corner of the screen, click the Start icon, and scan the programs. Choose the Add or Delete Program function. The Applications & features window will open this way.

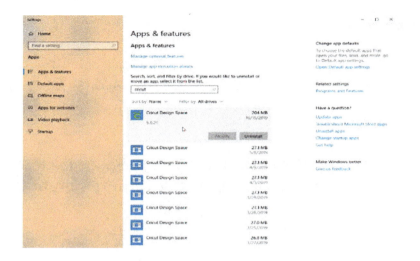

4. Pick Cricut Design Space from the folder, and then select the Uninstall option. Use the search field to check for Cricut.

5. Confirm that you would like Cricut Design Room to be uninstalled.

6. This will finish the uninstallation of the device. Restart the computer if requested.

Installing for MAC

1. Install and activate Design Space for Desktop on your Mac computer to download.

2. Open a browser on the internet and navigate to design.cricut.com.

3. Choose Download. When the Programme file is downloaded, the screen will shift. In every browser, it will look different. In this illustration, Google Chrome is used.

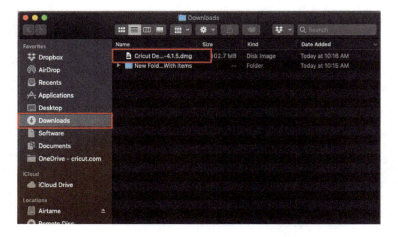

4. Double-tap the .dmg file in the browser or in the Downloads folder once the download is completed.

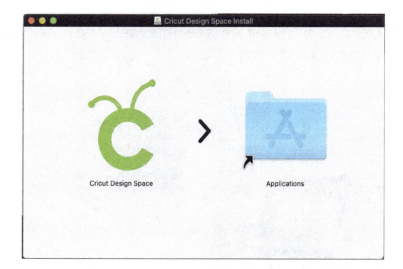

5. To start the installation, drag the Cricut icon onto the Applications folder icon. It automatically adds Design Space for Desktop to your Apps folder.

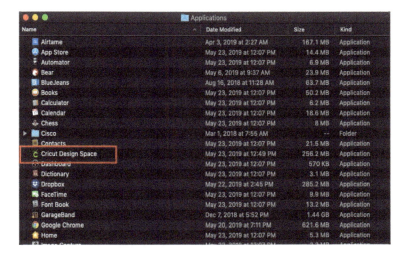

6. Double-click the Cricut Design Space in the Apps folder to launch Design Space for Desktop. Drag the Programme into your dock to create a shortcut.

7. It may appear that a Mac note asks whether you want to access the Programme that was downloaded from the internet. To proceed, select Open.

8. Log in with your ID and password for Cricut.

9. Enjoy using the Desktop Design Space feature.

10. Use a Feedback tab at the end of the Design Space menu to exchange feedback.

Things to Know

- Your sign-in is recognized by the app. Any time you launch, you would not have to sign in until you have signed out of the last session.

- It does not auto-save the app. Save the projects frequently as you plan the project and until you exit.

Uninstalling

1. Open the Finder key and choose Apps.

2. Locate the application of Cricut Design Space.

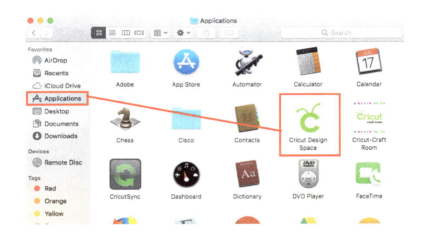

3. Move the Cricut app to the Trash folder.

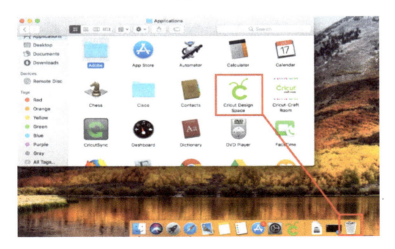

4. Then open the Trash icon and choose a gear key, then select Clear Trash.

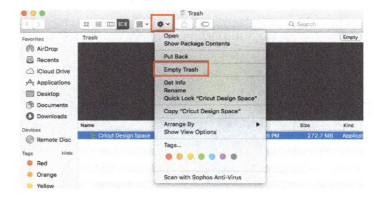

5. Verify that you want the things in the trash to be removed forever.

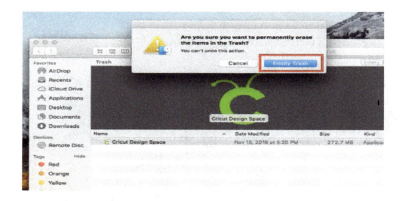

6. This will finish the uninstallation of the application. Restart the computer if requested.

Installing for IOS

1. Cricut Design Space can be used as an app on your congruent iOS device rather than using your user's Internet browser. Follow the instructions below to download the Design Space iOS app.

2. To open the app store, click the App Store icon on your device's home screen.

3. Cricut Design Space Search. The icon of the app will be shown in the center as a white square with a Cricut "C" green logo.

4. To download the app, press the download button and, if asked to enter, verify it with the iTunes password.

5. The software will open after the download is completed and will show options to complete the Latest System Configuration or to continue to the App Summary.

6. To get to the landing page, sign up, and start creating on the go, simply press the 'X' in the upper right corner if you do not want to do either.

Uninstalling

1. Click and hold the icon of Design Space until it buzzes.

2. To remove the application from the iOS device, click 'x' then.

Installing for Android

1. On your Android device, Cricut Design Space can be used as an app rather than on your device through the internet browser. Follow the steps given below to install the Cricut Design Space for Android.

2. To open the Play Store, press the Google Play Store icon on the device's home screen.

3. Cricut Template Room Quest. The Cricut Design Space software appears in the middle as a white square with a Cricut "C" green logo.

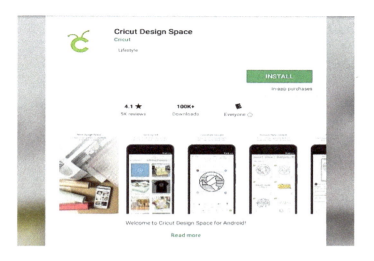

4. To download and install the app, click the Install button.

5. The app will display on your App Home Screen until the installation is completed.

6. To open the app, simply tap on the icon, sign in, and begin creating on the go.

Uninstalling

1. Open the app Settings.

2. Tap either 'Apps' or 'Applications.'

3. Swipe through to the Downloads tab or tap Application Manager.

4. Locate and tap on the app that you want to uninstall.

5. Press the button for "Uninstall".

How to Fix Error Codes?

Follow the instructions below to troubleshoot the problem: if you receive a warning in Design Space stating "an error has occurred,"

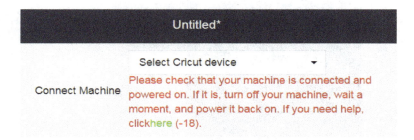

1. Sign out, and then sign back in, from Design space. In certain situations, the Design Space session can wait and provide this error rather than the prompt to log in again. Proceed to step 2 if this doesn't succeed.

2. You would need to re-create the design if the error just happens in one specific project. If you have used Connect, Weld, or Slice, this is an error message triggered by one or more of these actions. You will also need to redo the last action in certain situations. You will need to re-create the design if it does not help. Proceed to step 3 if the problem occurs in several projects.

3. Do you use machine fonts in the project? If so, consider using a new font and see if the dilemma can be fixed by that. Proceed to step 4 if it doesn't.

4. In certain situations, when you no longer have access to the Cricut Access plan you previously had, this notice will appear. If you have an activated Cricut Access plan, you can contact Member Care for asking help in ensuring the correct activation of your Cricut Access plan. If Cricut Access has not been subscribed through, proceed to step 5.

5. Make sure the code complies with the minimum required system specifications for Design Space to operate. Try cutting on a device that satisfies the requirements if your system does not fulfill the minimum requirements.

6. If you have an issue in Design Space as you attempt to submit the project to the system, you can help identify the problem with the number preceding the error.

Pick the particular error message that you get from the links below and adopt the suggested troubleshooting steps.

(0)

(-2)

(-3), (-10), (-19)

(-11)

(-18)

(-21)

(-24)

(-32)

(-33)

(0):

- Restart your desktop and your device (by powering the machine off and back on again). When you're using a Mac, make sure that by holding and pressing the device power button, you execute a Hard Reset before the screen goes dark and the desktop shuts down totally. And, to reset, click the power button.

- Make sure the device reaches the minimum specifications for Design Space operating.

If it does not, use a machine that fits the criteria to start the idea.

- Clear the cache, history, and cookies in your computer and check that you have a compatible browser and that it is updated. Continue to the next move if this does not succeed.

- Is this mistake happening in several projects? If the concern is limited to one project, it would be appropriate to recreate the project.

- Try a cut in another browser or on another device if neither of the above helps.

- Ask Member Care for help if the concern is addressed by neither of the following steps.

(-2):

- This is an error named "Not Supported."

- Be sure that with an Explore or Maker device, you are attempting to cut. Other devices are not Design Space compliant, which may allow this error to happen. If a compatible computer is in use, move to the next phase.

- Make sure your browser is updated; complete any updates required. Proceed to the next move if it doesn't succeed.

- Try using a browser that's different. If the dilemma is not fixed by this, continue to the next stage.

- Make sure the device satisfies the minimum specifications for Design Space working. Try a machine that satisfies the minimum criteria, if it does not.

(-3), (-10), (-19)

- (-3) This is an error named "Device Already in Use."

- (-10) This is an error named "Device Not Open."

- (-19) This is an error named "Device Already Open."

Perform the following actions:

- To refresh system contact, press the Retry or Reset Attachment button and attempt the cut phase again.

- Make sure that the New System Initialization process has been completed. If you have missed some portion of the method, this can allow this error to occur.

- Test your power button's color:

  o **Green:** The power button light of Maker/Explore will never be green because if the power light of your machine is green, you are trying to utilize Design Space on a system for which it is not appropriate. Instead, you may need to pursue a cut with an Explore/Maker device.

- o **Solid or Steady Red:** Take the troubleshooting measures.

- o **Blue:** This implies that by Bluetooth, the computer interacts with Design Space.

- o **White:** For Explore power button lighting, this is the standard hue. Suppose the light on the power button is white.

- o Please link to another USB port on your device.

- Make your user "forget" the Cricut Bluetooth device and then pair it again while you are attempting to use Bluetooth instead.

- If that doesn't fix the problem, instead, link to the device via USB cable and try cutting. Proceed to the next move if this does not improve.

- Disconnect the device from the console and switch it off. Finish a restart on the monitor as the unit is disabled and turned off. Reconnect the device to the system and wait for a few seconds, then open the Design Space and try the procedure again. Proceed to the next move if it does not help.

- Using a new browser to attempt the break. Proceed to the next move if it does not help.

- Using a separate USB cord to attempt to sever it. Typically, a normal printer cable is a correct setup, but try a printer cable if you don't have an external Cricut USB cable. Contact Member Care if you do not have a printer wire, who can give one to you.

- If none of this support fixes the problem, please contact Member Care for more assistance.

(-11):

- This is an error in "Device Authentication."

- Any Programmes running in the background, such as the backup Programmes, may trigger this to occur (Click Free, Caboodle, etc.). Please get the service discontinued and try again.

- Make sure your browser is up to date. You should go to the Menu> Support > About segment for Google Chrome and Mozilla Firefox to upgrade the browser.

(-18):

- This is an error called "Device Timeout."

- Switch off the Maker/Explore device.

- Shut Down the Design Space

- Re-launch the design space

- Power back on the Explore machine and try again for your cut.

- If the concern continues, approach Member Care for help.

(-21):

- This is an error in transferring data.

- Vacate the history of your browser, cookies, and cache.

- Close the browser and re-launch it to start and cut again.

- Try to cut with some other browser if this cannot fix the problem.

- You will notice a decrease in internet speed if it does not help, leading to this error.

- For assistance in fixing slow Internet speed, call the Internet Service Provider.

- This will also happen if the following are found in your project:

- A scoreline that has been modified or flattened to Print or Cut

- Unflatten the layout and disassociate the scoreline to fix it. Pick and flatten the printing layers, then re-attach the scoreline to them. Scorelines can only be added after the flattening phase.

- Writing Style font which has been modified to Print or Cut or has been flattened.

- Adjust the font style to fix it.

- The shape which is not completely enclosed (cut-path gap; lines do not match)

- When grouping, adding, and flattening, this may be induced by the sequence of operations. Ensure that before flattening, nothing in the layout is clustered or attached.

(-24):

- This is an error named "Ping Timeout."

- It may be because the project is too huge or not saved properly. You would need the project to be re-created. Proceed to the next stage if the problem arises with all projects.

- Try using another USB port on the device to connect the Maker/Explore machine to the device.

- Try connecting with a USB cable if you are using Bluetooth to see if the cut is completed.

There might be too much information to be processed through Bluetooth.

- Try a different USB cable to cut it. Typically, a normal printer cable is a correct setup, but try a printer cable if you don't have an external Cricut USB cable. Contact Member Care if you do not have a printer wire, who can deliver one to you.

- The minimum criteria could not be fulfilled by the internet speed. At www.speedtest.net, you can easily test the internet speed by clicking on Start TEST after the page has completely loaded. Design Space needs 2 Mbps to download and a minimum of 1.0 Mbps to upload. If your speed is weaker than this, on a different network, you would need to try your cut.

- If the minimum criteria are fulfilled by the internet speed, you may need to consider cutting it on a different computer.

(-32):

- This is an error named "Firmware Not Available."

- Making sure you are using a computer called Cricut Creator or Explore. These are the only Design Space compliant machines. If you are trying to use another Design Space unit, you may find this bug.

- For assistance, contact Member Care if you are using a compliant computer.

(-33):

- This is an error in the "Invalid Material Setting."

- Monitor the Dial for Smart Set. If set to Custom, make sure you've picked material from the Material Creation Space drop-down menu. This error will occur if the key is set to 'Custom,' but no material is chosen. Continue to the next stage if the key is not set to "Custom,"

- Try having a different setting for the material. If this mistake results in only one specific setting, feel free to contact Member Care for guidance.

Cricut Subscription Access

Cricut Access is a premium subscription that allows you immediate access to an awesome and vast library full of over 90,000 pictures, hundreds of fonts, and projects ready to be cut. You will get other perks, including discounts on approved images, fonts, and physical materials, based on the package you have.

Cricut Design Space and Cricut Access

The differentiation between Cricut Design Space and Cricut Access seems to be that the first is the FREE software where you import, edit, and eventually submit your designs to be cut to your Cricut Machine. The second is a premium subscription full of designs that can be used inside the Cricut Design Space that are graphics, fonts, and ready to cut.

Even if you don't have a Cricut Access membership, you are allowed to see and get all of the graphics that they provide within Cricut Design Space. When you submit your idea to be cut, you may need to pay for those digital data, however.

All Plans of Cricut Access Provide Access to

- Unlimited usage of 50.000+ photos, graphics, and projects ready to cut.

- 400+ Fonts Limitless use

- 10% Savings for all physical objects and items bought on cricut.com

- 10% Savings from products like Disney, Sesame Street, Hello Kitty, etc. on pictures, cartridges, cut ready projects on fonts.

- Member Priority Care Line (50 percent less wait time)

Monthly

- Pay $9.99 on a monthly basis and have unrestricted access to over 400 fonts and 75,000 photos for each font you love; no need to pay a la carte rates.

- 10% off all Cricut.com purchases and 10% off authorized pictures.

- The helpful dandy little green flag that warns you of all photos, cartridges, fonts, and projects included with your membership allows it easy to check for Cricut Access images.

Yearly

Exactly the same goodies as the monthly membership, purchase, save when you spend for a whole year.

Premium

Exactly the same benefits as monthly and annual packages, plus an extra discount perk such as FREE delivery on orders above $50.

You'll have limitless access to a lot of material and more than ample excuses to start crafting either way you go. If you have a Cricut Explore Air or Cricut Maker, then the only way to go is Cricut Access.

All the money you've invested in an amazing machine, then you'd better use it. Don't let it stay in the corner and transform it into an accessory for a decorative rack. It will amaze you, and you will be addicted within hours.

You're going to discover images you never imagined existed, and you're going to have fun utilizing them in imaginative ways.

And don't overlook that you're going to get 10% off all the materials from Cricut.com, which contains mats, blades, vinyl, machines, and tools of Easy Press, among several other items.

Overview of Cricut Design Space

The homepage and canvas are two portions of the design space. The homepage is where you discover projects that are new, fresh, and protected. Canvas is the area where the designs will be arranged or designed.

Home/Main Page of Design Space

The 1st page you see when you open Cricut Design Space is the homepage. The header, the banner, my projects, and highlighted content are four sections of the home.

The four sections of the Homepage

- Header

- Banner

- My Projects

- Ready to make/ Prepared- projects

BrooklynBerryDesigns.com

The Header

The menu symbol, also known as the hamburger, lets you move between the canvas and the home screen.

New system configuration, setup, account info, connection cartridges, Cricut availability, setting, and support are also included in this Menu.

The tab of the setting is where the lattice in the design space can be switched off, or the units displayed can be changed.

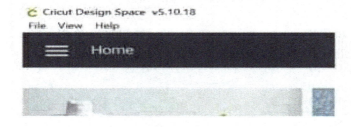

Banner

The carousel zone scrolls through several slides that are included. It's where it will feature updated information, promotional deals, maintenance notifications, or new items.

My Projects

This is where the designs, organized by most newly opened, are shown; in order to view them together, click on VIEW ALL. That is where to scan on a particular project you will browse through.

Ready-Made Projects

The next several banners are able to generate designs organized into categories. For e.g., projects included in Cricut Access, tasks by material, or projects by the system will be presented in this area

The Canvas

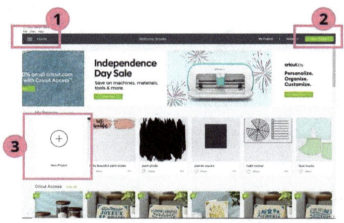

BrooklynBerryDesigns.com

You may access the canvas on the homepage from 3 separate areas, seen here.

In the Canvas area, there are 3 sections with toolbars. (1) The header, (2) the design section, and (3) the toolbar for the layers.

The Header

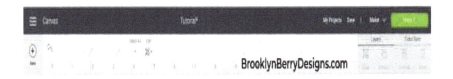

The header includes the Menu, the name of the project, the Menu for machine selection, and the green Mark It symbol.

Make sure to choose which machine model you are going to use so that you can reach the right menu and tool settings.

Panel of Design

New

This will display a page on a fresh blank canvas.

Templates

The templates provide you a scale and size guide.

This image is not going to be cut; it simply tells you how wide the shirt or object to be modified is on the canvas so you can design the template appropriately.

Projects

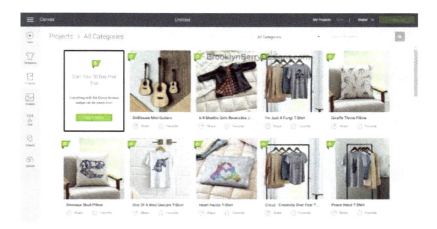

Look for inspiration for projects and already prepared designs. Tasks/Projects may be divided into several categories, including the type of project, seasons, or occurrences. Cricut access, infusible pigment, cards, Christmas, iron-on, stitching, knife blade, and planners are examples of featured projects.

Pictures

Browse, pick, and paste images comprising your own submitted images from the Cricut Picture Library onto Canvas.

Text

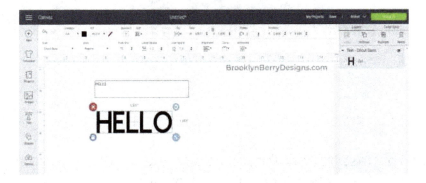

Apply words to the canvas and add sentences. The Edit Text toolbar emerges when text is inserted.

Shapes

Insert simple shapes to the canvas, including squares, circles, rectangles, lines, and triangles.

There are a number of stuff that you can fix with simple shapes to build and modify your designs. In a separate tutorial, we can go into depth on that.

Edit, Upload

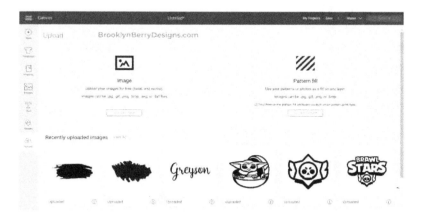

Cut images of your own by downloading .jpg, .png, and .gif .svg, .bmp, or .dxf document files for free usage.

Panel, Layers

The panel of layers will display every object on your designs' own layer. Each layer's color option is essential since it will assemble any layer on the same cutting surface with the same color.

Each design appears within the same sheet of paper as a teal with a cut. The layers enable you to individually change the parts and modify the line type (if it will cut, lure, engrave, etc.).

You will like the card, the scoreline. Then cut both from the same sheet and attach them together if you have a card that may have a design cut out along with a scoreline.

Cricut Cartridges

A cartridge is a basic device placed into your Cricut machine so that you can select templates to cut your machine. Your machine is worthless without a cartridge from Cricut. The more styles you have access to, the more cartridges you can do on your machine, the merrier the crafter.

The collections of fonts, pictures and graphics are contained in these cartridges that can be loaded into the devices. Each cartridge has a theme, so you can purchase Hello Kitty, baseball, elephant and winter-themed cartridges.

The concept is to use the pictures over the cartridges to make the pattern you want to cut with your Cricut machine. While on each cartridge, there are a limited number of photos, there are also a variety of attributes that enables users to create various designs from only one cartridge.

However, with the new machines, you can make your own photos and import pictures using Cricut Design Space tools.

Although using the Cricut cartridges may sound restricting to your imagination, they are a fantastic choice for crafters who cannot stop thinking about making their own cuts.

Also, you can merge and combine photos from all the various cartridges you possess with the Design Space software, also opening the artistic value of these add-ons.

All cartridges, normally in a tiny slot on end, can plug directly into the machine.

- In order to work with them in the software, you'll need to attach your Cricut cartridges to Design Space with the Explore, Explore Air 2, and Explore Air machines.

- You'll need to launch a new Design Space project.

- Click the 'insert photos' tab, and then pick the' Cartridges' option at the uppermost portion of the project menu.

- If the cartridges are connected to the computer, you will be able to access all of the cartridges on this page, following the steps, and you can select the one you would like to use.

- If they will be hooked together, you will automatically access the cartridges through Design space, so there will not be any need to take the cartridges around with you.

- You'll need to search the Cricut cartridges in the Craft Room software for the older machines, such as Expression 2, the counterpart to (design space is the) Craft Room.

- With the help of Explore machines, that is just as easy. You'll need to connect them back into the machine and connect them to the account in the craft room.

- A small menu can show up in the lower-left corner of the machine when you launch a new project in the Craft Room. The first tab here is 'Cartridges/Images,' and the cartridge you choose to deal with can be picked here.

- The cartridges with large typeface are the ones that will be added to your account successfully. Any non-bold cartridges would force you to insert them into the device or are actually cartridges that you have not yet purchased.

Cricut Cartridge Types

About the different types of cartridge:

Font – If it's a card you create for a friend or a sign you put together; this choice will help you get the work. You should choose a new kind of font for every day of the month for all the different letters and numbers to pick from.

Imagine – Imagine is great that with each picture you choose to cut away, you do not have to run out and get a different color of paper. The fictional cartridge would actually print on white paper the color template you want and then cut it out. On your Cricut cartridge list, this should certainly be a must.

Project – The project cartridges can be a lot of fun, whether you are organizing a group or creating a shirt.

Shapes – With any project you are working on, there are thousands of various shapes to select from.

Solutions – Cricut Solutions allow it much smoother to decorate and enjoy the numerous holidays during the year. To support you enjoy your favorite holidays, each cartridge includes basic shapes. These individual cartridges are classified as "simple" since they typically have just one or two cuts to choose from and are usually very affordable.

Cricut Cartridges: Disney

With some companies, Cricut has managed to secure some awesome licensing deals that contribute to creating cartridges based on certain movies and superheroes.

Sesame Street, Hello Kitty, and even DC Comics, for instance.

However, some of their popular cartridges come from Disney. These awesome cartridges will encourage you to make cuts for your dreams' frozen party or even a picnic for Winnie the Pooh.

Cricut Cartridges: Fonts

The range of Cricut cartridge fonts is also super common.

Cricut got you covered if you like fancy adorned lettering or monogram pattern fonts.

Chapter 2: Models of Cricut Design Space

All Cricut devices have some features which are similar to other devices. You would be capable of doing all of the given activities, no matter what Cricut model you choose.

Features of Cricut Design Space

Cut & Compose

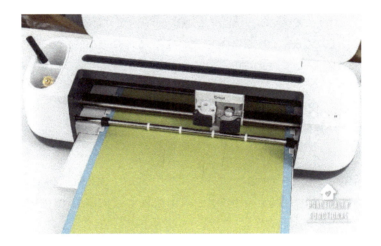

Each Cricut machine is capable of cutting and carving (or draw). It may emanate with the usual sharp-Point Blade for cutting a broad range of common crafting products, no matter which machine you purchase, and all the Cricut machine models are compliant with Cricut pens and pointers.

Carve/Cut along a Range of Products

Every Cricut machine model will cut numerous materials; creativity is the actual limit! Cricut's page mentions hundreds of various products that may be cut on all devices using the same Sharp/Fine-Point Blade.

Some of the devices, however, have the option to use substitute blades or trappings that enable you to cut or carve many more items, such as cloth material, leather, wood, etc.

The Design Space Software

Many Cricut machines use Design Space software to allow you to design and create designs for the machine.

The Design Room is available for all to use and can also be found on a Desktop or Laptop or an iOS or Android device. No matter what device you have, Design Space works the same way, and you always use this to upload tasks to your device for cutting or drafting. Trying to seek pre-made photos or posting pictures of your own.

A massive library of already made pictures, typestyles, and graphics that you can practice for the projects is part of Cricut Design Space. Or you should insert your own picture for the Cricut machine to use. It doesn't matter which computer you have; the very same method with both of them would be to search for photos from Cricut Design Space or upload your own.

Cutting Wirelessly Via Bluetooth

You could be requested to connect it to the computer using a USB connection when you first set up your new Cricut machine (particularly if you set it up using the computer rather than a smartphone or tablet device). But all Cricut machines might be used wirelessly after the setup process, so you don't need to be linked to the machine with a wire.

Differences between Machines

Quick description of the main parts in which the machines vary.

Size of Machine

The Cricut Maker and the Cricut Explore Air 2 are desktop machines; they are around 2 inches high and 8' to 10' tall, and 8' to 10' deep. The Maker is around 24 lbs., and the Explore Air 2 is around 16 lbs., but they are really designed to be set up and stable anywhere on a table or desk.

It seems that the Cricut Joy is much smaller and intended for portability. It is 8 inches wide, 4 inches high, 4 inches deep, and less than 4 pounds in weight. You can pick it up, take it around, and easily make it anywhere you want; no room for design is needed.

Mats and Mat-Less Cutting

Both the Maker and Explore Air 2 involve the usage of a mat for cutting. For these devices, there are currently four discrete cutting mats.

The Light Grip mat for sensitive materials such as tissue paper, the Standard Grip mat for standard materials such as paper & vinyl, the Strong Grip mat for heavier materials such as cloth, and the Fabric Grip mat for fiber. All of the other four mats come in 12 "x12" or 12 "x24".

Contrasting the greater devices, with or without a mat, the Cricut Joy will cut. The Joy has a slenderer cutting frame, but the mats Light Grip and Standard Grip even come with a smaller scale that fits with the Joy devices (4.5''x6.5'' and 4.5''x12''.)

Smart products that are spools of material intended to be suckled straight into the system and cut devoid of a mat may also be cut by Cricut Joy. Smart Vinyl, Smart Iron-On, and Smart Labels are currently developed by Cricut (a writable vinyl.)

Size of Cutting

Since a cutting mat is needed for the Maker to Explore Air 2, the biggest sole portion of product they can scratch is 12'' x 24'' (24'' long is the maximum cutting mat possible.) The Cricut Joy will cut unusual patterns on material that is 4.5'' wide-ranging and about 4 foot long while cutting without a mat, or it can cut a repeated pattern on reels of material approximately 20 ft. long. (The Joy will cut items for about 4.5" x 12" while cutting with a mat.).

Holder for Sole vs. Double Tool

On a carriage that moves back and forth when you raise the cover of a Cricut device, you will see the primary tool holder. There is a double tool carrier for both the Cricut Maker & Cricut Explore Air 2, which ensures there is a brace to hold the blade and another clamp to protect things like pens or the scoring trackpad. This makes anything to be released and cut by the device in one step! The Cricut Joy seems to have a sole tool holder, which means that if you want to write on the project and cut it out, you'll have to change out the tool for a pen halfway along the process.

Adaptive Tool Framework

A modern invention is the Adaptive Tool Framework, which is only usable on the Cricut Maker.

The tool container carriage will only go up and down on the Explore and Joy devices. That means that the posture is moreover "down" and hitting the material below it on the Mat, or it is "active" so that before moving "down" again to cut, the whole posture will shift to a new point.

In 4 aspects, the Adaptive Tool Method is different:

1. For about 4 kg of the depth of cut, it provides far more strength, 10x more than most devices.

2. To swap and transform the Blade, it uses a steering mechanism that actively regulates the position of the Blade throughout all times.

3. For each cut move, it automatically changes the Blade's pressure to get a sparkling cut even though tough material.

4. An entirely new set of accessories and tools (such as the Rotating Blade, Knife Blade, Debossing Tool, Engraving Tool, etc.) enables the machine to be used so that you can deal with thousands of new products.

Generally, the Adaptive Tool System allows even more power on top of the tools, facilitating much more difficult cuts, cutting heavier materials, the freedom to extend and employ new styles of tools, and any time smooth, crisp cuts.

To see which model is better, compare Cricut machines.

Insert Mat Cards with the Card

The capacity to configure Insert Cards with the use of the Card Mat is another aspect that is exclusive to the Cricut Pleasure.

Typically, when making cards using a Cricut, you can insert a single layer of material into the device to chop it down to card size, and then you will fold the cut card into an envelope to match it.

To allow the Fun to cut out just the front of the card even if it is folded, you can load a pre-folded card on the Mat with the Card Mat!

Again, this means you can customize greeting cards for a small device where a flattened-out card normally won't go through the system.

Printing and Cutting

The Creator and Explore Air 2 will use Print Then Break, which enables the projects to incorporate particolored images or pictures. The picture will be sent to the home printer by Design Room, and you can then load the published image into the Cricut to get it cut out; no scissors are necessary!

To help the machine to line up the cuts on your printed template, the Cricut Joy machine does not have an "eye" feeler that orates the process points, so the Print Then Cut function can't be used.

Method for Quick Cutting

While writing or cutting standard paper products, cardstock, iron, and vinyl, the Cricut Maker and Cricut Explore Air 2 can use "fast mode" to enable the machine to cut and begin writing twice as fast!
When you make a variety of variations, like cards or party favors, of something, this is incredibly beneficial. There is no "fast mode" alternative for the Cricut Joy.

Connecting Physical Cartridges

Unusual Cricut machine models (such as Cricut Word, Cricut Personal, and Cricut Create) used actual cartridges for cuttable pictures, illustrations, and fonts that were beavered into the system and housed digital files. Instead of traditional cartridges, the latest set of Cricut machines utilizes images and fonts from the interactive Production Space catalog.

The Cricut Explore Air 2 machine has a slot where you can plug a cartridge in. Then you must "link" the physical cartridge to the digital Design Space account so that you can always manage the cartridge graphics. The Cricut Maker and Cricut Joy do not have physical cartridge slots, so you would have to buy a separate USB cartridge adapter for your device if you wish to use cartridge material for your Maker or Joy so that you can connect your cartridge to your Design Space account.

Bundles, Sizes, & Price

Another huge distinction between devices is the tones they come with if extra materials and attachments are included with the machine and the cost.

Rates differ from vendor to vendor (particularly if anyone has a sale), but the Cricut Maker is extremely costly in general, and the Joy is the most inexpensive, right in there along with the Cricut Explore Air 2.

The machine packages are great for someone just starting out, so you can get some additional features for the machine and cut off supplies at a discount, all in one go. There are a variety of great package options available, so just see what looks good to you when you are about to buy a machine.

As far as color goes, Cricut also comes up with numerous choices for the devices, although some of those colors are unique to certain outlets or certain special edition models. But after you've decided the Cricut machine is perfect for you, you should browse online for the available colors before purchasing.

Cricut Models

1. Cricut Joy

The Cricut Joy is the newest device of Cricut. Cricut calls it a great little device for carving and writing that makes almost everything easier to customize. At a super cheap price, it is an eminence automated croak cutting machine that makes it a perfect entry-level choice for those who just begin. It will cut fifty-plus materials from vinyl, iron-on, and more from plain paper or cardstock.

There are actually only two tool proficiencies for the Cricut Joy: the perfect Blade and Cricut Joy pointers & markers. But there is practically no limit to the number of tasks that can be achieved with just splitting/cutting and writing. The Cricut Joy will do what you need for fast and easy ventures, cards, and customization.

The Pros

- It automatically carves and writes. No need to do anything on your own; you can do everything with this machine.
- Cut more than 50 products. In a broad range of items, the regular Sharp-Point Blade enables sharp, crisp cuts.
- Cutting Mat-less. Smart fabrics, which fall in large rolls that automatically feed into the device for long, consistent cuts without having a mat, can be cut by the Cricut Joy.
- Mat's card. The card mat makes for swift convention cards that, even when folded, can be carved out and customized.
- Compact sizes. The Cricut Joy is tiny and lightweight, so it's super versatile and easy to put in a hutch or on a bookshelf for easy access.
- Inexpensive. At an entry-level price, the Cricut Joy is a completely integrated digital die-carving device.
- Bluetooth built-in. For quick cutting, attach it without wire to the machine.
- Free software of Design Space. Over 100,000 cuttable patterns and fonts plus thousands of prepared projects are accessible, or your own project can be made easily.
- Use pictures of your own. Simply upload your particular photos, and they will be automatically transformed into curtail-able images by Design space.

The Cons

- Max width of material. A maximum material diameter of 4.4 inches is accessible for The Joy. You're safer off using the bigger machines if you choose to perform big or complicated tasks.
- Single holder for tools. You have to temporarily turn out the Blade as well as the pen partly along with the cut if you choose to compose and cut with the Cricut Pleasure.
- No flashy tools. This system just operates with the sharp-point Blade of Cricut Joy and the pens and markers of Cricut Joy; you cannot measure, engrave, smash, etc., as you could with the larger devices.
- No Print and Cut Then. The Cricut Joy does not have the "eye" sensor needed to declaim the registration marks printed for a project named Print Then Cut.
- The fabric can't be cut. The Cricut Joy isn't meant for cloth cutting.
- No designed space for cartridges. To connect the external cartridges to your Design Space premium profile, you must buy a separate adapter.

End Result

For persons who would be capable of doing fast and simple ventures without much hassle, The Cricut Joy is great. It gangs up almost instantly, and its small size guarantees that it can be set up everywhere; no craft room is needed.

2. Cricut Explore Air 2

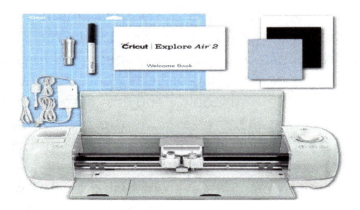

A full-size cutting device (maximum material thickness of 12 inches) at a fair price is the Cricut Explore Air 2. It arises with the regular sharp-Point Blade that enables thousands of materials to be cut and is compliant with the Deeper Point Blade & the Concocted Blade (sold independently) to help you to split even more items.

It too has a Quick Function, which enables the device to cut and write on basic materials such as cardstock, vinyl, and iron-on up to 2x faster. For persons who create several copies of the projects (like instructors) or persons who create stuff to trade who will value the period of time they preserve, this is very useful.

The Cricut Explore Air 2 has a dual tool tray, unlike the Cricut Joy, ensuring it can keep both a blade and an optional auxiliary. The 2nd loop is familiar with accessories such as the Scoring Stylus & Cricut Pens, ensuring that without needing to move tools in the center, you can cut and compose or test entirely in one step.

There is also built-in Bluetooth functionality in the Cricut Explore Air 2 so that you can cut without wire/cable.

The Pros

- Automatically cuts, writes, and scores. No need to do anything on your own; you can do everything with the machine.
- Double holder for tools. Without getting to switch off tools, cut and compose everything in one move.
- Can cut more than 100 materials. A large range of products are cut from the regular Fine-Point Blade. Suitable for cutting additional items with the Dense Point Blade plus Concocted Blade.
- Bluetooth built-in. For ease of cutting, attach wirelessly to the machine.
- Speedy Mode. On cardstock, plastic, and iron-on, cut and write about 2x quicker.

Free software of Design Space. About 1 million cuttable graphics & fonts plus thousands of prepared projects are available, or your personal project is designed easily.

- Print and Cut. Easily combine the designs with printed images or illustrations.
- Using pictures of your own. Easily share your own photos, and they will be instantly transformed into cuttable photos by Design space.
- Built-in Cartridge Slot. Connect your external cartridges using your device to the Design Space profile.

The Cons

- Not meant for fabric cutting. Prior to cutting, you should secure the fabric with a backing fabric. The Blade keeps dragging along the cloth, triggering holes and clefts.
- Non-compliant with adapters for the Adaptive Tool System. Unable to utilize Rotating Blade, Knife Blade, Scoring Wheels, or all other attachments for the potential Adaptive Tool System.
- Not accessible. The device is too huge to be conveniently portable.
- A cutting/carving mat is needed. Prior to inserting it into this device, you must place the product on a cutting mat.
- Subject to cuts of 24''. Since a cutting mat is required for this machine, it will not cut anything longer than 24''.
- No space for a card Mat. The card mat is currently available only for the Cricut Joy.

End Result

For persons who create a lot of things with their Cricut (tutors, company owners who export their artistries, etc.) who can enjoy how ample time Quick Mode saves for them, the Cricut Explore Air 2 is a decent fit3.

3. Cricut Maker

Cricut's expert machine is the Cricut Maker. It is called the supreme nifty cutting machine by Cricut. It's the - level automated die-cutting device at the price of a private machine that produces work quality. From the greatest and precious material and paper to matboard, balsa wood, and leather, hundreds of items may be cut.

The whole new Adjustable Tool System is used by the Cricut Maker, which provides more direct power over the tools,' like rotating, raising, and changing pressure during the whole cut. When Cricut extends its tool offerings, the Adaptive Tool System often helps the device to use new styles of tools later on.

The Maker can also use the following tools associated with the Adaptive Tool System, in addition to the Sharp-Point Blade, Deep Cut Blade, and Bonded Textile Blade, which are well-suited with all Cricut machines:

- Rotating Blade: This helps you to cut cloth with a Cricut Maker, and the basic sharp-Point Blade is a major upgrade. Tough materials such as burlap or denim and finer materials such as crepe paper or satin may also be cut. Without staining or clumping, this Blade helps you to create complex cuts on cloth (that is why you requisite stabilizer support while using the sharp-Point Blade).

- Knife Blade that helps you to quickly cut heavier and thicker materials like balsa wood, leather, mat board, and Cricut Chipboard. Without fearing if the Blade will crack, you may manage some incredibly intricate designs.

- Scoring Wheels: On small, heavy, and also coated paper fabrics, these tools create crisp ridges. They enable you to create excess scorelines on every material that, when you pleat it, does not crack.

- Engraving Method: This tool helps you to produce exquisitely engraved (human beings or canine) dog tags, nameplates, artwork and decoration, accessories, logotypes, keepsakes, and much more.

- Puncture Blade: This blade offers consistent, precisely corrugated lines that provide you with smooth, even rip up without first folding. It's great for pages of tear-out booklets, raffle passes, handmade newspapers, curved forms, or some projects that need an unsoiled tear.

  This tool helps you to produce crisp, accurate debossed templates. It is a Fine Debossing Tool. The rotating ceramic ball's extensive variety of motion allows you full control to make your own personalized decorative embellishments, designs, monograms, labels, closures, and more.

- Wavy Blade: This blade offers you an amusing spiky edge on a range of common materials; use it on any substance that can be cut by the Maker.

As they depend on the Adaptive Tool System, the Explore Air 2 and the Joy will not use these blades & tools. In the other machines, the regular tool holder gait just doesn't have the accuracy or control necessary.

Like the names imply, the Adaptive Tool Framework is programmed to seamlessly move between tools, modifying the enterprise system to what apparatus is loaded into it. This helps TONS to build different styles of tools in the upcoming to do the latest kinds of crafts for the machine.

The Pros

- Automatically cuts write & rates. No need to do anything of it on your own; you can do everything with this machine.
- System of Adaptive Tool. The modern drive system helps the machine to have more power on the tools. The greater the strain, the more nuanced cuts!
- The extensible toolset. The Adaptive Tool Framework is designed to allow in the future different kinds of hewing tools apart from simple blades.
- Cut more than 250 materials. A large range of materials are cut from the regular Sharp-Point Blade, and the Rotating Blade and Knife Blade may cut much further!
- Access to patterns for sewing. Gain access to thousands of prepared to cut stitching patterns using the machine.
- Double holder for tools. Without trying to switch off tools, cut and compose everything in one move.
- Bluetooth built-in. For quick cutting, attach wirelessly to the machine.
- Quick Mode. On cardstock, vinyl, and iron-on, cut and write about 2x quicker.
- Free software of Design Space. Around 1 million cuttable graphics and fonts plus hundreds of prepared projects are available, or your personal project can be designed easily.

- Print and cut. Easily combine the designs with printed images or illustrations.
- Using pictures of your own. Upload your private pictures quickly, and Design Space would automatically transform them into cuttable/carve-able pictures.

The Cons

- Cost. The MSRP is $389.99, the highest cost of any machine from Cricut.
- Not being portable. The device is too heavy to be comfortably portable.
- A cutting mat is needed. Prior to loading it into this device, you must place the product on a cutting mat.
- Restricted to cuts of 24″. Since a cutting mat is required for this machine, it cannot cut material lengthier than 24″
- No Mat Card. The card mat is actually eligible only for the Cricut Joy.
- No integral space for cartridges. To connect the external cartridges to your Design Space profile, you must buy a separate adapter.

End Result

The Cricut Maker is ideal for persons who want their machine to be able to do something (particularly sewists, quilters, craftsmen, or everyone else who cuts a huge amount of fabric or heavy materials), and those who want their purchasing as much as feasible to be 'future-proof.'

Best Cricut Design Space Machines for Beginners

1. Cricut Explore One

The Cricut Explore One is perfect for someone who is just starting to cut and craft effectively. The variations this one exhibits with Cricut Explore Air 2 would be noticed by someone who is acquainted with these devices. This version, though, is much affordable. While it lacks Bluetooth technology, consumers can install the wireless Bluetooth transmitter of their preference. Using a Mac, iPad, PC, or iPhone, it is simpler to cut.

The fact that the computer cuts broad-ranging materials is one of its biggest attractions, though. However, the appealing qualities don't stop there. The machine's Smart Set technologies may also be used for multiple things, such as:

- Providing quality cuts on every material
- Design of a tailored setting for broad materials

- Makes clean cuts in numerous types and sizes

The Pros

- Supporting cartridges, perfect for starters

- The software of Design Space is not only simple to use but also free.

- Provides access to the projects through different gadgets, including iPads, PCs, Macs, and iPhones

- It deals with more than 50 free photos and 25 designs with a single click.

- Enables users to share cost-free custom fonts and photos

- Users may search it for pre-made designs and templates

- The storage containers and the standard-grip cutting mat are extremely convenient.

- It's one of Cricut's cheapest devices.

The Cons

- The lack of incorporated Bluetooth technology induces consumers to purchase adapters

- The inclusion of only one holder inhibits users who choose to cut, craft, and publish everything at the same time.

- Its cartridges are very pricey.

2. Cricut Air Explore

One of the best Cricut entry-level devices for beginners is the Cricut Explore Air. It has everything you'd like to craft and cut various materials in certain kind of machines to decorate your townhouse and turn it into a vibrant area.

With incredible precision, it cuts all kind of materials. What's more, more than 60 different material forms are cut by this machine, including:

- Paper

- Vinyl

- Vellum

- Iron-On

There are some other attractions on the machine that involves a double carrier, which you can use as a blade and marker. Simply put, personalized messages may be cut and written concurrently.

On account of that, it has a double tool holder, which you can use to guarantee you are still close to your pen and Blade at all times. This version comes with Bluetooth technology, unlike the Cricut Explore One, which supports the needs of someone who loves rapid and successful wireless cutting.

The Pros

- Cuts and writes numerous materials in a single phase,

- Includes long-lasting blades

- Has a resilient structure

- The machine is really simple to set up.

- Also, it's simple to use

- Provides support for cartridges

- It's incredibly easy,

- It is compliant with the iPad app

- Contains orange grid lines to keep core designs

- Great for wireless cutting activities

The Cons

- Unable to operate without a connection to the Internet

- The software of design is not as responsive as it should be.

Necessary Tools for Cricut

Cricut Tool for Weeding

The Cricut Weeding Method is perfect for poking out little parts of cut-out material, which looks a little like anything you'd see in the dentist's office (or other substances).

It is also good (so they don't adhere to the fingers) for picking up things with adhesive on it. And while you're doing intricate designs, reap the benefits of the angled part of the hook to tie down pieces. When the nail or the floppy end of a scissor is too wide for the task, you'll enjoy this tool. This tool may be used on any project affiliated with Cricut.

Infusible Ink Pens by Cricut

Using these markers to generate transfers such as t-shirts, tote bags, coasters, and more that can then be used on Cricut blank pieces, such heat-transfer inks conform absolutely to the end product, so you would never have a rigid line or sagging edge around a transfer like you will for a transfer of iron.

The colors are vivid and rich.

Cricut Adhesive Basic Grip Cutting Mats

There's a mat for your Cricut. But you'll love the ease of making several available while you're really churning on a job. It is not unusual to ask for upwards of 15 mats for projects. And though you can take the paper off as it runs thru the Cricut machine, so reuse the Mat, it's a lengthy process, and it's a big time-saver to have more mats accessible.

With the Cricut Maker and Cricut Explore devices, such mats may be used. Every three-pack is meant for a certain purpose, such as for cloth or cardstock, to choose the Mat that is perfect for your needs.

Cricut Scoring Stylus

Use this stylus to scorelines in the Cricut Explore machine-great it's if you create stuff you want to fold up, such as a greeting card or something three-dimensional.

You will love this time-saving tool if you are creating several cards (hello, winter holidays or wedding invites!) and that it will protect you from frustratingly inconsistent folds. Just remember that the stylus did not score deeply enough, some reviewers thought.

Cricut XL Scraper

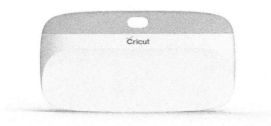

With the aid of this scraper, make smooth a breeze, which scoops up small pieces of paper with comfort. Plus, you can use it to clean out (bubble-free!) vinyl as well.

It is considerably bigger than the scraper that comes with or could have preceded your machine in starter packs. When it's time for bigger tasks with tones of little parts floating about, it particularly comes in handy.

Armor Etch Cream

Do you like to see the drawings appear on glass? Bring the pint glasses and windows on! You may apply patterns on glass surfaces with the assistance of Armor Etch Cream.

The very first step is to use your Cricut device to make a stencil. Move the pattern to the glass and place a coat of Armor Etch Cream on top of it. After making it stay for a moment, you'll extract the cream.

Brayer Cricut

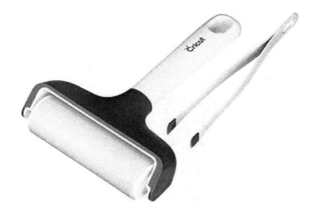

You want to ensure that everything is spread fully flat on the Mat when you start a project with a synthetic material, such as vinyl or fabric, to prevent crinkles and bubbles from damaging the designs.

To smooth lines and transfer air bubbles after you lay down your stuff, push the Cricut Brayer along the top of the products on your cutting pad. It has a perfect size in hand and is extremely quick to use

Bright Pad Cricut

While weeding, do your eyes ache as you try to find out what to erase? An important convenience is the Cricut Bright Pad.

The backlight allows it easy to spot the scores in the paper, so you can quickly take your weeding method to get to work. This list pad has an adjustable LED light so you can weed and trace with ease.

Cricut Explore Housing & Blade Deep Cut

You'll need one of these blades if you choose to hack into balsa wood or tougher materials. When you have a Cricut Explore, go for the Cricut Explore Deep Cut Blade. Per Cricut, it is able to cut more than 50 items, including several 1.5 mm thick materials. (But note that you may want to do some test cuts to get a sense of the appropriate settings on your machine).

Go for the Cricut Knife Blade + Drive Housing if you have the Cricut Maker, which can slash through tougher substances, such as balsa wood and leather, like the Deep Cut Blade. Reviewers enjoy the sharpness of the weapon but notice that it is not sufficient for complex, tiny projects.

Cricut Quick Swap + Housing Engraving Tip

Is everyone dreaming of creating an engraving of their own with initials, titles, or a cool logo? Without anything but your Cricut Maker device, this instrument makes it simple to engrave glass, cloth, metal, and more. Unfortunately, the Cricut Explore or the Cricut Joy may not work on this instrument.

Cricut Pen Set

Cricut Explore devices, such as the Cricut Joy, operate with this collection of 30 pens.

Note: An adapter is required for the Cricut Explore One device, per supplier.

Use these pens to move drawn designs to paper through the design software of your Cricut, or just use them without the machine to freestyle draw. These pens are odorless, as per Cricut, and after curing, the ink will remain permanently in place.

Chapter 3: Cricut Projects and Selling Ideas

There are several things when it refers to the Cricut machine that you can do about it. If you've ever dreamed of earning money with your crafts, here are a couple of ideas you should create and sell for additional income.

Some DIY Cricut Crafts

There are as many ideas for Cricut as there are people, twice the amount of materials that you will use. You can create wonderful DIY projects for every event if you have a Cricut Explore (existing, Air or Air 2), Cricut Maker, or the charming Cricut Joy.

Here's a sample of the most recent Cricut machine projects you might make.

1. DIY Raindeer Plaid Gift Tags

A reindeer flannel Christmas gift tag is a project that must be created by Cricut! This gift tag is a fast and simple project that you can design and make by printing and cutting. Insert your own text, change the plaid design with your own favorite and even switch the reindeer about as much as you like to create a gift tag.

Materials

- Explore machine Cricut

- The software of Cricut Design Space

- Jen Goode's Gift Tags and Reindeer Cut Patterns

- Standard Grip Cricut mat 12'' x 12''

- Cardstock

- Cricut's Gold Glitter pen

- Twine

- Glue

- A printer

Directions

1. To print, design, and cut gift tags, follow on-screen guidelines.

2. Glue the head of the reindeer against the tag.

3. Across the front of the gift tag, write the to/from names in the space given. If you'd like, create a little message.

4. Insert twine through the gift tag's top hole and tie it to your gift.

Tip: The tag pattern may be modified. To adjust the template for printing, just unflatten all the parts and pick the tag border. Make sure that all the parts are re-flattened.

For fun: apply some red glitter to the nose of the reindeer, and you'll also have a cool Rudolph gift tag.

2. Cute and Quick Cricut DIY Pumpkins

To make potentially thousands of variations, mix and match the pumpkin face parts cut with your Cricut machine. To make an adorable pumpkin that is specifically their own, you should pre-cut all the face shapes and let the children choose their favorites. For all sorts of DIY and decor, this Halloween project has a free SVG file that you can use.

Materials

- Free download: Jen Goode's Halloween Faces SVG file

- Machine to Cricut

- Black vinyl

- Pumpkins

- Scraps with ribbons or fabric (optional)

- Materials to create Jen Goode's Cute and Fast DIY Pumpkins

Directions

1. With a damp cloth, clean your pumpkin and pat it dry.

2. SVG file download. To Cricut Design Space, upload it. Ungroup and resize each face of a pumpkin to the size you like.

3. To cut out the pumpkin faces, follow the on-screen guidelines.

4. Apply each face to the single pumpkin.

5. Finish the pumpkin with pieces of ribbon or cloth twisted and bound across each pumpkin's stem.

Tip: To verify it holds to the pumpkin well, use outdoor or permanent adhesive vinyl.

Options for customizing the DIY pumpkins:

All aspects of your DIY pumpkins can be mixed and matched. Paint it or draw on it first for a fancier pumpkin, then add the vinyl face parts.

For all ages, sticker faces are preferred; even preschoolers and kids will love rearranging a pumpkin without paint or carving tools. For more bling, use Shimmer Vinyl.

3. DIY Puzzle Element Necklace

You can make a cute little DIY Puzzle Element necklace in about 30 minutes with your Cricut. To match your own color and theme, you can customize this pretty Cricut project. Apply paint or also some sort of fun fabric accent with glitter. It's up to you completely.

Materials

- Cricut Explore Cutting Machine

- The software of Cricut Design Space

- The Jen Goode-designed Puzzle Piece Necklace design

- Standard Grip Cricut mat 12'' x 12''

- Cardstock-White

- Glue

- Glitter

- Chain necklace

Directions

1. Print and cut puzzle parts according to the directions on the screen.

2. Depending on how dense you like the jewelry pendant, repeat cut to produce 4-7 puzzle pieces.

3. Remove the middle heart from all the pieces of the puzzle.

4. Layer pieces of the puzzle, adding glue between layers. To ensure a strong seal between layers, push firmly. Allow it to dry out.

5. On half of the section of the puzzle, add glue and spray with glitter.

6. Add it to a chain necklace.

Tip: Optionally, one basic heart can be glued to the front of the pendant for another look.

4. DIY Spring Gift Tag with Your Cricut

With a beautiful spring style, create your own gift tags. For all your spring festivities, you may use such gift tags to decorate preference bags or adjust the text to create tags to add to presents.

Materials

- Cricut Explore machine

- The software of Cricut Design Space

- Jen Goode's Garden Birthday Day Party and Tiny Tag Cut Designs

- 12'' x 12'' Standard Cricut mat Grip

- Cardstock

- Cricut pens

- Glue

- Ribbon

Directions

1. To print and cut tag pieces, follow on-screen directions.

2. Layer different components of the tag and glue them into place.

3. Attach a ribbon around the tag and tie it to the gift tag.

5. Penguin Funny Christmas Card

Materials

- Machine for Cricut Cutting

- Jen Goode's Reindeer Penguin Art

- StandardGrip Cricut mat 12'' x 12''

- Cardstock in colors of holidays

- Cricut Pens in Silver and Red

- Glue

Directions

1. Cut the designs according to the directions on the screen.

2. Layer all the penguin cutouts with glue and top with the print art, then cut the penguin template to make a dynamic accent for your card.

3. Within the front of the card, glue the square cutout to ensure that the square cutout window is fully protected.

4. Optionally, split a second square inside.

5. Within the window area, glue your penguin accent.

6. Assembling the envelope.

7. Paste the mini heart to the middle of the cutout pattern of the snowflake and use it to secure the envelope as a sticker.

6. DIY Fancy Floral Planner

With your Cricut, customize your planner with fancy flower cut pages that you make. It is easier to create this DIY planner accent than you would expect. You just need a Cricut and the design of the SVG

Materials

- An account of Cricut Machine and Cricut Access

- A page for flower planner SVG file

- Cardstock with your preference of colors.

Directions

1. To Cricut Design Space, upload the SVG file.

2. To fit your particular planner, resize. If there are separate spaces for your planner loops, you may easily cover the contour of the provided holes and incorporate your own.

3. To cut the separate layers, follow on-screen directions.

4. The stylish cut and backing cut layers are stacked. If you'd like, glue them together.

How to Make Money with Cricut Crafts?

The simpler the craft, the more competitive it would end up being while selling crafts. Smaller implies that when it is time to deliver, fewer material to create the item and less weight is equivalent to more benefit.

The primary factor in designing a Cricut business plan is the cost of goods, overall size and shipping factors, time and commitment from beginning to end (because time is money!) and popularity in this list.

Materials Cost: Material expenses normally incorporate into pricing; however, overhead costs are something you might want to know. Many consumers have to bring resources first to buy materials. There will also be some surplus supplies and material for bulk sales. You should still attempt to acquire as much product as you may like, but it is never optimized perfectly.

Shipping: There have been several claims that while shipping is easy, customers just purchase more. This is typically achievable for the vendor by folding the delivery costs into the price of the goods. If you have a high-cost point product, this is good, but if the product's natural price is $5 and delivery costs $50, that really doesn't sound right for the end customer.

Effort: It is mostly a labor of love to many crafters selling their items. Although, when creating crafts for demands takes over life, it takes away from the joy.

In the world of business, the days you have to postpone the family picnic, turn down the offer to drink with the boys, or wait up all night because you have a delivery deadline to follow is a reality. It's simply something to bear in mind.

Popularity: Trends come and go; riding one never hurts. That's the beauty of selling homemade; the supply chain and practices appear to be more flexible such that even if the winds switch direction, you can pivot. You should turn modes and start ramping out what people want, whether it's new movies and songs, events, or some other element that sparks a new trend.

How to Use a Vinyl Cutter to Earn Money?

For Cricut's company sellers, vinyl is the right material. It's pretty cheap, lightweight, and really easy to ship, and there are so many items you can make, most notably.

Wall Art

The options here are infinite. As with the display not actually running, cottage wall decoration is always going high with Fixer Upper.

On Pinterest, there are more than half a dozen searches monthly for cottage wall art. Don't skip the acts out there.

Personalized Decals

Personalized stickers are perfect as they apply from events to home decor and so many ultimate uses. It's a difference that the major retailers will not contend with as you provide personalized service.

Stickers

Related in nature to vinyl decals, because of the modification opportunities and their delivery rates (as it does not cost much), stickers are a popular commodity.

The Highest Selling Cricut Projects Segment May Be Wedding Decor and Favors

The demand for weddings is strong and breathing. It's not a surprise. Back yard ceremonies are on the rise. The quest for them has risen by 441 percent. Individuals manage to save a bit for their wedding.

Although individuals have smaller affairs, they cut down on the information. A more personalized touch is needed for small intimate occurrences. The best items for today's wedding are artisanal items, tailored wedding party gear, and personalized favors.

How to Use a Cricut Air 2 to Earn Money?

Using the Cricut Explorer, there are too many items to market.

Flowers of Paper

The trend of paper flowers is at an all-time peak, much as farmhouse decor, with more than half a million monthly searches on Pinterest for it. From Mother's Day to celebrations to baby showers, they are perfect for all times. No surprise they demand so much.

Cricut Cake Toppers

Customization is important when it comes to selling Cricut ideas. The simplest and most cost-effective items to create could be cake and cupcake toppers.

Parents are still looking at elevating their game with all manner of tailored decor and favors at children's birthday parties.

Business Ideas via Cricut

The options are now completely infinite with the top-notch cutting machine, such as the Cricut Maker.

There are so many things to deal with, from paper to fabric to wood.

Flowers of Felt and Fabric

As per Pinterest, Cactus designs queries are up 235 percent. Get on with this succulent theme of Felt Succulents.

Projects of Wood

There are far more than a million queries a month for rustic decor on Pinterest. By chance, with the Cricut Maker, you can cut wood! A good thing is customized wood signs.

Certain Products for Leather and Imitation Leather

With the Cricut Explorer, you can definitely hack both leather and fake leather, but with the Knife and Rotary cutter, it's certainly smoother. There are plenty of the finest decorative and colorful fake leathers that are super luxurious.

Some of the easiest items to manufacture and sell with the Cricut are cards because they impress everybody.

Cards merit their specific category since they are very cost-effective to create, and from birthdays to marriages, there is a need for one on each day to thank you. Plus, they really don't get any cheaper shipping cards.

Where to Sell Your Cricut-Made Goods?

Here are some sites you may like to sell your awesome Cricut designs so that your Cricut will earn money!

- By word-of-mouth locally

- Fair for Local Crafts

- At the church, college, retailer, regional pop-up shop

- Facebook Personal Profile

- Company page on Facebook

- Groups on Facebook (make sure you have permission from the moderator)

Online shop of your own through:

- Shopify

- WooCommerce

- Space Square

- Etsy

- Handmade Seller Platform of Amazon

- eBay

- Instagram

Tools of Marketing

Here are a few strategies you may want to try if you need to raise up some business:

Marketing's Word of Mouth

If you have created things for friends and they enjoy them, check if they can post a link to the shop or email address with the other friends or on their social networking feeds.

Marketing on Platforms

A number of times, on your sales website, like Etsy, there are ways to "boost" or "feature" your content. Bear in mind that during the busier periods of the year, you can have greater competition, but fewer people purchase during the slow periods of the year.

Tips and Tricks of Cricut

It's not difficult for Cricut Design Space, but certain aspects are surely not as spontaneous as all of us will want them to be. And it may also seem like even the utmost straightforward methods are unnecessarily complex while you are really getting started. However, you can eventually see that Cricut Design Space really contains all you want to make awesome projects once you get moving on the first few projects and that there are around tones of great hacks that make it not just easy to design but really effective.

Cricut Design Space Tips

1. Weld, Contour, and Carve – Customize the Projects. Using the three key editing tools: Welding, Contour, and Carve, every file, whether it's one from the Design Space Picture Archive or you upload directly, can be modified, customized, and personalized endlessly.

All 3 of these methods are found along the toolbar at the bottom end on the right-hand side and will only be highlighted when a particular template has the functions available.

These devices might not look like they are doing anything at first sight. Even so, they are extremely strong and are the basics to the formations being entirely customized. Go detailed and read about each tool's ins and outs here: Weld | Contour | Slice

2. Your Search Words Experiment. In the Design Space Picture Library, the search feature may be slightly specific. A fairly common word that often won't generate all kinds of pictures. Yet whenever a single phrase or a specific letter is tweaked, more pictures instantly populate.

If you type the word "dots" into the bar for search, it provides around 115 photos. Parting off the "s."

3. Synonym Search. Searching for different synonyms is another smart practice since each picture is marked with different check words.

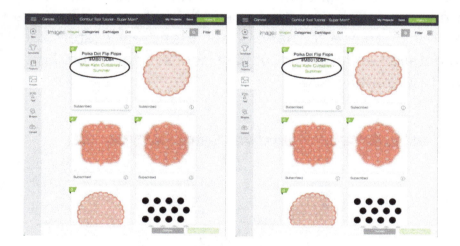

4. See the Similar Cartridge for More.

You will locate one picture you love in the center of a whole host of other photos that you don't when you use the search feature. The best way to begin is by the cartridge (set) from which it emerged.

Just click the tiny details circle in the bottom end, right of every image inside the Graphic Space Image Library, to navigate the cartridge quickly and conveniently (below left).

With a clickable (green) link, it will open the picture info that will yield you to the complete range of photos (below right)!

5. Free Pictures & Text Access.

Be sure to use the FREE tools inside Cricut Design Space, whether you are just finding your mode around, wanting to see your device in motion, and/or want to hold your designing costs low.

Using the Filter in the Design Space Picture Library to locate FREE images... just select the option "Free" to see an assortment of photos you can incorporate at zero cost into the projects.

To discover FREE fonts... every font you have built on your device can be cut from your Cricut machine. This not only ensures that you can cut every pre-installed font on your device, but even any great font that you can locate and grab from any of your favorite free websites, such as Font Squirrel or DaFont.

Simply select 'My Fonts' from the font menu filter to locate the fonts you will use without sustaining extra charges. This can display ALL fonts that are loaded on your device, and also the Cricut fonts that you might have bought (either separately or from a Cricut Access pass), which is a perfect way to make sure you don't have to recompense for fonts!

6. Quickly Re-Color. The Color Sync tool is a perfect way to preserve time for the projects and verify the multiple designs utilize the same colors.

You can close with various colors of a similar hue as you put multiple designs on the Design Canvas (for example, three diverse greens, four diverse blues, etc.).

As an alternative to picking each layer to re-color it, move down the right-hand tool section to the Color Sync tool.

7. The Tool for Hiding.

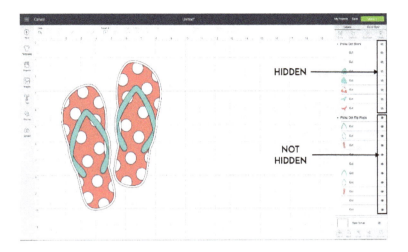

Any picture "hidden" is not deleted from the canvas, but when you submit the project to be cut, it will not be used.

The "Hide" icon pins on/off, rendering it is so simple to cut out what you require and/or hold your concept canvas clog without losing a trail of photos in which you might always want to perform.

8. Change Cut, Score, or Draw to Any Line.

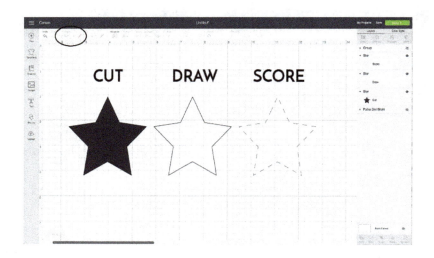

Once upon a time, you had to find a template with certain particular characteristics if you needed a line to be strained or scored (rather than cut).

A new update to Design Room, however, now enables every line to be conveniently modified from cut to score to draw with the quick drop-down menu for Line type on the top toolbar: As a "Cut" template, most designs can settle on the canvas—Although you can quickly adjust the outline (using the pens) of the picture to be drawn or graded (using the scoring tool or scoring wheel).

In order to modify how your template can eventually be formed, just make sure your levels are un-fastened and un-attached.

9. Patterns Manipulate. Now you can adjust how the picture is filled by using the latest Fill feature at the top of the toolbar. You may switch out colors or allocate a pattern inside of the picture with a layer chosen.

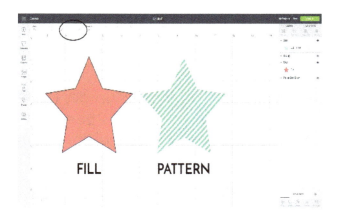

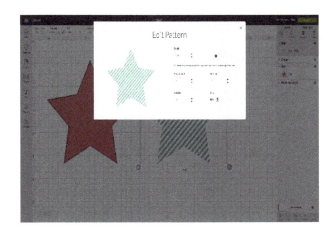

Without depending on patterned scrapbook paper or cardstock, satisfying the pictures with one of the already loaded designs is a nice way to add curiosity to your designs.

In accumulation to the myriad designs available, the size and direction of the pattern can also be manipulated by clicking on "Edit Pattern" in the Pattern toolbar (under Fill).

10. Using Keys for Keyboards. For about any order you might think of, there are keys on the Design Space canvas (e.g., Repeat, Erase, Copy, Cut, Print, etc.).

The buttons appear on the picture corners themselves, in the upper toolbar, and in the Layers panel on the right. Try utilizing several of the keyboard keys that function with other computer programs, however, to save time.

In specific, these shortcuts are really helpful and will protect you a lot of time while working on major projects: Copy (Control C) | Paste (Control V) | Erase (Delete button) | Undo (Delete button) (control Z).

11. Using a Crop Cut. A crop tool is a tool that might seem to be absent from Cricut Design Space. There is a solution, though.

In combination with the unrestricted shapes (e.g., circle, square), you will use the Slice Method to do what a traditional Crop Tool can do.

Conclusion

Machines from Cricut have influenced the world of crafts. For crafters, these devices are pretty popular because they are enjoyable, easy to use, and save time. Such machines are a must-have if you love to craft and customize. There are many versions of Provo Craft Cricut machines.

Expression, Expression 2, Visualize, Personal Cutter, Mini, Gypsy, Construct, Cake, Cake Mini, and Martha Stewart Crafts Version are all included. There is a die-cutting machine that fits you and your kind of carving process.

Every time, these devices can give you specific die cuts. No cutting and crafting further through the hand. This saves a massive amount of time, meaning that you can get working on other tasks that you have not had the time to get into. If you like, you can also work at the same time on several tasks.

Cricut Paired Devices with the thousands of designed Cricut cartridges accessible from Provo Craft, the artistic side gives you infinite opportunities.

You can make a note as to what components are included with it until you select the one that is perfect for you.
In addition to the machine, you would sometimes need to buy tools such as cutting pads, spatulas, new blades for the project, cartridges, and, of course, some cutting materials.

As you can see, these devices are a big expenditure, but over the years to come, these can be really satisfying and enjoyable. No matter whether you are a novice or an experienced crafter, any crafter can prosper from time-saving crafts and professional-looking designs.

Amaze your family and acquaintances with your innovation. Again, make crafting with Cricut machines enjoyable and innovative.